THE GARDEN-TO-TABLE

How to Grow Your Own Food,
Put It Up,
and Serve It in Over 300 Savory Ways

COOKBOOK

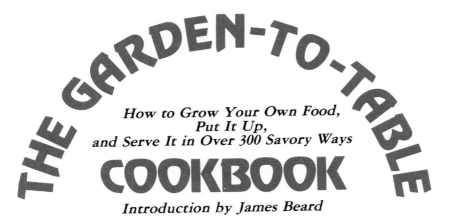

THE GARDEN-TO-TABLE

How to Grow Your Own Food,
Put It Up,
and Serve It in Over 300 Savory Ways

COOKBOOK

Introduction by James Beard

A James Beard · Milton Glaser · Burton Wolf Book

Edited by Helen Witty and Burton Wolf

BEARD GLASER WOLF LTD.

McGraw-Hill Book Company

New York   St. Louis   San Francisco   Toronto
Düsseldorf   Mexico

Book design by Milton Glaser Studio.

Illustrations by Norma Erler Rahn.

1 2 3 4 5 6 7 8 9 D O D O 7 9 8 7 6

Library of Congress Cataloging in Publication Data

Main entry under title:

The Garden-to-Table Cookbook.

"A James Beard-Milton Glaser-Burton Wolf Book."
Bibliography: p.
Includes index.
1. Cookery (Fruit)   2. Cookery (Vegetables)
3. Canning and preserving.   4. Vegetable garden-
ing.   5. Fruit culture.   I. Witty, Helen.
II. Wolf, Burton.
TX811.G33   641.3'5   76-3331
ISBN 0-07-023715-8

For
Richard, Anne, and George—H.W.
Andrew, James, and Stephen—B.W.

Editors and Contributors
The Garden-to-Table Cookbook

Editors
Helen Witty and Burton Wolf

Helen Witty, after a career in editing scholarly and reference books and textbooks, combined an interest in culinary matters with her publishing experience and now specializes in editing, consulting, and writing in the food field. She has written on both food and gardening for magazines and has been most recently a principal editor of *The Cooks' Catalogue*. She has prepared Part Three, to which she also contributed a number of her own recipes.

Burton Wolf is the managing director of a group of companies which have extensive interests in the areas of publishing, food, and photography, among them Beard Glaser Wolf Ltd., a firm in which his associates are James Beard and Milton Glaser. He has been principal architect, in both the conception and the editorial direction, of a number of books, including most recently *The Cooks' Catalogue*.

Part One: Growing Your Own . . .

Marjorie J. Dietz

Marjorie J. Dietz is associate editor of *Plants & Gardens*, the quarterly publication of the Brooklyn Botanic Garden. She is the author of numerous articles in magazines and of many books, including *The Concise Encyclopedia of Favorite Wild Flowers* and *Landscaping and the Small Garden*. She also edited the massive two-volume *10,000 Garden Questions* (1974). Mrs. Dietz is herself an avid gardener and writes from experience in growing plants of innumerable kinds and varieties.

Part Two: Putting Up Food

Marie Roberson Hamm

Marie Roberson Hamm edited the 23-volume *Woman's Day Encyclopedia of Cookery*, has written many cookbooks, including most recently *Gifts from Your Kitchen* and *The Crockery Cookbook* (1975), and has contributed food and travel articles to numerous magazines and newspapers. Cooking is not only Mrs. Hamm's profession, but a hobby she shares enthusiastically with her husband. She has contributed two of her favorite recipes to Part Three.

Part Three: Recipes

Helen Witty

Helen Witty, co-editor of this book, whose background is described above, prepared Part Three. This section includes scores of recipes devised or shared by the contributors named in the list that follows.

Recipe Contributors

Barbara Acosta, long active in publishing, was recently a member of the staff of *The Cooks' Catalogue*. As a cook, she is particularly noted for her skill in preparing and freezing dishes for guests at ski weekends at her country house.

Michael Batterberry has, with his wife, written several books, including *On the Town in New York Since 1776: A History of Eating, Drinking, and Entertainments*, and his articles and recipes have appeared in leading magazines. He teaches at James Beard's New York City cooking school.

Grace Zia Chu, author of the extraordinarily successful *The Pleasures of Chinese Cooking*, has recently published *Madame Chu's Chinese Cooking School* (1975). Acknowledged to be the foremost authority in the United States on the cuisines of China, she has long taught Chinese cooking, both in her own school and at the China Institute of America in New York City.

Ruth Ellen Church, a syndicated wine columnist for the Chicago *Tribune*, had been food editor of that newspaper for more than thirty years when she recently retired. Author of seven cookbooks, she is at work on her second wine book, *Entertaining with Wines*, and two other new books—one on the wines and cheeses of the Middle West, the other on microwave cooking.

Elizabeth Susan Colchie is a noted food consultant who has done extensive recipe development and testing as well as research into the history of foods and cookery. She was on the editorial staff of *The Cooks' Catalogue* and has written countless articles for such magazines as *Gourmet* and *House & Garden*.

Carol Cutler, who has been a food columnist for the *Washington Post*, is a graduate of the Cordon Bleu and L'École des Trois Gourmands in Paris. She is the author of *Haute Cuisine for Your Heart's Delight*, and will shortly publish her new book, *The Six-Minute Soufflé and Other Culinary Delights*.

Florence Fabricant is the food editor of the East Hampton (New York) *Star* and also writes on food for the Long Island edition of *The New York Times*. She has contributed to various magazines and was on the staff of *The Cooks' Catalogue*.

Maria Friedlander, while describing herself as "not a professional in the cooking field," is nonetheless a serious cook with special interests in the cuisine of her mother's native region in Italy and in the Finnish-derived cuisine of the family of her husband, the photographer Lee Friedlander.

Edward Giobbi, a painter of international reputation, is the author of *Italian Family Cooking* and has had his recipes published in national magazines and newspaper features. He raises his own fruits and vegetables and puts them up in quantity, and is known in the culinary world as a master Italian cook.

Marcella Hazan is the author of the acclaimed *The Classic Italian Cookbook*, and her recipes have also appeared in numerous magazines and newspapers. She is at work on a second cookbook. Since 1967 she has taught Italian cooking in her home in New York City, and plans also to teach in Bologna, the gastronomic as well as political capital of her native province in Italy, Emilia-Romagna.

Helen McCully is food editor of *House Beautiful* magazine and the author of many books on food, among them *Nobody Ever Tells You These Things About Food and Drink*; *Cooking with Helen McCully Beside You*; and most recently, *Waste Not, Want Not: A Cookbook of Delicious Foods from Leftovers*, 1975. She was a consultant on the staff of *The Cooks' Catalogue*.

Glenna McGinnis was food editor of *Woman's Day* magazine for more than thirty years and served as the food editor of the original twelve-volume *Woman's Day Encyclopedia of Cooking*. She has conducted cooking schools throughout the United States and is currently editing, writing, broadcasting on radio, and conducting her own business, Home Economists Unlimited, in Connecticut.

Jane Moulton, a food writer for the *Plain Dealer* in Cleveland, took her degree in foods and nutrition. As well as reporting on culinary matters and reviewing food-related books for the *Plain Dealer*, she has worked in recipe development, public relations, and catering. She has long had a special interest in preserving.

Gloria Pépin doesn't leave all the cooking at home to her husband, the internationally known chef Jacques Pépin. She is a devoted gardener, cans and freezes as much as possible of her crop, and is especially interested in Chinese and Spanish, as well as French, cooking.

x

Editors and Contributors

Monoroma Phillips, food consultant and originator of Monoroma's Tandoori Mix, is credited with introducing tandoori chicken to New York City. She is the author of *Everyday Recipes*, a small book on Indian cooking written to convince Americans that all Indian cooking is not hot. She is at work on a new cookbook.

Felipe Rojas-Lombardi, a native of Peru, is an executive chef, teacher, lecturer, food columnist, and author. His books include the *A to Z No-Cook Cookbook*, a cookbook for children, and *Game Cookery*. He was also an author of *The Great Cooks Cookbook*, and is currently working on two new books on culinary subjects, *The Traveling Potato* and *Everyone Can Cook Book*.

Allianora Rosse is considered the best botanical artist in America, and has illustrated innumerable articles and books on horticultural subjects, including seven volumes of the Time-Life *Encyclopedia of Gardening*. She is also the author of books on crafts and needlework and is a devoted gardener and a cook noted for her knowledge of varied cuisines, including the Indonesian.

Paul Rubinstein, son of the world-famous pianist Artur Rubinstein, is a stockbroker by profession but has written three cookbooks, *Feasts for Two, The Night-Before Cookbook*, and *Feasts for Twelve (or More)*, 1975.

Cammy Sessa is a staff writer and fashion editor of the *Virginian-Pilot* newspaper in Norfolk, Virginia. She conducts a weekly newspaper column, based on the use of natural foods, that arose from her interest in vegetarianism.

Harvey Steiman, food editor of the *Miami Herald*, writes weekly columns that cover food and its preparation as well as wine and restaurant reviews. He has taught cooking classes and lectured on wine and restaurants at the food and hotel school of Florida International University.

Pilar Turner is the founder and co-director of the International School of Cooking in New York City. She began her culinary studies as a child in her native Spain, and has also studied at the Culinary Institute of America. Her repertoire of recipes includes many handed down in the oral tradition of Spain since the seventeenth century, as well as many which she has created herself.

Maggie Waldron has been a member of the food staff of *McCall's* and has worked most recently with the commodity accounts of a large advertising and public-relations firm in California. Dealing with the fresh-fruit accounts led her to develop a lively interest, reflected in her recipes, in canning and freezing.

Nicola Zanghi is the owner-chef of Restaurant Zanghi in Glen Cove, New York. He started his apprenticeship under his father at the age of thirteen, and is a

Editors and Contributors

graduate of two culinary colleges. He has produced and performed on his own television program and has instructed at the Cordon Bleu school in New York City.

Associate Editors:
Emily Aronson and Susan Lipke

Illustrations:
Norma Erler Rahn

Garden Plans:
Derek Fell

Beard Glaser Wolf Ltd.

James Beard, one of the world's most distinguished food experts, conducts cooking schools in the United States and Europe, writes a syndicated food column, contributes to many magazines, and appears on television. His many cookbooks have earned him a world-wide reputation.

Milton Glaser, is the design director of *New York Magazine*, co-author of the "Underground Gourmet" magazine series, restaurant guides, and cookbook, and is one of the world's outstanding graphic artists.

Burton Richard Wolf, co-editor of this book, is described on page vii.

Contents

Part Three: Recipes

Introduction

by James Beard

Americans in greater numbers are plucking their food straight from the earth and rediscovering the meaning of "fresh." What is more, they are preserving again, in the tradition of earlier generations—canning, pickling, making jams and jellies, even smoking and drying. It all makes good sense, because properly home-grown and home-canned food is apt to be healthier, cheaper, and more satisfying than commercial equivalents. The cook who lovingly tends his vegetables through the cycle of growing before they reach the stove has an extra feeling of achievement and a certainty about the produce he is using. The finer the raw vegetable, the finer the finished dish will be. Homemade chutneys, pickles, and relishes can give a lift to a simple meal. Nicely done jars of jellies and jams make wonderful gifts.

This delightful book will show you how to join the movement. It will not only turn you into a sophisticated gardener, but it will make you a better cook—in addition to its many detailed recipes and directions for canning, pickling, preserve making, and freezing, there are hundreds of recipes and suggestions for preparing for the table the canned and frozen foods you have put up.

I grew up in an age when there were few acceptable canned fruits and vegetables on the market. My mother would allow tins of French peas, mushrooms, and truffles into the house, and that was about it. If you took pride in your table, as Mother did, you canned five months out of the year, as each food came into season. She had strong opinions as to which things were worthy of being immortalized. I can recall long discussions between Mother and her friends about the best peach varieties for canning. Some held out for Elbertas; she insisted on Muirs and Crawfords.

The household canning started in the spring, with asparagus. At that time we had almost nothing but white asparagus on the West Coast, which Mother preferred anyhow. She would order crates of it. I can still see those jumbo specimens, with perfect tips and ivory stalks, which came packed in moss. After processing in wide-mouthed jars, every spear of asparagus uniform in size, 150 quarts were ready for storage. They were beautiful to look upon and were brought out for luncheons, dinner parties, and special occasions.

Next in line for processing were strawberries, raspberries, and apricots. During the summers at the beach, wild huckleberries and blackberries were preserved. Then came apples—Gravensteins from our own trees—corn, prunes, plums, pears, peaches, grapes, and finally, tomatoes, not to mention twenty kinds of pickles and relishes, made all summer long. Along with cured meats and various staples, this gave us a handsomely stocked larder to see us through the winter.

Although I do little canning of the basic kind these days, I do enjoy doing certain special things like pickles—mild pickles, and the tiny *cornichons* that the French use and that are so costly to buy. (You'll find a recipe for *cornichons* in this book.) I also like to make chutneys, and in the fall, when I can find them, I preserve ground cherries (an earlier generation also called them "husk tomatoes"), a luscious fruit a little like the gooseberry, which makes an excellent topping for ice cream. And in my wanderings I often find fruit that is so good, I am compelled to turn out a few jars of jam, to prolong the memory of it.

As I have said, the pleasure of all kinds of preserving is greater if you grow your own food to begin with. Those fortunate enough to have a small garden patch can supply themselves with the choicest vegetables and berries—items hard to find in the local market or too expensive to buy on a daily basis, like Bibb lettuce and raspberries. If you are a city dweller, you will be astonished to learn what you can grow on your terrace or in a sunny window. Even if you lack room for many vegetables, you can always find space for a tomato plant or two and a few herbs. My own herb garden in New York City keeps me in fresh tarragon, rosemary, basil, and thyme for a good part of the year. As my students have found in tasting sessions, herbs can make a dramatic difference in a dish.

We are lucky to have a quick method of food preservation that our grandparents never knew—freezing—which makes it a much easier matter to store the harvest. Not everything lends itself to freezing, of course, but many frozen vegetables and fruits are better than if they had been canned. And freezing can be used in surprising ways. Last summer, for example, I made uncooked, frozen raspberry jam. It was sensational, and took no time to prepare. But if you get hooked on good old-fashioned preserving— and I predict you will—nothing can ever replace the comfortable rolling boil of the jam kettle.

A "Black Thumb" Note:

It is difficult for us to imagine a reader who, by following the simple instructions in Part One of this book, would not wind up with a perfectly respectable food garden. However, there is a rumor that some amongst us were born with the gardener's black thumb, instead of a green one, and that no seed of their planting will grow. If that is true, or if you (for some sad reason) are unable to grow your own vegetables, Part Two and Part Three of this book can still be used effectively with purchased vegetables and fruits.

However, in order to come up with something reasonably like the quality of home-grown vegetables and fruits at a bearable cost, we suggest that you look into the following possibilities:

1. Almost every city in the United States has a wholesale produce market—perhaps one not quite on the level of the old Les Halles in Paris, but usually one that is large and full enough to supply you with just about every fruit and vegetable you could want for canning and preserving. Of course, what you buy at the wholesale market is not the same as home-grown food, not in taste or price: there is nothing so low in cost or so high in quality as the fruits and vegetables that come from a good home garden. But the nice thing about big wholesale produce markets is that they are available for your harvesting each day of the week, all year round, and the fruits and vegetables are fresher than any you can buy at retail stores. Just drive in and fill up your car with whatever looks good: strawberries, zucchini, asparagus, and just about everything else that is in season in *any* growing area, not just locally—from garden to packer to trucker to wholesaler to you. Not the real thing, but not bad. Most wholesale dealers welcome "retail" customers, so long as they buy in wholesale units—bushels, boxes, and so on. Don't be put off by this unit-buying requirement: most of the time, the wholesale unit is just the amount you'd want for putting up.

2. Join a local food co-operative, or organize one. Such co-ops can purchase all kinds of food—not just produce—at wholesale prices and divide the wholesale lots up into smaller units for distribution to the members, who get the advantage of low prices without the need to accept wholesale quantities individually. With

today's rising food prices, a co-op makes good sense. There are a number of books on the subject of forming and operating co-ops, and some include a national directory of existing co-ops.

3. Make a special arrangement with your greengrocer for the fruits and vegetables you want to put up in quantity. More often than not, a local retailer of produce is willing to give a special price on specific units of fruits and vegetables. If you explain that you are about to undertake some preserving and that you need some wholesale units of various items, he may well quote you a price only slightly above wholesale. It's important to do this in advance—ask him how much notice he needs—so that he can make the purchase to your order during his next visit to his wholesale source.

4. If you live anywhere near farming or truck-gardening country, don't overlook the farm stands—especially those that are family-run. They often have produce you would be proud to have grown yourself. One of our editors, with a country house but limited gardening space, regularly buys from such a stand, the owners of which will even allow customers to pick their own strawberries, green beans, tomatoes, and other crops.

During recent years another of our editors had access to ample land for gardening, but has since taken up temporary residence in a small house with virtually no space for growing things. So that canning and preserving might continue, if not gardening, a search was made for a source of good fruits and vegetables at reasonable prices. It turned out that the Hunts Point wholesale produce market, in New York City, offered an outstanding selection, including many fruits and vegetables not often seen in retail stores in the metropolitan area. Because of the many hundreds of kinds of fruits and vegetables brought into the New York wholesale market, new preserving horizons were opened. Many of these delicacies are shipped in for resale to fine restaurants and specialty food shops, and never reach local supermarkets and greengrocers.

So, our temporarily gardenless editor has been provided with a wide variety of quality produce to be put up through the entire year, including a number of things that either the climate or limited space would make impossible or difficult to grow locally. Wholesale produce markets and good farm stands exist throughout the United States and Canada, and they can turn a black thumb, if not green, at least peachy.

Part One
Growing Your Own Vegetables, Herbs, and a Few Small Fruits

Logically enough, anyone interested in good food and its preparation soon begins to dream about growing and harvesting the full-flavored vegetables and seasoning herbs so essential to the good life. This section—Part One of this book—will tell you how to grow them and a few fruits as well. Sometimes, though, the cart comes before the horse: the successful food gardener may be an indifferent cook who needs help and inspiration. Parts Two and Three of this book offer both, telling you how to freeze, can, pickle, and otherwise preserve your surplus, and also how to prepare for the table in delicious ways the food you have grown and put up.

Who Can Grow Vegetables?

Today, thanks to improved knowledge about plants and to improved gardening techniques, it is a fact that just about anyone can grow some kinds of vegetables—and just about anywhere. A second fact is that many of the rigid rules of vegetable gardening have vanished. The rules have become flexible, and growing techniques abound that were unknown only a few years ago. There are many ways to garden, and often many different methods to follow for growing each vegetable.

A third fact is that no matter how you choose to garden, the harvest that results is bound to be superior to its supermarket counterpart in freshness, flavor, and, very likely, in nutritiousness too. Never mind whether your vegetables look as pretty as those in the market bins. The chances are that yours will be pretty, too, but if they have a blemish or two, remember that much of the apparent beauty of a commercially grown fruit or vegetable is only skin deep—the result of a deliberate breeding program to toughen the produce for mass harvesting by machinery, for rough handling and long shipping, and finally, for a long shelf life in the marketplace—and never mind how the produce tastes when it reaches the table!

No Land? Make a Portable Garden Indoors

People who live in apartments and houses that lack growing space outdoors can grow *some* vegetables, but here no miracles can be promised, nor can vast harvests be expected. Yet isn't it miracle enough that a sunny window sill can become a miniature food garden? A garden with, perhaps, a few pots of the small-fruited 'Pixie' tomato, a flat of lettuce, and any number of herbs in boxes or pots, to be used to freshen the taste of the produce brought from the supermarket? Much more than that in the way of home-grown foods for feasting can be expected by the city dweller who has access to a roof, a penthouse, a terrace, or a balcony. Here there will be more sunshine and more space, some of which can be used vertically by planting climbing beans and such vining vegetables as cucumbers, melons, and the winter squash variety called 'Butternut.'

Fluorescent lights have revolutionized the growing of many plants indoors, where rooms in both apartments and houses are otherwise often too dim for growing anything except philodendron.

Fluorescent lights are no use outdoors, but they can sometimes be arranged in such a way as to supplement the available light inside a window that receives only a few hours of sunshine a day. Don't expect to grow pots of fruiting tomatoes under fluorescent lights alone, but you can grow quite decent lettuce, herbs, curled and upland cress, mustard, and some other leafy vegetables, in either summer or winter. Joan Means, of Massachusetts, recently wrote in *Horticulture* magazine that she grew 'Salad Bowl' lettuce all winter in her basement under fluorescent lights.

You will find, though, that the best use of fluorescent lights in vegetable gardening is for starting seeds indoors in early spring to produce plants to be set outdoors when the weather warms, either in containers or in the open ground. (See "Indoor Seed Sowing," farther along in this section.)

Instant Outdoor Gardens in Containers

The easiest and quickest way to introduce a beginner to the pleasures and promises of vegetable growing is through container gardening. This is about the only means that most city people have for such enjoyment, yet it's a method that also appeals to suburbanites who may have extensive terraces but not much else in the way of usable space. Container gardening is also a good method for vacationers who reach their summer properties late in the spring, or who have beach or country houses with lots of sunny deck space but only inhospitable sand dunes or rocky outcroppings beyond. In short, container gardening offers something for everyone.

Getting Started: Containers to Consider

One of the refreshing developments in gardening today is the tremendous increase in the variety of containers that can be used for growing plants. They range from the sublime—expensive, often custom-designed containers and antiques that were formerly only dust gatherers—to the mundane: discarded receptacles of many kinds, flue tiles, bushel baskets, plastic pails, and the usual clay

pots. You can build your own rectangular or square wooden plant-ers, or have a carpenter do it for you if you are not handy in that direction. Garden centers offer a dazzling supply of both standing and hanging containers, but keep your eyes open for other possibili-ties. This is an obvious area for creative projects using wood, cement, plastic, or cast-offs.

Anyone who hears the ordinary bushel basket championed as a container for growing vegetables is likely to be dubious, as we were before seeing one planted with two kinds of lettuce and some herbs, and another with a large single plant of zucchini squash loaded with baby fruits. The effect was most attractive, and the practicality of bushel-basket gardening was proved. Note that before you fill a bushel basket—or any other basket—with soil, you should line it with a thick layer of newspaper, or, better, with heavy plastic sheeting. Make holes in the plastic to allow drainage of excess water.

Among the best tomatoes—both for size and flavor—we have ever harvested were grown in wooden boxes from the grocery store, placed on the sunny roof of an apartment house in the city. (Today most groceries are shipped in cardboard cartons, but liquor stores sometimes have surplus wooden boxes of about the right size and depth.) Three or four seedling tomatoes were stuffed into each box, and though the plants were crowded, they were kept productive by a weekly fertilizing with liquid fish emulsion after the fruits began to appear.

Plants and Soil for Containers

If you limit the kinds of vegetables you grow to the young plants available at nurseries and garden centers, and if you fill your containers with one of the various packaged synthetic soil mixes (Redi-Earth and Jiffy-Mix are two brands), available at the same sources, you eliminate seed sowing and fussing with mixing your own soil. You will find an engaging variety of seedlings, or vegeta-ble transplants, at your local outlets. Beyond the obvious ones—tomato, cabbage, eggplant, and pepper plants—you should find seedlings of lettuce, broccoli, celery, cucumbers, perhaps melons and squash, and often herbs, all ready to go into containers. They will be in neat little trays or flats, or in individual pots. (Some of the pots may be composed of peat, in which case you simply dig a hole, place the pot in it so its rim is just below the surface, and fill in around and over the pot with soil.)

Feeding Your Container Garden

The synthetic soil mixes usually contain fertilizers (however, read the label to be sure), so no additional fertilizing is usually necessary for quick-maturing vegetables such as lettuce. However, you will want to use a liquid fertilizer (to be found at garden centers, and often also in hardware and dime stores) for the long-season, heavy-producing fruiting vegetables such as tomato, pepper, eggplant, squash, and cucumber. Apply in the strength recommended on the container, and make the first application after the first fruits have begun to form, not before. Frequent but light applications of fertilizer are best for plants in containers.

Container-grown vegetables have the same requirements for sun and good light as plants growing in the open ground. However, an advantage to using some containers—those that are portable—is that they can be moved to follow the sun's path, and, if you use one of the synthetic soil mixes, the containers are lighter to move than they would be if they were filled with garden soil.

Watering Is Vital

Another requirement of all plants is adequate water. Watering correctly is the major pitfall awaiting a beginner, and neglecting a pot or tub that is dry can kill the plant or damage it severely. A slower death is the prospect for plants in containers that are continually overwatered—this is killing your plants with kindness, so to speak. A wilting plant is not necessarily showing signs of drought—waterlogged soil, as well as bone-dry soil, can cause this condition. So the best way to determine the need for watering is to *feel the soil.* If it is dry or on the verge of dryness, give the pot or tub a thorough soaking until water runs out of the drainage hole; then leave it alone until it needs a good soaking again. (See the box on the next page for more on watering.)

Planting Ideas for Container Gardens

Almost any vegetable can be grown in containers. Well, almost any—we wouldn't recommend asparagus, for instance, and we were doubtful about melons until hearing about a couple who grew them successfully on a sunny deck, two plants each in redwood boxes measuring 18 inches by 14 inches and 16 inches deep. Every time they watered their plants they added 20-20-20 fertilizer, a half-teaspoon to a gallon of water. (Fertilizer formulas—such as 20-20-20—are explained under "The Chemical Fertilizers," page 16.)

Tomatoes are everyone's favorite, and they are well suited to growing in containers. A plant of a standard-sized variety will need from 2 to 5 gallons of soil or synthetic mix, but the small-fruited varieties, sometimes also grown in hanging containers, can get along on 1 gallon of soil—an 8- to 10-inch pot would be about right for these. Eggplant, pepper, and all other vigorously fruiting vegetables have about the same needs as to soil quantity, so don't stint on the size of your container.

More About Containers and Their Water Requirements

- Small, shallow containers need more water than large, deep ones, such as planters and tubs. Containers for growing most vegetables should be at least 8 to 10 inches deep.
- Containers dry out faster in summer than in spring or fall, and fastest when the weather is windy and dry.
- As plants enlarge and begin to fruit and as the roots fill the containers, they need much more frequent watering than while they are in the seedling stage.
- The synthetic soil mixes tend to retain moisture well because of their high peat content. At the same time, excessive water drains from them readily, a built-in safeguard against overwatering for the beginner.
- On sunny, open rooftops and terraces, a daily soaking of containers may be necessary. But this is not a rule! Only you can judge when watering is needed in your situation—feel the soil to be sure.
- Humid weather slows down the drying-out process. On windy, clear days, twice-a-day watering may be necessary.
- Be sure all containers have drainage holes at the bottom.

If you have the space for a good-sized planter, you can grow a miniature vegetable garden in it. You won't be able to move it once it is filled with soil, so place it in the sunniest spot you have. Dimensions of the planter can vary, of course, but the depth is important—about 8 inches is the minimum, and 12 to 15 inches is much better. The width of the planter box can be from 18 to 36 inches and the length as great as your space permits. Such a box can support all the ingredients you need for salads—lettuce, onions (grow from "sets"—see the growing directions for onions), small-fruited tomatoes such as 'Tiny Tim' and 'Pixie,' herbs such as chives, basil, and chervil.

If you don't want to build a planter, ready-made window boxes are available in various sizes. A rooftop, a city balcony, or a terrace will have space for several such purchased boxes.

FOR A VERTICAL CROP, POLE BEANS

Although buying started plants is a great convenience for city gardeners who are limited to containers—for one thing, it's hard to use up all that seed if you buy packets—you may be itching to sow seeds. In that case, beans make a good crop to experiment with. You can grow two or three plants of a pole-bean variety in a tub or other container holding about 6 gallons of soil. The vines will need support to twine around. Improvise with string stretched between the container and a handy nearby surface—the effect can be artistic as well as practical.

Whether you prefer to buy started plants or to grow your own vegetables from seeds, before deciding on what to grow, turn to the alphabetically listed discussions of vegetables beginning on page 36 and check the growing suggestions for each kind you're considering. Much of the information there applies to plants grown in containers as well as in the open ground.

A Backyard "Farm" in the Suburbs or Beyond

Even greater than the satisfaction that comes from picking your own ripe tomatoes from a tub on a terrace is the joy of gathering a whole basketful of tomatoes, *plus* snap beans, squash, cucumbers, beets, carrots—enough fresh vegetables to serve immediately, plus a surplus for freezing and canning. As the season progresses, corn, broccoli, winter squash, and finally kale can be added to the basket. And even potatoes. (*Potatoes?*—Yes. See page 73 for a unique way to have your own potato patch.)

Space and a Place in the Sun

Space is the first consideration when you begin to plan your vegetable "farm." As recently as thirty-five years ago, a plot of ground about 50 by 100 feet was suggested as the ideal size for a family vegetable garden—and this well before the advent of home freezers! Few of us today have access to so much space, but if you happen to be one of the lucky ones, hurrah for you. With a vegetable garden of that size, you and your family should be able to grow most of the year's vegetable-food requirements.

Finding a place to grow vegetables on today's limited properties may require determination and imagination, but some space does exist on most suburban (and even some city) lots. Gardens in oblong or square shapes are traditional and are perhaps the easiest to plan, but there's no rule that says your vegetable plot can't be circular or oval. If you don't have space that measures 40 by 30 feet, or 20 by 20 feet, or 30 by 10 feet, settle for what you have, which may be a spot measuring 10 by 10 feet, or even 5 by 3. Whatever the size, you can still have a vegetable garden.

And you can grow vegetables even if most of your property is a landscape architect's paradise. Tomato, pepper, eggplant, and summer squash are ornamental plants that mix well with flowers. Snap beans and such leafy vegetables as lettuce, spinach, and Swiss chard are possible subjects for edgings along shrub, rose, and flower gardens; the low-growing herbs, especially thyme and chives, also make ideal edgings, and any herbs can be spotted among permanent plantings.

Before you decide finally on your garden location and pick up a spade, remember the need for adequate sunshine. Without a place in the sun, vegetables, especially the fruiting ones like tomato and pepper, will not grow or mature properly. The minimum amount of summer sunshine your garden plot should have is about five to six hours daily. The leafy vegetables—lettuce, spinach, cabbage, beets, carrots—will perform better than fruiting vegetables under the handicap of limited sunshine, but even they do their best in full sun. If the space is shaded in part, use the area in the shade (and this, for vegetables, means *light* shade only—never such dense shade as the north side of a house) for leafy rather than fruiting crops.

Drainage

Vegetables will grow well in a number of kinds of soil, in the open ground as well as in containers, so long as the soil is well drained. Good drainage is as essential to the health of your vegetables as sunshine. If pools of water stand long after the last rainfall on the surface of your chosen plot, or if the soil is generally as soggy as a bog, you can be sure the drainage is faulty. Find another location, or grow your vegetables in containers.

The Good Earth: Organic Matter

Generally it is safe to say that any soil that has been supporting a healthy growth of grass, flowers, or shrubs (or even weeds, for that matter) will be suitable for vegetables. But very sandy soils tend to dry out fast, so they need the addition of large quantities of humus-forming materials—called organic matter—to bind the soil particles together and thus help retain nutrients and moisture. The same materials—organic matter—are added to clay soils to lighten them and improve their physical texture. Organic matter has been described as "the life of the soil," and there's hardly a garden or crop that won't benefit from its presence.

PEAT MOSS, MANURE, AND OTHER SOURCES OF HUMUS

The most accessible source of organic matter today is peat moss, available everywhere at garden centers in 4- or 6-cubic-foot bales. One 6-foot bale is the usual recommendation per 100 square feet of ground. Other good sources of organic matter are all animal manures. Manures can be spread over the soil "fresh" in the fall or winter, when they can't burn (that is, damage) plant growth, but should be in a rotted or semi-rotted state when added to soil in the spring. Then there are rotting or half-rotted leaves or leafmold, the valuable residue of leaves that accumulates on the forest floor; rotted sawdust or wood chips; "spoiled" hay (available in rural areas from farmers); rotting straw; grass clippings; kelp and seaweed (it's unnecessary to wash these before adding them to soil); and other materials that may be available locally.

COMPOST AND COMPOST-MAKING

A cheap but valuable source of organic matter, and one that responds to current environmental concerns to recycle our used resources rather than destroying them, can be your own compost pile. This is a heap or pile of various organic materials, built up layer by layer and including such things as vegetable trimmings and table scraps, grass clippings, weeds, leaves, the contents of the cat's litter box, animal manure (if only small quantities are available), seaweed, and any healthy plant trimmings that come to hand.

To make your pile, alternate each 4- to 6-inch layer of organic matter (which can be a mixture of kinds) with a thinner layer of soil (diagram). The materials decay slowly, losing their individual char-

acteristics as they become a dark, rich, humusy mass. The time required for usable compost to form ranges from a few months to a year, and the compost needn't be completely broken down to a fine texture before it's used. The process of composting is speeded and the compost is improved by the addition of a generous sprinkling of fertilizer (5-10-5, for example) to the top of each layer of organic matter.

You can spread any of the organic materials discussed above over the garden in a 2- to 4-inch layer and till or fork them into the soil in either fall or spring. Or you can add organic materials generously to the holes when you are setting out individual plants, such as tomatoes or peppers, or add them to a small plot when you are preparing it for a particular crop, such as lettuce.

Preparing the Soil

If you have any choice, fall's brisk weather makes it a good time to prepare your soil if the spot has not been used previously to grow vegetables. The interval after cultivating it until planting time in spring will permit the soil to settle, and freezing and thawing action, if you live in a cold climate, will also help to improve the soil texture. If you have a heavy clay soil, fall preparation largely eliminates the danger of damaging its consistency and causing compaction by digging it too early in spring, before it has dried out properly. Fall is a good time to improve the soil of *any* garden, too—especially that of a vegetable garden that was prepared hastily or late in the preceding spring, or a garden whose soil simply needs renewal.

THESE TOOLS WILL HELP

The easiest and quickest way to prepare a garden is with a rotary tiller. If you own a tiller, you already know that it can be used in quite limited space as well as in open plots—some gardeners use their tillers to help in digging planting holes for trees and shrubs—but if you have a postage-stamp plot, it's probably simpler to spade or fork it over to a depth of 8 to 10 inches instead of buying or renting a tiller. (See "How to Dig" a little farther along.)

Any organic matter that is being applied at the time of digging should be mixed into at least the top 6 inches of soil, and deeper if possible. If you're using a tiller you may need to make several passes to reach this depth; and if you're digging by hand,

turning over the bed a second time, this time using a digging fork, will help to mix in the material.

Although garden centers and outlets specializing in agricultural implements are filled with all sorts of alluring mechanized equipment as well as the good old "self-propelled" hand tools, the average backyard garden can be worked very well with a wheelbarrow, a long-handled spade, a digging fork, a hoe, a rake, and a couple of trowels, one narrow, one wider. You might want to toss into your tool kit an old kitchen knife, and a Dutch hook—a weeder that looks something like a miniature scythe blade—or some other hand-

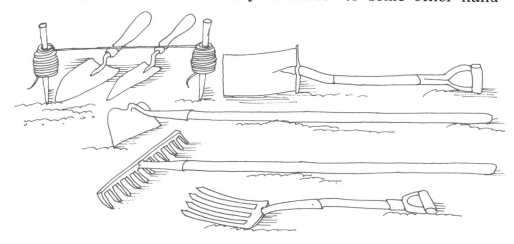

weeding tool will come in handy. A sturdy line with two stakes attached is useful for laying out paths or making straight lines for seed sowing—get a ball of mason's cord from the hardware store and it will last for years. After you have bought the basics, you can think about purchasing or renting a tiller, and perhaps you will want eventually to consider a shredding machine—a worthwhile

investment for those with good-sized gardens who have access to quantities of leaves, small branches, and other organic materials that can be chopped into usable mulch or composting material.

Feeding the Plants That Feed You

Adding organic materials to the soil of the vegetale garden will improve its physical condition and, especially when animal manures are added, will add to its fertility, too. Usually, though, commercially formulated fertilizers are the most reliable and quick-acting sources of the three vital elements needed for plant growth—nitrogen, phosphorus, and potash. These fertilizers are most often added when you dig the garden. Further plant feeding is sometimes done later in the season—see the alphabetical entries for the specific plants farther along in this section. Other, relatively minor, elements are necessary in addition to the big three, an important one being iron. Most of the minor nutrients are either present in the soil, or are brought in when you add organic matter, or are present as trace elements in added fertilizers. Not all soils are necessarily deficient in the three major elements, but since these are used up in large amounts in vegetable gardens, where close planting is often necessary, a further boost from fertilizers is usually required. Sometimes one element, such as potash, may be in low supply. For example, beets and carrots and other root vegetables require more potash, while lettuce, spinach, and other crops grown for greens need more nitrogen. On the other hand, too much nitrogen given to tomatoes can result in leafy, lush plant growth but few blossoms or fruit. The same fate can befall bean plants that are overfed with nitrogen.

THE CHEMICAL FERTILIZERS

How much more do you have to know about fertilizers to grow good vegetables? While the subject of soils and nutrients is a complex one and dear to the hearts of scientifically minded gardeners, the average vegetable gardener can get along quite well with a bag of 5-10-5 chemical fertilizer, applied in the spring at the rate of 4 pounds to 100 square feet. The dry 5-10-5 mixture can be spread by hand or by a lawn-fertilizing machine (spreader). The designation "5-10-5" indicates the amounts of the three vital elements present: 5 percent of nitrogen, 10 percent of phosphorus, and 5 percent of potash. Other fertilizer formulas can be, for example, 10-6-4, or 5-10-10, or 20-20-20, depending on their specific uses (read the label). Or you can buy bags of a single element, such as superphosphate or muriate of potash.

CONCENTRATED AND ORGANIC PLANT FOODS

Also available at your garden center are containers of highly concentrated fertilizers, in dry or liquid form, which must be mixed with water before they are applied to soils and plants. Some are designed for foliar feeding—direct application to the leaves. For all these liquid plant foods, follow label recommendations and don't strengthen the application—just enough is plenty, and an overdose can damage plants, just as too-strong fertilizer mixed into the soil can "burn" roots.

There are also fertilizers of purely organic origin. Fish emulsion, available in several brands, is an organic fertilizer in liquid form that is mixed with water before use. Dried blood or blood meal, an organic fertilizer from the packing houses in stockyards, is very high in nitrogen—about 13 percent.

DO PLANTS KNOW THE DIFFERENCE?

Whether you choose to join the organic gardening movement and stick to compost plus organic fertilizers only, or simply use compost or organic matter plus both chemical and organic fertilizers, you should understand that the plants can't tell the difference! All nutrients, whether from organic or chemical fertilizers, must be broken down into the same inorganic forms before plants can absorb them.

Sweet or Sour Soil: The Role of Lime

One other aspect of soils and fertility that vegetable gardeners should know a bit about is lime. Probably most beginners are aware that soil can be "sweet" (alkaline) or "sour" (acid), and that lime, in the form of ground limestone, is the agent applied to soils to reduce acidity. Knowing whether your soil is too acid (or too alkaline) can be important in maintaining the availability of nutrients for proper plant growth. Extreme acidity or alkalinity can release toxic elements in the soil, and either condition also encourages certain diseases.

THE pH SCALE

Actually there is a precise system—called the pH scale—for measuring the degree of acidity or alkalinity of soil. The scale goes from 1 to 10, with 7 as the neutral point—at this reading a soil is neither acid or alkaline. All soils rating above 7 are in the range of alkalinity, with 7.1 to 7.5 being considered slightly alkaline. Soils below 7 fall into the acid range, with those testing at 6.5 to 6.9 being slightly acid. Medium-acid soils are in the 5.2 to 6.4 range.

Most vegetables grow best in only slightly acid soils, so if your soil tests medium acid (5.5), you will want to add ground limestone at the rate of 35 pounds per 1,000 square feet in order to raise the pH reading to 6.5. Every two or three years, you'll want to retest your soil and add lime again as needed. Lime has other functions in the soil besides adjusting the pH: it supplies calcium, and it changes a heavy clay soil to a more crumbly texture.

If your soil is very alkaline, your County Agent (see below) is the best source of advice on improving it.

The best way to find out if your soil needs lime and other

special improvements is to have a sample of it tested. This is one of the aids to homeowners and farmers alike rendered by the Federal Extension Service in every state. Call your County Agent, listed in the telephone directory under the name of your county plus "Cooperative Extension Association," for information on preparing the sample; what the cost, if any, will be; and where to send the soil sample for testing.

In addition to County Agents and the soil-testing service they offer, you can sometimes find garden centers or other commercial sources for testing. Do-it-yourself soil-testing kits are widely advertised and are reasonably useful to the experienced gardener. They have their limitations, however, and for accurate analysis plus specific recommendations for improving your soil, it's worth it to seek out the help of professionals.

How to Dig

This is a section to skip if you have spent much time on the business end of a spade, digging fork, rake, or hoe. But if you haven't, read on.

As we have mentioned, fall is a good time for the basic preparation of garden soil, especially if the spot hasn't been under cultivation for a long time, if ever. But you can dig your garden in the spring, too, if you wait until the soil has dried out enough not to stick together when you squeeze a handful. Dig it when it's wet and the texture will be damaged, to your grief.

Drive in your stakes and string your mason's cord to outline the garden area, and begin by making a clean cut along the line you've marked, taking small spadefuls and tossing them inward, toward the garden-to-be. For this one row only you'll be facing into the garden—the rest of the time you'll be digging backward. (If you are making a garden with curved edges, by the way, you can establish the shape by laying a garden hose on the ground.)

With your neat edge-cut made, dig your second row, working straight back along one side of the garden, backing up with each step; or else dig across the width of the garden, making sure you leave no undug spots between your first, or edge-marking, row and your second one. Drive your spade as straight downward as you can and dig as deeply as possible. Don't try to make your "bites" too big, and turn each spadeful over completely and give it a thwack with the back of the spade before moving on.

If your soil is in good condition, and if you have first spread organic materials, lime, and fertilizer, or whatever else your soil requires, on the surface, a single digging may be enough. But it's a good idea to go over the bed again with a digging fork. This second turning mixes in the added elements more thoroughly and improves the texture, especially if, as you did with the spade, you give each forkful a good bash with the back of the tines after you turn it.

If you use a tiller to prepare your garden, follow the manufacturer's instructions for using his machine; these vary from one make to another.

If you don't plan to plant your garden at once, you can leave it rough—this works especially well if you have dug it in the fall. When planting time is near, rake it smooth, moving backward and taking long, easy sweeps, leveling the surface while winnowing out stones or other rubbish. If time permits, let the soil settle for a few days, then level any high or low spots before planting.

To make a guide line for setting out plants or for marking a furrow, use your stakes and cord again. The easiest way to make a furrow is to use one corner of the hoe, moving backward and guiding the blade along the taut cord. If the resulting furrow is too deep, use the straight edge of the hoe to fill it in from one side before sowing.

If the weather seems likely to be dry for a while, you might try the California trick of running a gentle stream of water into the furrow, soaking the bottom well before sowing the seeds. Cover the seeds with soil that has stood above the irrigation line—obviously you don't want to cover them with mud-pie material.

Planning and Planting

The real fun of vegetable gardening begins when you plan what you are going to grow. If you have time, order a few seed catalogues from mail-order firms (see page 97) and start your vegetable list with their help. Take a poll in your family for vegetable likes and dislikes—and bear in mind that "dislikes" can change to "likes" when really fresh, home-grown vegetables are served in imaginative ways. Consult the alphabetical entries on individual vegetables farther along in this section, and see also Parts Two and Three of this book for recipes and ideas for using the foods you can grow.

Making a plan on paper before it's time to plant is a help, so you can be sure you're including everything you want to grow and that you're placing it where it will do well—tall plants where they won't shade low ones, sun-lovers where they will get the most sun,

←————————10 ft.————————→

Tomatoes (Staked)	2 ft.
Snap Beans (Bush)	1½ ft.
Snap Beans (Bush)	1½ ft.
Lettuce (Head)	1 ft.
Lettuce (Loose-leaf)	1 ft.
Carrots	1 ft.
Beets	1 ft.
Onions	1 ft.

10 ft.

and so on. As you plan, too, make a note of the best planting date for each vegetable, whether you intend to sow seeds or purchase started plants. Figure out succession planting, too: when early vegetable crops are gone—spinach, for instance—you'll have space for another vegetable that should get its start in warm weather.

Spring planting can begin in the garden sooner than you might think. This is because several vegetables—and their seeds—

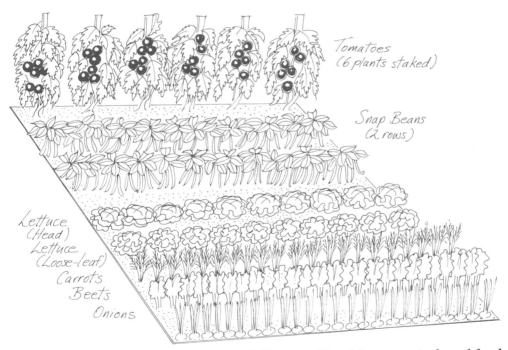

Tomatoes
(6 plants staked)

Snap Beans
(2 rows)

Lettuce
(Head)
Lettuce
(Loose-leaf)
Carrots
Beets
Onions

Only 10 by 10 feet, this garden will yield a considerable amount of good food. You could substitute a row of pole beans for the bush beans, or have a row of summer squash instead of either. Broccoli or cabbage could replace the lettuce, or the lettuce could be succeeded by a planting of a warm-weather vegetable to mature in the fall. This plan, like the others in this section, indicates typical spacing: variations in spacing that are feasible are stated in the text.

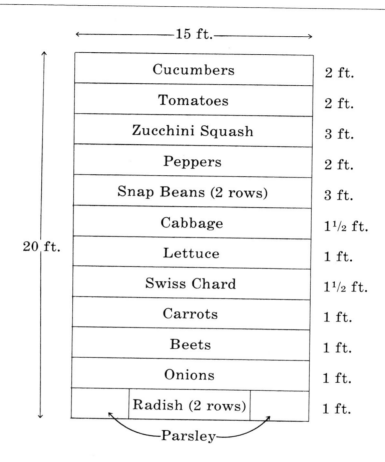

This garden, occupying 15 by 20 feet, is an ideal size for the beginning gardener, as it can be dug by hand but will supply a generous crop of vegetables. The varieties in the top half of the garden are tender vegetables, to be planted after the danger of frost has passed. Those in the lower half, from radish to cabbage, are hardy and can be planted well before the last date of frost in your locality. Any other kind of summer squash can be substituted for zucchini; and if you'd like a longer season of yield, replace the bush beans by staked pole beans.

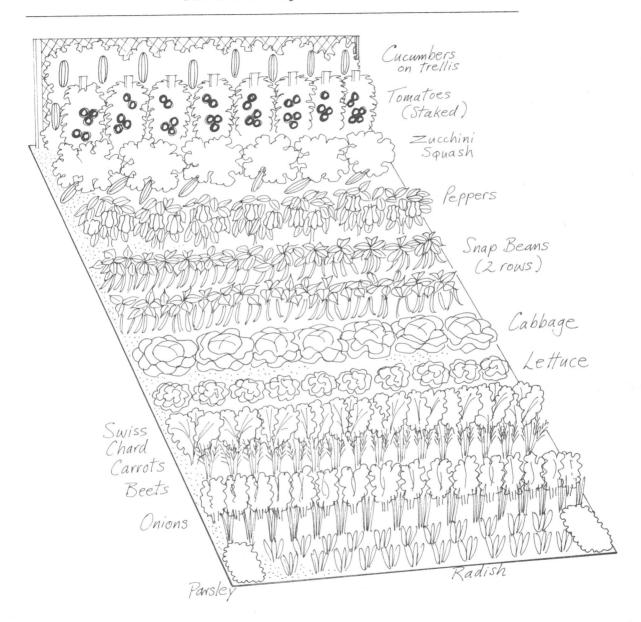

Cucumbers
on trellis

Tomatoes
(Staked)

Zucchini
Squash

Peppers

Snap Beans
(2 rows)

Cabbage

Lettuce

Swiss
Chard
Carrots
Beets

Onions

Parsley

Radish

The Garden-to-Table Cookbook

	30 ft.		
4 ft.	Asparagus (2 rows)	Corn (3 rows)	6 ft.
4 ft.	Strawberries (2 rows)		
3 ft.	Rhubarb	Tomatoes	3 ft.
2 ft.	Herbs	Summer Squash	3 ft.
2 ft.	Peas (double row)	Peppers	2 ft.
7½ ft.	Melons	Snap Beans (2 rows)	3 ft.
		Cabbage	2 ft.
		Lettuce (2 rows)	2 ft.
		Swiss Chard	2 ft.
7½ ft.	Cucumbers	Root Crops	4 ft.
		Broccoli	1½ ft.
		Cauliflower	1½ ft.

30 ft.

A garden as large as this—30 by 30 feet—allows space for melons and cucumbers, and for tomatoes to grow without staking. Additional space could be found if you use trellises for the melons and cucumbers, stakes for the tomatoes. The perennial crops—asparagus, strawberries, rhubarb, and herbs—are placed where they won't be disturbed by annual tilling or digging. If you'd like to grow blueberries, you could place a row of them across the far end of this garden, and run the asparagus in front of them. You could adjust the space for the corn and tomatoes, perhaps by eliminating the least-favored of the other vegetables shown. If you're not fond of root vegetables—turnips, parsnips, and so on—choose other vegetables instead.

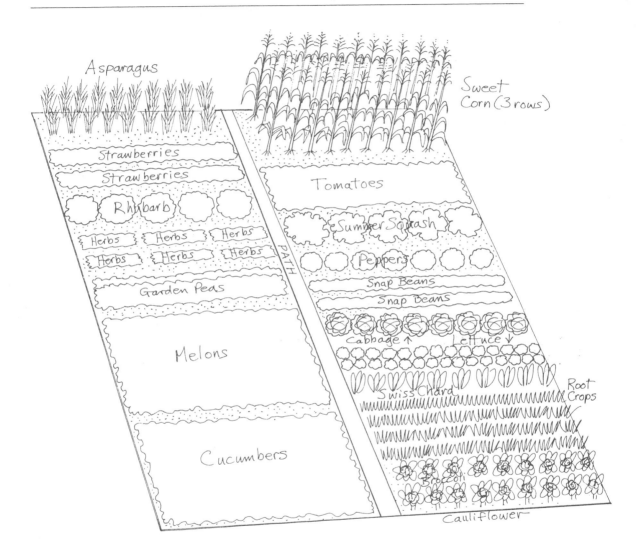

Asparagus

Strawberries

Strawberries

Rhubarb

Herbs Herbs Herbs

Herbs Herbs Herbs

Garden Peas

Melons

Cucumbers

PATH

Sweet Corn (3 rows)

Tomatoes

Summer Squash

Peppers

Snap Beans

Snap Beans

Cabbage ↑   Lettuce ↓

Swiss Chard   Root Crops

Broccoli

Cauliflower

are exceptionally cold-hardy, even to withstanding freezing temperatures. Such vegetables should be planted outdoors a good four to six weeks before the last killing frost can be expected in your region (again, ask your County Agent, as this date can vary widely from region to region). This means that these vegetables will make most of their growth during the cool, moist spring, with harvesting taking place during late spring or early summer. These same hardy vegetables are the ones recommended for planting again in midsummer to fall for the last harvests of the growing year.

Examples of cold-hardy vegetables are peas, spinach, broad beans, onions—sets, transplants, and seeds—cabbage, and radishes.

Tomatoes, sweet corn, snap beans, and squash are examples of favorite vegetables that make their best growth after the soil and atmosphere have warmed—they should be planted after the time frosts cease in your area. Close behind them come eggplant, melons, cucumbers, and peppers. The United States Department of Agriculture, in its tabulation of planting times for common vegetables (see chart), recommends that these last four be planted about a week or more after the frost-free date, but spring can move so fast in some regions and in some years that tomatoes, eggplant, corn, and cucumbers all end by being planted at the same time.

Sowing Seeds

Before sowing seeds, if you have applied fertilizer, be sure it has been incorporated with the soil and is not sitting on the surface. Sow the seeds *thinly*—seed packets give the correct spacing. This takes more time than sowing thickly, but you'll be glad you have sowed with restraint during the weeks ahead when you'll be thinning the seedlings. If you lack patience for spacing seed correctly, buy seed tapes, ribbons of water-soluble material that have been impregnated with seeds at the correct spacing. The tapes are about 15 feet long and are simply laid in the furrow and then covered with soil.

Planting depths and spacing for each vegetable are usually given in seed catalogues as well as on the seed packets themselves. This information is also given in the alphabetical entries on specific vegetables that begin on page 36. If you cheat too much on suggested spacing, especially between rows (and many home gardeners must do *some* cheating because of limited plots), you may

Part One: Growing Your Own

Some Common Vegetables, Grouped According to the Approximate Times They Can Be Planted. (Adapted from the United States Department of Agriculture "Chart of Common Vegetables .")

Cold-hardy Plants for Early-Spring Planting		Cold-tender or Heat-tolerant Plants for Later-Spring or Early-Summer Planting				Hardy Plants for Late-Summer or Fall Planting*
*Very Hardy**	*Hardy**	*Not Cold-hardy**	*Requiring Hot Weather**	*Medium Heat-tolerant**		*(Not suitable for extremely cold regions)*
Broad (fava) beans	Beets	Beans, snap	Beans, Lima	Beans, all except fava		Beets
Cabbage	Brussels sprouts	Okra	Eggplant	Chard		Broccoli
Lettuce	Carrots	New Zealand-spinach	Peppers	Soy beans		Collards
Onions	Cauli-flower	Soy beans	Sweet potatoes	New Zealand-spinach		Kale
Peas	Chard	Squash	Cucumbers	Squash		Lettuce
Potatoes	Mustard	Sweet corn	Melons	Sweet corn		Mustard
Spinach	Parsnips	Tomatoes				Spinach
Turnips	Radishes					Turnips
*Plant 4 to 6 weeks before frost-free date.	*Plant 2 to 4 weeks before frost-free date.	*Plant on frost-free date.	*Plant 1 week or more after frost-free date.	*Good for summer planting.		*Plant 6 to 8 weeks before first fall freeze.

find there is no room for the all-important harvesting. Once the seeds have been covered to the correct depth, press the soil firmly over them.

Moisture and Mulches

Once you have finished sowing seeds or setting out transplants, don't neglect their immediate moisture requirements. Most newly sown seeds—and all transplants—benefit from a generous

Pointers on Planning and Planting the Vegetable Garden

- Place long-lived plants (asparagus, rhubarb, strawberries, raspberries, and perennial herbs such as thyme and sage) at one end or side of the garden, where they will not be disturbed by annual tilling or spading.
- Run your rows north and south, if possible, to permit the plants to receive the maximum amount of sun. If your garden slopes, run rows across the slope to prevent erosion.
- It's a good idea to keep salad crops (radishes, lettuce, cress, roquette) in one area. If your garden has any shade during the day, these and other leafy plants will tolerate it the best. Transplants of lettuce can be moved from the salad-garden area and planted among your asparagus or your young tomato or pepper plants, as they will mature long before the space is shaded by developing asparagus and tomato plants.
- When you plant early-maturing vegetables, such as spinach, peas, broad or fava beans, or collards, plan ahead for what you will plant in their place. Suggestions: snap beans, lima beans, or soy beans; or, if space permits, summer squash, eggplant, tomatoes, or peppers. This succession planting makes the best use of space, especially in the small garden.
- If you plant pole beans, try to place them on the north or west side, so they will not shade lower-growing plants.
- A complaint among both experienced and first-time gardeners is that everything in the garden ripens at once! This is true to some extent—though there are freezing, canning, and preserving to take care of the surplus—but the harvest glut can be cut back by planning. First of all, check the number of days from planting to harvest when you select your vegetable packets. This information is usually included with catalogue descriptions, besides being on the seed packets; see also the chart on page 34. Harvesting dates can differ among varieties of the same vegetable, so you can choose several varieties for a longer season. Plant pole beans and snap beans at the same time: the pole beans will begin bearing ten days or more after the snap beans.

watering—a fine misty one for the seed rows and a good soaking around the entire plant for the transplants. Repeat this watering as the soil dries out in succeeding days. It's vital not to allow the soil to crust over seed rows; if it does, the seedlings may not come up.

One way to retain moisture in the soil and eliminate weeds is to mulch around and between large plants, such as tomatoes and eggplant, and between rows of carrots, bush beans, and other row crops. Most mulching materials are of an organic nature (pine needles, leaves, leafmold, straw, seaweed, bulky compost, rotted sawdust, rotted wood chips, newspapers, peanut hulls, and the like) and have the advantage of providing humus for the soil as they decompose. A synthetic mulching material is black plastic. Authorities differ on whether the plastic warms the soil, an advantage for melons and eggplants that revel in warmth but a disadvantage for cold-tolerant plants such as lettuce or spinach.

One more word about moisture: When you water your garden, do it thoroughly, being sure that moisture soaks deeply into the soil. If you use a sprinkler, set a jar or can in the garden and keep the sprinkler running until at least an inch of water has been caught in the jar. And don't work among your beans when the foliage is wet; to do so is to encourage disease.

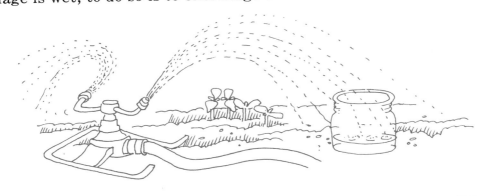

Living with Pests

As spring departs, your vegetable-garden paradise may be marred by various plagues and pests. The answer is to have a handy plunger-type duster and a supply of an all-purpose vegetable dust ready. These are sold at garden centers and may be ordered from seedsmen's catalogues. The worst pests in our garden are always cabbage worms—not on the cabbages, but on broccoli plants—and squash borers. The cabbage worms are pretty well controlled by hand-picking and by dusting with rotenone, one of the most benign of insecticides. The squash borers remain a problem, but Sevin is supposed to prevent them, if applied at 10-day intervals, starting in early summer. Most gardeners can learn to live with a few pests rather than dousing their plants with poisonous chemicals.

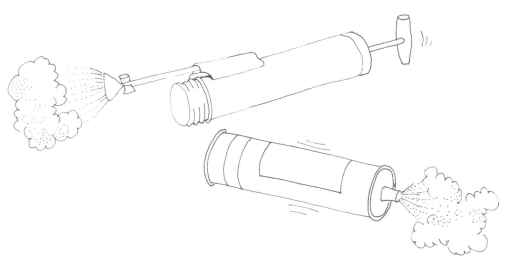

Of course if a really serious plague or horrendous horde of pests appear, drastic measures are needed. This is a good time to call your friendly County Agent in the Federal Extension Service (see page 18).

Final advice on the summer garden: Don't give it up too soon. In mid- or late summer, plant lettuce and other quick-maturing crops that will mature during fall and even until early winter in some regions. Cresses, roquette, and other salad plants also grow well in the late summer and into fall.

Controlling Weeds by Cultivation

We've already talked about controlling weeds by the use of mulches—our favorite method, and one that has the additional advantage of conserving soil moisture. But there are some situations where mulching may not be feasible. If it isn't, you'll have to choose between hand weeding (sometimes the only way to remove weeds that have sprung up among seedlings) and cultivating with a hoe or other tool.

An ordinary hoe, used with a scraping motion (don't chop or dig) is fine for removing weeds alongside your rows of plants and in paths. Or you may want to acquire such a specialized tool as a scuffle hoe (long-handled) or a Dutch hook (a hand tool), which you push or pull along just under the soil surface to cut off weeds at their roots. However you cultivate around plants, do it shallowly: deep digging is sure to injure the roots of your vegetables.

Indoor Seed Sowing

Starting seeds indoors is placed here, after the general gardening information, not because it is unimportant, but because it's very possible for the first-time gardener or any gardener to have a complete and perfect vegetable garden without sowing a single seed indoors.

Transplants of such long-season, slow-developing vegetables as tomato, eggplant, and pepper, as well as many other vegetables, are always available from local garden centers, nurseries, or greenhouses, and most of the other major vegetables—beans, for instance—are easily grown from seed sown in the open ground.

Yet starting some of your vegetables indoors from seed can be fun—almost a hobby in itself—and it also allows a greater selection of varieties than is offered locally. While indoor seed sowing isn't as easy as, say, planting a row of snap beans in the garden, there are many aids and innovations today that can help toward success.

Using Artificial Light

Fluorescent light units are a major help, especially for those who lack sunny window space. The tops of the growing seedlings must be kept close to the light tubes, about 4 inches, for proper development. Move the light upward—or the seedling containers downward—as the plants grow.

Soil and Soil Substitutes

Other important helps include the various synthetic soil mixtures, such as Jiffy-Mix and Redi-Earth, which eliminate the nuisance of sterilizing the soil in the oven, otherwise necessary because of certain soil-borne diseases that attack seedlings. Most synthetic mixes contain fertilizer (but read the bag or container to be sure), so that eliminates another fuss. The mixes can be put in various flats or pots that you can buy, or you can improvise containers from milk cartons, plastic food-storage boxes, and such kitchen discards as aluminum foil baking pans.

Pot Innovations

Another clever, step-saving innovation today is the peat pot. There are two kinds, the Jiffy-7 pellet and the original peat pot, which is available in 2½-inch, 3-inch, and larger sizes, just like the regulation clay and plastic pots. The Jiffy-7 pellet is just that—a pellet—until it is soaked for a few minutes in water, when it expands in the most amazing way to a little peat pot measuring 1³/₄ by 2 inches, already filled with a growing medium and fertilizer. If you don't think *that* is a modern miracle, try it. You'll be impressed.

What is so remarkable about both kinds of peat pots is that a couple of seeds (in the case of the Jiffy-7) or more (depending on the size of the peat pot) can be planted in them and left until it is time to plant the seedlings outdoors. Usually the weaker or weakest of the seedlings is pinched off a week or two after germination, leaving a single plant in each pot. At transplanting time pot and plant both go into the ground, where the pot soon decomposes. While the seedlings are indoors, there is no need to transplant them into larger containers, as the roots simply penetrate the peat walls as they grow. No transplanting shock is suffered by the plant at any stage.

The Plastic-Bag "Greenhouse"

Another modern aid to indoor seed sowing is the ordinary clear plastic bag. Pots or small flats, after the seeds have been sowed and the soil has been watered, can be slipped inside them, or can be covered, if they are too large to fit into a bag, by sheets of kitchen plastic, held in place by rubber bands. The plastic prevents the soil from drying out; and, as the seeds begin to germinate, the enclosure is gradually opened to admit air, being removed entirely

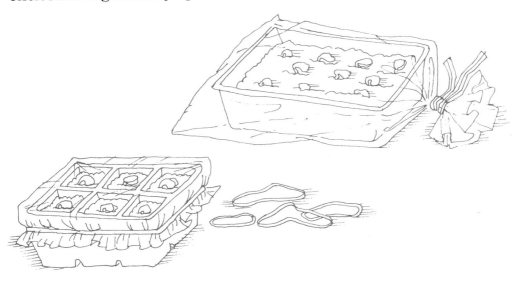

Approximate Number of Days from Planting to Harvest.
(Source: United States Department of Agriculture.)

Vegetable	Early Variety	Late Variety
Beans—green pod (bush)	45	65
Beans—green pod (pole)	56	72
Beans, lima	65	78
Beets	55	80
Broccoli*	70	150
Brussels sprouts*	90	100
Cabbage*	65	110
Chinese cabbage	70	80
Carrots	60	85
Cauliflower*	55	75
Celery	90	115
Collards	70	80
Corn, sweet	65	90
Cucumbers	55	75
Eggplant*	70	85
Kale	55	70
Kohlrabi	55	62
Lettuce (head)	45	76
Lettuce (leaf)	45	50
Muskmelon	75	110
Okra	55	60
Onions	90	130
Parsnips	110	130
Peas	58	75
Peppers (sweet or bell)*	62	80
Potatoes	90	120
Radishes	23	30
Rutabagas	80	90
Spinach	34	45
Squash (summer)	50	60
Squash (winter)	95	110
Tomatoes*	65	90
Turnips	42	55
Watermelon	80	95

*Days from transplanting. Additional time is needed from seeding to transplanting. For indoor growing-time requirements, see discussion beginning on page 35, and see also the entries for specific plants.

when germination appears to be complete. As the seedlings are being gradually weaned from their enclosure, pay attention to their need for moisture. While encased in plastic, seedlings must be kept out of direct sunlight or nearby incandescent light, or they will be cooked to death. Fluorescent lights—which are cool—will not harm them.

Indoor Growing-Time and Temperature Requirements

Eggplant and pepper need a six-to-nine-week growing period indoors before they are of good transplant size for outdoors. Tomatoes are faster-growing, requiring from four to seven weeks, depending upon variety. The hardier, faster-growing vegetables, such as lettuce, require less time—three to five weeks. (See the alphabetical entries for specific plants for their indoor-growing requirements.) The best temperature range for indoor growing is between 70° and 75° F. during the day and 60 and 65 degrees at night.

THE HARDENING-OFF PROCESS

The major problem with indoor-grown seedlings is getting them in shape to endure the transition from the windless, often less well lighted but warmer interior to the shock-filled great outdoors. Unless the seedlings have been grown in unusually cool and sunny rooms indoors, a week of hardening-off, as the process is called, may be necessary before it's safe to set the seedlings in the open ground. The plants are moved outside for a time each day, the first day receiving only a few hours of exposure to the sun (or, better, to a mixture of sun and shade), and then brought indoors. The exposure time is increased gradually, as is the exposure to direct sun, and finally the plants are left out at night. A day or so later they are set into the ground—a relief to all concerned.

An Alphabet of Home-Garden Vegetables, Fruits, and Herbs

Artichokes (Globe Artichokes)

The globe artichoke is a perennial. The prized edible part is the leafy flower bud, plucked before it becomes a purplish thistle-like flower. (The tuber is the edible part of the Jerusalem-artichoke, an unrelated plant that belongs to the sunflower tribe but is often called just "artichoke.") Commercial globe artichoke production is confined to favored, cool coastal sections of California. Home gardeners in that region and in some other places with mild winters and cool summers can grow this vegetable. Where winters are severe, as in Maine, Michigan, and Minnesota, for example, forget it. Adventurous souls in the more benign regions of the North and South have had some success with globe artichokes—Thomas Jefferson is known to have grown them at Monticello, his home in Virginia, from plants or seeds imported from France. We know of two plants that have produced for three years running in a garden on Long Island, New York.

Growing Suggestions for Artichokes

EXPOSURE AND SOIL: Sun or partial shade (the partial shade where summers are excessively hot and dry). A rich, well-drained soil that does not dry out. Add peat moss, compost, or rotted manure to the soil before planting. Seek a protected position if you don't live in one of the favored growing areas, so the plants have a chance to survive winter and to escape disturbance when the garden is dug.

WHEN TO PLANT: In the spring.

SOWING AND PLANTING: West Coasters have no trouble finding dormant plants in local nurseries. For planting elsewhere, young plants are offered by a few mail-order nurseries (Gurney Seed & Nursery Company, Yankton, South Dakota 57078, and California Nursery Company, Niles, California 94536 offer plants), and seeds are sold by most mail-order houses. It takes two years from seed for plants to reach bearing size. Sow seed indoors in early spring in peat or Jiffy-7 pots, about six weeks before frosts will end outdoors. Plant the seedlings 3 feet apart in the garden. In late fall, cut back the top growth and tie the remaining growth together over the crowns. Mulch the plants with straw or hay and pray that they will survive the winter.

HARVESTING: Harvest the buds—the artichokes—while they are still tight. Even if the "leaves" of the buds are too tough to eat—a common complaint in Northern regions with hot, dry summers—the delicious hearts should be tender and flavorful.

Asparagus

The merit of asparagus in the home garden is its permanence. Once established, the roots send up succulent shoots spring after spring, making this one of the longest-lived of food crops as well as one of the most delectable. Asparagus needs space, if you are to have enough spears for fresh use in spring and for freezing or canning. Fifty well-established plants will supply an asparagus-eating family of four, leaving some surplus for freezing, or 10 plants per 15 running feet of row will supply one person. An asparagus planting does not reach maximum yield until about its fifth year, but after that you can count on from 10 to 15 years or more of harvesting. The best position for an asparagus planting, which must not be disturbed when routine digging is done, is at one end or along one side of a vegetable garden. If your plot is pint-sized, another location, outside the vegetable garden, may be feasible. Asparagus plants, after harvesting ends, shoot up quickly, become feathery-foliaged and tall, 3 to 5 feet or so. The effect is as ornamental and densely green as a row of shrubs. So you may want to sacrifice a strip of lawn and make an asparagus hedge or border. Lower-growing plants, either flowers or other vegetables, can be planted in front of your handsome asparagus row.

Growing Suggestions for Asparagus

EXPOSURE AND SOIL: Sun. A well-drained, deeply prepared and humus-rich soil. Rotted manure, rich compost, seaweed and/or peat moss will help supply the necessary humus. Add to the soil 4 to 5 pounds of 5-10-5 fertilizer per 100 square feet. If your soil tests very acid (below 6.5 pH), ground limestone should be added, too, at the rate of 3 to 5 pounds per 100 square feet.

WHEN TO PLANT: In early spring. Buy one-year-old dormant roots from mail-order nurseries or local garden centers.

SPACING AND PLANTING: Set asparagus plants from 12 to 18 inches apart in rows from 3 to 5 feet apart. Where space is limited, you can use the lesser planting distances, but don't be fooled by the small size of the one-year crowns or roots received from nurseries—each single crown will increase to many, and asparagus plants in the summer develop into tall bushy plants—hence the need for widely spaced rows.

Place the crowns or roots, with the center bud at the top, in wide trenches about 8 inches deep (the depth can be less in heavy clay soils). Then cover with about 2 inches of soil. As strong new growth appears, continue to add soil a little at a time until the trench is filled. Deeper planting, once customary, is unnecessary.

Feeding asparagus with 5-10-5 (2 to 3 pounds per 100 square feet) or a similar fertilizer once a year—in spring or after cutting has stopped (see "Harvesting," below)—and adding compost and rich organic materials are aids to keeping the plants in top shape for their annual spring production.

When weeding asparagus, cultivation must be very shallow, or the roots will be harmed.

HARVESTING: One year after planting, you can harvest spears for about three weeks. In the following spring and thereafter, harvesting can continue over a two-month period, so long as the spears remain chunky. Rather than cutting, snap the spears off at ground level with your fingers when a height of about 6 inches is reached. This is better than using a knife beneath the soil level—that can injure the buds of future shoots. Most, if not all, of a home-grown asparagus spear is tender and edible—which is not, alas, true of the spears of commercially grown "grass."

Beans

The snap beans you serve from your garden will be crisp yet tender, full of flavor and nutrition. Snap beans have green or yellow pods that can be nearly flat or rounded, according to variety, and they grow on bushes or climbing plants. How do you decide whether to grow bush varieties or the climbing or pole kinds? The choice depends mostly on the size of your plot: average or larger gardens have room for both, but the postage-stamp plot gains space for other vegetables when pole varieties are chosen—these use vertical rather than horizontal space.

Bush snap beans are just about the easiest of all vegetables to grow. From seeds-in-the-ground to harvest time takes 50 days or so. Pole snap beans are not difficult to grow, either, but you must provide support for the vines—sometimes a nuisance for a busy weekender. Pole varieties usually need about 60 days to produce pods ready for picking, but then their harvest season lasts much longer than for bush beans.

LIMA BEANS. Snap beans are most people's favorite, but lima beans, fresh-shelled from pods of home-grown plants, offer a surprising taste treat. Lima beans are available in both bush and climbing or pole varieties, but they require a longer growing time than snap beans. If your garden is small, forget lima beans, but consider them if you can sacrifice row space to a vegetable that takes from 65 to 70 days before harvesting begins. (The variety 'Henderson Bush Lima' takes 65 days.) Pole lima beans need an even longer growing season before pods can be picked—about 85 days—but this is no problem if you live in the South or another warm-climate region.

BROAD OR FAVA BEANS. The broad bean is a vegetable novelty only to Americans—it is well known on the Continent and in Great Britain. Also known as the fava bean, it is a possibility for cold-climate gardens because the large seeds must be sown in late winter or very early spring—at a time when space is abundant in all gardens, though you may have to wear gloves against the cold as you sow the seeds. From seed to harvest requires about 65 to 80 days, with the plants making their major growth during cool weather. Harvesting is in late spring or early summer, after which the plants quickly succumb to hot weather, leaving space for a succession crop such as snap beans, Swiss chard, or what-have-you. Broad beans form unique, even ornamental, plants, tall and bushy, with glossy bold foliage and pods about 6 to 7 inches long. The pods are filled with large, flat beans which must be shelled like lima beans. The plants can become so heavy with pods that some sort of support is suggested—one or two horizontal cords stretched between two posts would be adequate.

SOY BEANS AND BEANS FOR DRYING. If you have plenty of garden space, you may want to consider growing soy beans. The tough pods are not ready to have their tender edible seeds shelled out until about 100 days after sowing. Soy beans can be used fresh from the pods while still green—pick them before the pods turn yellow—or, as with lima beans and most other beans, the pods can be allowed to mature on the plants and then picked and shelled for use as dry beans or to produce bean sprouts. Other beans to grow for drying are kidney, white marrow, and dwarf horticultural (cranberry) beans. If you have the space for these long-season vegetables, they are well worth growing and storing for the winter to come, after they have been well dried out in an airy place and separated from the pods and trash.

Growing Suggestions for Beans

EXPOSURE AND SOIL: Sun. Well-drained soil of average fertility. Sprinkle on about 2 pounds of 5-10-5 fertilizer per 100 square feet and work into soil before sowing. Broad or fava beans prefer a soil rich in organic matter, such as compost or rotted manure. Prepare the soil for broad beans in the fall, rather than waiting until early spring, when the soil may be too wet to work.

WHEN TO PLANT: Broad or fava beans must be planted early—between March 15 and April 1 in the latitude of New York City—or, in other words, when you sow peas, whether you live to the north or the south of that latitude. All other beans are heat lovers and like warm weather and warm soil. In most Northern areas, the first sowing would be about May 15. Then make a second sowing in about two weeks.

SOWING AND PLANTING: All bean seeds are large, so they are a pleasure to sow. If they're planted at the correct distance, no later thinning is required. Make a furrow about 2 inches deep and space the seeds in the row about 3 to 4 inches apart and cover with soil. If your space is limited, allow 15 inches between rows; 18 to 24 inches would be better.

Since climbing beans are twiners, poles make the best supports. These should be firmly set in the ground before sowing, so that they protrude about 5 to 6 feet above the ground. Space the poles from 18 to 24 inches apart and plant 2 to 3 seeds per pole. Or you can make teepees of 3 poles apiece, tied together at the top; space the teepees about 4 to 5 feet apart. Or use a single pole, but create a teepee with pieces of heavy cord radiating in Maypole fashion to short stakes set in the soil.

A later sowing of pole beans can be made around sunflower plants, which will serve as supports. There are many ways to train beans—use your ingenuity. But avoid wire supports, as they get too hot for the plants.

HARVESTING: Pick snap beans before the seeds swell in the pods, while the pods are tender. And keep picking, daily if necessary, for as soon as any pods are allowed to mature, the yield slows or stops. A single sowing of bush snap beans should produce abundantly for 20 days, sometimes longer. Pole snap beans yield considerably longer. Lima and fava beans, which have a shorter harvesting period, are ready when the beans are prominent in the pods.

PITFALLS: If bean plants fail to appear above ground after sowing, you may have planted them too early. Cold, wet springs can cause the seeds to rot. The opposite is true of fava beans. Too late a sowing, and the plants just sulk.

Slugs sometimes feast on bean seedlings. Dust with rotenone if beetles appear on the foliage. Avoid handling bean plants when the foliage is wet; to do so will encourage disease.

Beets

You may think of the beet as a rather "neutral" vegetable for the home garden, but before passing it by, consider succulent, tender beet greens or tops, cooked with the small sugar-sweet beets still attached. This can be a special treat from the small garden, since beets do not require a lot of space. A 10-foot row should be enough for two people, a 20-foot row for a family of four.

Growing Suggestions for Beets

EXPOSURE AND SOIL: Sun. A well-drained soil containing humus (add compost, peat moss, rotted manure, etc.) that is never allowed to become bone-dry.

WHEN TO PLANT: Beets are cold-hardy. Seeds can be sown early, even while there are still frosts, which can be about April 1 in many Northern regions. Follow, where space permits, with successive sowings up until about July 1.

SOWING AND PLANTING: Sow the seeds in a furrow about 1 inch deep, spacing them 1/2 inch apart, and cover with soil. Allow 12 to 15 inches between rows. No matter how carefully you sow the seeds, you may be alarmed at how crowded the seedlings seem. This is because each beet "seed" is really a seed "ball" that contains three to five or more potential plants. So the rows must be thinned, but if you enjoy eating fresh beet greens, wait to do the job until the tops are large enough to fill the pot. Continue the thinning process as the roots enlarge. Be sure to water the plants during dry spells.

HARVESTING: For beet greens, eat both tops and roots. The most tender beet roots are those 2 inches or less across, which will be ready for harvesting within 48 to 50 days.

PITFALLS: Woody, tasteless beets are often the result of a check in growth caused by drought. Watering when the rains fail insures good quality.

Blueberries

On suburban properties where space is lacking for a proper "fruit garden," blueberry bushes can be planted for year-long enjoyment, the berry harvest in summer being a bonus. The shrubs, which grow eventually to about 5 or 6 feet, make a fine hedge or background for vegetables or flower gardens, or as a boundary between properties.

For a family of four, ten bushes (two plants each of five varieties) will provide sufficient berries for fresh use, with a surplus for freezing and preserving. (A mixture of varieties, usually two of each variety, is required for pollination so berries will set. Most nurseries offer a collection of varieties selected for cross-pollination.) By planting early-to-late varieties, a harvest of berries from early to midsummer can be expected.

Growing Suggestions for Blueberries

EXPOSURE AND SOIL: The best berries are produced from plants in full sun, but quite good harvests can be gathered in half shade. The soil should be acid (around pH 5) and rich in humus. You can hardly overdo the organic matter for blueberries. Peat moss is a good source of organic matter and should be mixed in generous amounts into the planting holes. If your soil grows rhododendrons, azaleas, camellias, and other plants that prefer acid soils, you'll have no trouble with blueberries. Otherwise, you had better consult a local nurseryman or your County Agent about the feasibility of your growing them.

WHEN TO PLANT: Early spring or fall.

PLANTING: See above. Set bushes about 6 to 8 feet apart. Then apply a thick mulch, from 3 to 6 inches deep, of decayed sawdust, wood chips, or half rotted leaves (leafmold) or compost. A mixture of all can be used. Maintain the mulch from year to year, adding more as needed. In spring, apply a complete fertilizer or an organic fertilizer such as cottonseed meal at the rate of about 1 ounce of fertilizer per plant for each year of age up to eight years. (Two-year-old plants are usually shipped from nurseries, so each plant would require 2 ounces of fertilizer the first year.) Usually a second application of fertilizer (use a nitrogenous one such as ammonium sulfate) is made about the middle of June, at the rate of $1/2$ pound for a plant that is over three years old. When sawdust is the mulch, twice as much fertilizer should be used—about $1\frac{1}{2}$ times as much as would be used when there is a mulch of leaves or wood chips.

HARVESTING: Pick only ripe berries, as the berries do not become sweeter—although they will become softer—after they are removed from the bushes. Partially ripe berries are sour. After the berries show color, wait a week before harvesting. However, the berries on a plant never ripen all at once, so frequent picking is necessary.

PITFALLS: The birds! They can decimate the crop, especially in seasons when there seems to be a lack of other food or during droughts, but in other years the birds may ignore most of the berries. Light-weight netting is available to throw over the bushes, and using it is the only sure way of saving the berries for yourself.

Broccoli

Even a few broccoli plants—as few as three or four—are worth growing, because each plant is a mighty producer through summer and the crisp autumn weather. The major edible portions are the clusters of flower buds, but all parts of the plant are good to eat except the roots and lower stems. Broccoli is a favorite for home freezing.

Growing Suggestions for Broccoli

EXPOSURE AND SOIL: Sun. Average garden soil. A complete fertilizer such as 10-10-10 at the rate of $1\frac{1}{2}$ to 2 pounds per 50 square feet, can be mixed into the soil before planting.

WHEN TO PLANT: In early spring for summer harvests, and early summer to midsummer for fall harvests.

SOWING AND PLANTING: In the spring, you have a choice of sowing seeds indoors about six weeks before the time for planting in the garden; or buying young transplants at a garden center for immediate outdoor planting; or sowing seeds directly in the garden at the time when you sow radishes. If you sow seeds indoors, press two seeds into each Jiffy-7 pot, and pinch off the weaker of the two seedlings a week or two after germination. In the garden, transplant the seedlings, either home-grown or purchased, into either rows or blocks, allowing 15 to 18 inches between the plants, 30 inches or so between rows.

HARVESTING: Begins 60 to 110 days from seeding, depending somewhat on the variety and on weather conditions. The big center cluster forms first—one cluster will often be enough for three or four diners. Cut the clusters while the buds are still tight and before they even begin to open into tiny yellow flowers. The many side shoots on the plants will continue to form clusters, so the harvest will last for a month or more.

PITFALLS: Cabbage worms and loopers, as green as the plants, almost always appear. Hand-picking these off, if you have only three or four plants, can work pretty well, but dusting or spraying with Sevin is the usual recommendation. A rotenone dust also gives quite good control. (Follow the container directions when using *all* sprays and dusts.)

Brussels Sprouts

The edible portions of this cold-hardy plant, the little "sprouts" that resemble miniature cabbages, reach their flavor peak in late autumn. Along with other cabbage relatives, they help keep many gardens in production after cool weather arrives. The sprouts are packed into the leaf axils up the thick main stem of the plant, and one plant may produce a hundred or so of them. Knowing this can help you decide how many plants to grow. The sprouts freeze very well.

Growing Suggestions for Brussels Sprouts

EXPOSURE AND SOIL: The same as for broccoli, above.

WHEN TO PLANT: Not too early, since the best sprouts form in the fall about 90 to 110 days after seeding. Start plants in late spring to early summer so that the sprouts will mature in the cooler days of autumn.

SOWING AND PLANTING: Sow seeds in a short row in the garden in furrows ½ inch deep; thin the seedlings and later transplant them to 24 inches apart. Allow 24 to 36 inches between rows. Or purchase seedlings—if you can—as 10 plants should be more than enough for most families.

HARVESTING: Sprouts begin to form in the fall as the weather cools. Harvest the bottom sprouts first; cut them off with a knife while they are still tight and firm. Remove the lower leaves from the stalk as the harvest continues. Sprouts and plants will withstand heavy frosts and even prolonged freezing.

PITFALLS: These are ungainly plants, sprawling and space-consuming in a small garden.

Cabbage and Chinese Cabbage

Some people eat a lot of cabbage, others hardly taste it from one year to another. Let's say that cabbage heads are often in good condition and good supply in markets—and are often a good buy, too. So perhaps it hardly pays the home gardener to bother—yet that garden-fresh cole slaw can taste delicious. Trying to choose among the various cabbages presented in seed catalogues can be a heady experience. You must decide whether to grow early varieties (60 to 70 days to maturity), or late or winter varieties (90 to 100 days), or a combination of both, which will give you a long season of fresh cabbage.

Chinese or celery cabbage is somewhat different, growing in large, tall, cylindrical heads. It has a much milder flavor and more delicate texture than ordinary cabbage. It, too, is hardy and frost-resistant and has about the same growing requirements as Brussels sprouts. Space the plants about 10 inches apart.

Growing Suggestions for Cabbage

EXPOSURE AND SOIL: Sun, or partial light shade, if unavoidable. Deep, humus-rich soil that does not dry out easily. Mix compost, rotted manure, peat moss, or other organic material, plus a commercial fertilizer (10-10-10, or 5-10-5) at the rate of 1½ to 2 pounds per 50 square feet, into the soil before planting. Do not plant cabbages and their relatives (broccoli, kale, cauliflower, and Brussels sprouts) in the same location year after year. Rotate their positions with those of non-cabbage crops to avoid disease problems.

WHEN TO PLANT: Sow seeds of early varieties indoors in March in the North for transplanting to the garden about four to six weeks later. Sow seeds of late or winter varieties outdoors in midspring.

SOWING AND PLANTING: Sow seeds in small flats and transplant into peat pots or Jiffy-7 pots. Grow the seedlings at an indoor temperature of about 60° F. At this temperature, plants will require only minimum hardening off before being set in the garden. Or buy seedlings from a garden-center nursery and set out. Small-headed cabbages should be spaced about 12 inches apart in rows 24 inches apart. Larger varieties need more room.

HARVESTING: Begins in 65 to 100 days from seed sowing, depending on the variety. Heads are ready to be cut from their stalks when they feel firm.

PITFALLS: Warm weather causes heads to split. Harvest any split heads at once. The same kind of weather can prevent head formation. Cabbage worms—surprise—like cabbages! Try sprinkling kosher or other coarse salt among the outer leaves when you see the worms. Two or three applications are usually necessary. If the salt doesn't work, there's always Sevin or rotenone, applied according to directions on the package.

Carrots

Young carrots, finger-long, are one of the great delicacies of a home vegetable garden and one you can't find in a supermarket. Carrots are also one of the few crops that you can grow to a larger size—with quality still better than that of the store product—for harvesting in fall and storage in winter. Carrots can be eaten raw in salads, cooked in butter, or frozen. They're used in cakes and tortes and jams, too.

Growing Suggestions for Carrots

EXPOSURE AND SOIL: Sun; however, a few hours of fairly light shade a day are acceptable. Very heavy clay or rocky soil does not produce the best carrots (see below for variety suggestions if you have such soil). Soil should be loose and well-drained. Add about 3 pounds of 5-10-5 fertilizer per 100 square feet, mixing it well with the existing soil.

WHEN TO PLANT: Same time as for beets. Since the seeds of carrots are slow to germinate, the time-honored custom is to mix radish seeds with them, so the quick-appearing radish seedlings mark the row and help space the carrots.

SOWING AND PLANTING: Sow seeds in shallow furrows about $1/2$ inch deep. Allow 8 to 18 inches between rows. When carrot seedlings are 2 to 3 inches tall, thin them to stand 1 to 2 inches apart. One to three sowings, the last about July 1, can be made if space permits.

HARVESTING: Pull carrots at any time the size suits you. For winter storage, you can keep the carrots, with their tops removed, in a box of moist sand in a cool part of the basement. Carrots can remain in the soil until late fall.

VARIETY SUGGESTIONS: Choose your carrot variety according to soil type. Short, stumpy varieties, such as 'Oxheart,' 'Short 'n Sweet,' and 'Goldenhart,' are recommended for heavy, rocky soils. Longer, slender varieties, such as 'Nantes Half Long' and 'Goldpak,' do well in deep, loose soil. Most other varieties are suited to average garden soils.

Cauliflower

The freshest cauliflower is what you grow yourself—unless you are as lucky as we are and live in a region famous for its commercial production, so that you can buy heads fresh-cut along the highway. However, success with this vegetable in the home garden can be elusive. It is a challenge to grow where summers are hot and dry. It also consumes precious garden space over a long period—90 days are needed from seed to harvest. If you want to try it, stick to the 'Snowball' and the purple-headed varieties, which should form heads in the fall. Ten or so plants can feed a family, with a surplus for freezing.

Growing Suggestions for Cauliflower

EXPOSURE AND SOIL: Sun. Humus-rich soil.

WHEN TO PLANT: In early summer.

SOWING AND PLANTING: Sow seeds in a short furrow about ¼ inch deep, then thin and transplant the seedlings into rows or blocks, with plants 12 to 18 inches apart, the rows 24 to 36 inches apart.

HARVESTING: To obtain pristine-white heads, you must fold or tie the large leaves over the heads to protect them from the sun, beginning when the head—the flower bud—is 2 to 3 inches in diameter. Do this when the plants are dry. No such procedure is necessary for the purple-headed varieties. Actually, blanching is only cosmetic and affects neither flavor nor nutrition, so you can eliminate this step if you wish. Heads are ready to cut when the individual florets or "curds" are firm and tight and have not begun to separate.

PITFALLS: The usual caterpillars that prey on members of the cabbage family—see "Broccoli." Hot weather may prevent head formation.

Celery and Celeriac

Celery and its close relative celeriac, or knob celery, or celery root, are not the easiest nor the most practical vegetables for home gardens. Both require a long growing period from the time of seed sowing to harvest—about 180 days for celery and 200 days or so for celeriac. Their soil requirements are also special. Although celeriac usually isn't harvested until its thickened, knobby base is about 2 to 2½ inches in diameter, celery is edible at any stage.

Growing Suggestions for Celery and Celeriac

EXPOSURE AND SOIL: Sun. Rich, moist soil that does not dry out. This means plenty of organic matter—compost, rotted manure, peat moss, and so on—and frequent soakings from the hose. Mix 5-10-5 or other commerical fertilizer (about 2½ pounds to 50 feet of row) into the soil before planting, and apply a liquid fertilizer to the soil about every three weeks.

WHEN TO PLANT: Sow seeds indoors in late February or early March.

SOWING AND PLANTING: Seeds germinate very slowly. Sow in small flats in Jiffy-Mix or Redi-Earth, 5 to 8 seeds to an inch, ½ inch deep. Keep warm (about 70° F.) and enclose the seed flat in a plastic bag so the planting medium will not dry out. Thin the seedlings to stand 1½ inches apart in the flats. Seedlings can be planted in the garden about 10 to 12 weeks after sowing, or after night temperatures outdoors no longer fall below about 45° F. Space the plants 6 to 8 inches apart all around. If you choose to blanch celery (to make the stalks whiter and less bitter), do it in the fall. Enclose each plant in a tall paper collar, or run black plastic or freezer paper along each side of the row, banking it with soil to hold it in place. (Banking with soil alone tends to rot the stalks.) The stalks should be well blanched after 10 to 20 days. Don't blanch more plants at a time than you want to harvest.

HARVESTING: Dig celeriac after its knobs are 2 to 2½ inches in diameter; dig or cut celery as needed (see blanching information above). Both vegetables can be stored after harvest by covering their roots with moist soil in a cellar or a coldframe that is cool but frost-free.

PITFALLS: If celery or celeriac form seed heads in early summer and do not develop properly, it means the plants were set out too early and suffered from the cold. Drought will also check growth.

Chard (Swiss Chard)

Chard is such a pretty plant that it's worth a place in the food garden, if only a short row, for its ornamental appearance. The edible parts are the broad white (or red) stalks and the juicy leaves which, like New Zealand-spinach, are gathered all summer and through the fall for greens. In fact, R. Milton Carleton, a good vegetable grower and one who appreciates good food, recommends cooking Swiss chard and New Zealand-spinach together for an intriguing blend of flavors.

Growing Suggestions for Chard

EXPOSURE AND SOIL: Sun. Average garden soil.

TIME TO PLANT: Early to mid-spring.

SOWING AND PLANTING: Swiss chard is actually a beet, so several seedlings will emerge from each "seed," which is more correctly a seed ball. Sow seed in furrows about 1/2 inch deep, allowing 12 to 24 inches between rows. Then thin the seedlings to 6 inches apart—wait to do this until thinnings are large enough to be cooked.

HARVESTING: Pick the outer stalks when they are about 6 inches long, beginning in early summer (60 days from sowing). Cut off at base with a knife, leaving the heart of the plant intact to go on growing.

Corn

The big garden plot, say 50 by 100 feet, is the best place to grow sweet corn, although it isn't ruled out if you have only 30 by 30 feet. Don't think you can just squeeze in a single row of corn somewhere. Corn should always be planted in blocks of at least three rows of the same variety in order for pollination, necessary to develop the kernels, to occur. (The pollen is spread by the wind, so imperfect pollination is bound to result when a single row is planted.) If you have the space, try to grow three different varieties, not only to stretch the harvest of corn for immediate use, but to supply ears for freezing and canning. You'll need about 5 feet of row for each corn-devouring member of the family.

Growing Suggestions for Corn

EXPOSURE AND SOIL: Full sun. Well-drained, fertile soil. Before sowing, spread 3 pounds of 5-10-10 or 5-10-5 fertilizer per 100 feet of row and mix it well into the soil. A second application at the same rate can be made alongside the rows when the plants are up to your knees. Don't neglect water during droughts—corn plants are very thirsty.

WHEN TO PLANT: When the weather and soil have become warm, and at 10-day intervals thereafter up to about July 1 in most Northern regions. Or plant all your corn at once, but select early, midseason, and late varieties to extend the harvest.

SOWING AND PLANTING: Sow seeds 1 inch deep and 4 to 6 inches apart in rows 2½ to 3 feet apart. Thin seedlings to 8 to 12 inches apart. Always plant at least 3 or 4 rows of each variety in a block to insure cross-pollination. Corn is one vegetable whose seeds don't keep, so buy fresh seeds each year.

HARVESTING: If you don't pick your corn at the right time, you might as well buy ears in the supermarket. The silk should be dried or beginning to shrivel; sample ears should be plump and the kernels, milky. Since the ears begin to lose their sugar as soon as picked, the sooner they can be served or processed, the better.

VARIETY SUGGESTIONS: There are many excellent hybrid varieties from which to choose. One of our favorites is 'Silver Queen' (92 days), a long, white-eared hybrid of extraordinary sweetness. Earlier varieties are 'Illini Xtra-Sweet' (85 days), recommended for freezing as well as table use; 'Honey and Cream' (78 days), an outstanding early variety with mixed gold and white kernels. Recommended for freezing as whole ears are two miniature corn varieties, 'Golden Midget' and 'White Midget,' which bear ears from 4½ to 6 inches long. They are possibilities for medium-sized gardens, since their stalks grow to only 3 feet. (Sow their seeds 6 to 8 inches apart in rows that are 2 feet apart.)

PITFALLS: Hybrid varieties are resistant to diseases, and some varieties are even resistant to such pests as the corn earworm. ('Honey and Cream,' for one, resists the corn earworm.) It's usually easier to cut out wormy portions of the ears than to follow a spraying or dusting program. However, Sevin can be dusted or sprayed on the foliage and silk, first when tassels emerge and every four to five days through the growth of silk; this is to control the corn borer and corn earworm. Poorly filled ears are result of incomplete pollination. Follow the block-planting recommendations above for good pollination.

Cresses

There are several kinds of cress that add zing to spring salads. Curled or garden cress is low-growing and fast—in the garden it's ready to eat in a week, and, it can be cut often thereafter until flowers appear and it becomes too peppery. Upland cress is similar to curled cress, except that its foliage resembles that of watercress. "Indian cress" is an old name for the nasturtium of flower gardens. Its leaves and flower petals have a pleasant and peppery taste when mixed in salads, or used in sandwiches with cream cheese.

Watercress can be grown in a garden—if you have moist soil, say near a brook or a natural spring or a spring-fed pond or a ditch; but alas, not many are so blessed.

Growing Suggestions for Cresses

EXPOSURE AND SOIL: Sun or light shade. Average garden soil, with the exception of watercress, which prefers to grow in shallow water, although it does well in moist soil.

WHEN TO PLANT: Upland and curled cress in early spring; or plant in late summer for fall use. Seeds of nasturtium should be sown in mid-spring after heavy frosts have ceased. This is a double-duty plant; enjoy its beauty in the flower garden, and pick it for the table. Sow watercress in small pots in spring and transplant when 2 or 3 inches high.

SOWING AND PLANTING: Sow in short rows in very shallow furrows, or scatter the seed in patches. The thinnings can be used in salads or sandwiches. Soak nasturtium seeds overnight in water before sowing them about ½ inch deep. Curled or upland cress can be sown in pots indoors for winter use. Keep the pots in a cool but sunny window.

HARVESTING: Cut as needed—usually within a week or so for curled and upland cress. These cresses have a short life, so several sowings can be made. Gather nasturtium leaves as needed all summer. Watercress is a perennial; gather it whenever it shows fresh growth.

Cucumbers

Although the cucumber is a vining vegetable that can use lots of space, it is worth growing in the smallest garden because there is such a world of difference between the tough-skinned, often wax-coated cucumbers shipped to markets and the cucumbers plucked at home. Cucumbers are so prolific and so quick to begin production (harvesting can begin in from 48 to 65 days) that five or six plants can provide a family with enough cukes to eat fresh and for pickling. Perfectly good pickles can be made from any variety, but if you plan a major pickle project, select varieties especially recommended for that purpose in seed catalogues. A few such are 'Tiny Dill' (55 days); 'Pioneer' (50 days); 'Burpless Hybrid' (62 days). The aforementioned 'Tiny Dill,' as well as 'Cherokee 7' (60 days) and

'Patio Pik' (48 days), are compact enough in their vining habits to permit them to be grown in the smallest gardening space, including boxes and tubs.

Space can be saved with all cucumber vines by training them upwards rather than letting them sprawl. Chicken wire, though often satisfactory, can burn the tendrils in very hot weather. Better is string netting, offered by most mail-order nurseries and seed houses, which can be stretched between two posts.

Growing Suggestions for Cucumbers

EXPOSURE AND SOIL: Sun. Humus-rich soil that is well-drained but retains moisture.

WHEN TO PLANT: Mid- to late spring, after soil and weather have warmed. Seed can be sown indoors in peat or Jiffy-7 pots about four weeks before outdoor sowing would be safe. After setting the plants in the garden, you may want to give them the protection of Hotkaps (see page 88).

SOWING AND PLANTING: Sow seeds 1 inch deep about 4 inches apart, if vines are to be trained upwards. Otherwise, thin plants to about 12 inches apart, allowing 3 to 4 feet between rows. Mulching cucumbers with black plastic, or with hay or another organic mulch, helps keep the shallow roots moist.

HARVESTING: When cucumber fruits are ripe (bloated, over-sized and yellowish or orange), it's too late! So pick them before their ultimate size is reached, when the skin is bright green and the spines are just starting to soften, and before the blossom end begins to show a large white patch. Pick often to prevent large fruits from dragging down vines trained to a fence or other support. In warm, sunny weather, the fruits grow fast, so vines need daily picking if production isn't to be checked by overripe fruits. For tiny sour pickles in the French manner (*cornichons*—see the recipe section), pick the fruits when they're a mere 1½ inches long.

PITFALLS: Today's hybrids seem remarkably resistant to troubles. The biggest problem is the fault of the grower—not removing fruits before they become overlarge or actually ripe.

Eggplant

The eggplant has skyrocketed in popularity in recent years. Even though it takes about 70 to 80 days from seed sowing to the ripening of the beautiful fruits, the wait does not seem to deter home gardeners. Three or four plants are about all that a small garden can support, but the plants are so attractive in flower and fruit that they can be grown outside the vegetable garden when space is limited there. Try them in a flower garden or in front of shrubbery, if there is ample sunshine. Eggplants do well in tubs on sun-drenched roof gardens or terraces. You can grow them from seed or buy transplants, always available from local outlets.

Growing Suggestions for Eggplant

EXPOSURE AND SOIL: Full sun. Humus-rich soil, enriched with about 2½ to 3 pounds of 5-10-5 fertilizer per 100 square feet.

WHEN TO PLANT: Sow seed early indoors (see below); plant outdoors after soil and weather have warmed.

SOWING AND PLANTING: Start seeds indoors about two months

before thoroughly warm days begin outside. Grow under fluorescent lights in peat pots. Plant outdoors about two to three weeks after danger of frost has passed. Space about 3 feet apart in each direction.

HARVESTING: The fruits can be cut off at any stage after they are large enough to handle, but always before the skin loses its shiny finish. The size of fruit varies among varieties, so consult catalogue descriptions for typical fruit sizes. Eggplants past their prime are generally very seedy. Try tiny-fruited varieties for preserving.

PITFALLS: Theoretically, if your garden produces good tomatoes, you should be successful with eggplant. This doesn't always follow, though. Setting the plants out too early in cold climates is a common mistake. In some seasons the weather, if unusually cloudy and cool, can hamper fruit production. Keep the dust gun loaded with an all-purpose vegetable dust and use it against flea beetles, which riddle the foliage with tiny punctures, mostly in early summer. Hand-pick and destroy any Colorado potato bugs that may appear on the plants.

Kale and Collards

These two members of the cabbage family are grown for greens, produced mostly in fall and winter, although collards sown early will be ready in summer. Though not everyone's favorites, they have merit and are excellent nutritionally. Both plants have their regional partisans, collards in the South and kale in the North. Both are hardy enough in their regions to be left in the ground, ready for picking as needed, throughout the early winter and sometimes even longer. Collards are more heat-resistant than kale, but this vegetable, too, seems to taste better after frosty weather arrives.

Growing Suggestions for Kale and Collards

EXPOSURE AND SOIL: Sun, although both plants will tolerate some shade each day. A humus-rich soil. About 5 pounds of 10-6-4 or a similar commercial fertilizer per 50 square feet can be mixed with the soil before planting.

WHEN TO PLANT: Collard seeds: Sow directly in the garden in early spring for summer harvest, or in early summer for an autumn harvest. Kale seeds: Sow seeds in midsummer for an autumn and winter harvest.

SOWING AND PLANTING: Sow seeds in furrows ½ inch deep in rows 18 to 24 inches apart. Gradually thin the plants to stand 8 to 15 inches apart. Removal of surplus plants can be delayed until the thinnings are large enough to eat.

HARVESTING: Kale matures in from 55 to 65 days from seed; collards are ready in from 70 to 85 days. Harvest the whole plants, or remove leaves as needed.

PITFALLS: Kale does poorly in heat. Don't plant too many of either of these vegetables until you have tried growing a sample of each.

Kohlrabi

The edible parts of this odd-appearing vegetable are the swollen or bulblike green section of the stem above the root, and the more tender of the leaves. The flavor of kohlrabi falls between that of a mild cabbage and a turnip. Kohlrabi is a cool-season crop, as are its relatives kale and collards. Although considered a novelty by most Americans, once tried, it may end as a welcome staple.

Growing Suggestions for Kohlrabi

EXPOSURE AND SOIL: As for cabbage, see page 48.

WHEN TO PLANT: For early to midsummer harvest in regions where summer nights remain cool, sow seeds in the open ground in early spring. For autumn harvests, sow seeds about 8 weeks before hard frosts are due. (Ask your County Agent—see page 18—for frost dates for your area.

SOWING AND PLANTING: Sow seeds in furrows about ¹⁄₂ inch deep, spacing the rows about 12 to 18 inches apart. Thin plants to about 4 inches apart.

HARVESTING: Cut the swollen portions of the stems when they reach 2 to 3 inches in diameter, about 50 to 55 days from time of sowing. Before cooking, peel and remove any woody portions of the "bulb."

PITFALLS: Harvest promptly, or "bulbs" will become woody.

Leeks

It's very satisfying to the good cook–good gardener to dig fresh leeks in fall or winter, rather than having to pay their market price (always high). The edible part of this mild-flavored onion relative is the fat, fleshy white stem and the tender lower portion of the green, straplike foliage. It's true that leeks require a little extra care and do take up a fair amount of space for quite a time before reaching maturity (about 130 days from seed to harvest). But leeks are very hardy and can be stored in place—they can be simply left in the garden through the winter in most regions, and dug and used as needed. Where winters are severe and snow cover is heavy, lift the leeks with some of the soil left around their roots and pack them close together, but upright in their original growing positions, in crates or boxes in a cool cellar or a coldframe. Fill the box with extra soil around the plants and keep the soil damp.

Growing Suggestions for Leeks

EXPOSURE AND SOIL: Sun. Humus-rich, well-prepared soil.

WHEN TO PLANT: Early spring.

SOWING AND PLANTING: Sow the seeds in the garden in furrows 1/4 inch deep, spacing the rows about 18 inches apart. Thin the seedlings to 4 to 6 inches apart. Young seedlings look discouragingly small for several weeks—they look, in fact, like newly germinated grass. Blanch the stems toward the end of summer, when the plants are about 6 inches high, by banking them with soil up to the point where the green replaces the white.

HARVESTING: Begins in midsummer, if the stems seem large enough, but it's usually fall or even winter before the stems are of a good size. (See above for storage.)

PITFALLS: Seedlings are tedious to thin and weed. Don't pull them up as unwanted grass.

Lettuce, Romaine, and Endive

Lettuce is surely one of the easiest vegetables for home growing, and one of the most rewarding: so many kinds of lettuce—

Bibb, for instance—found only in carriage-trade markets at high prices can be grown readily in the home garden. Although lettuce is a cool-season plant—it's mostly grown in the spring in the North and in the fall and winter in the South and in other mild climates— there are heat-resistant varieties that can extend the season. Some good ones are 'Ruby' (47 days), 'Salad Trim' (60 days), 'Oak Leaf' (40 days), and 'Deer Tongue' (80 days). A high-class variety for spring sowing is 'Bibb' and it now has several variations offered by seedsmen—including heat-resistant kinds—that are all beautiful as well as flavorful. Other outstanding varieties are 'Buttercrunch' (75 days); 'Tom Thumb' (65 days), perfect for limited space, such as window boxes; and 'Green Ice' and 'Salad Bowl,' both 45 days from seed to harvest and of the loosehead type, meaning that individual outer leaves can be taken as needed while the plant continues to produce new leaves.

Romaine or Cos lettuce (about 70 days) is the lettuce used in Caesar salad. It is self-blanching, growing in tight, upright heads with firm, crisp midribs.

The avid salad gardener may want to try endive or escarole and curly endive (these two are chicory rather than lettuce) for fall and winter.

Growing Suggestions for Lettuce

EXPOSURE AND SOIL: Sun or partial shade. Humus-rich soil that retains moisture. Mix organic matter very generously with your soil for lettuce; and also add a complete fertilizer, such as 5-10-5, at the rate of 2 to 3 pounds per 100 square feet.

WHEN TO PLANT: Throughout spring, and again from midsummer to early fall for late harvests.

SOWING AND PLANTING: Begin sowing lettuce in early spring in short rows, about 3 to 4 feet long, and continue with a succession of sowings every 10 to 20 days with different varieties, so salads can be varied and harvests extended. Switch to heat-resistant varieties as summer and warm weather approach. Don't plant lettuce seeds too deeply—about 1/2 inch or even less is sufficient—or too thickly, as thinning can be tedious. We prefer to sow the seeds in short rows; then we transplant the young seedlings, spacing them about 5 to 10 inches apart for heading varieties, closer for loose-leaf types. The extra time needed to transplant lettuce seedlings pays off in prettier plants that are also of better texture and longer-lasting than plants growing where they were sown. If you don't transplant your lettuce seedlings, be sure to thin them according to specifications for the variety given on the seed packet.

Lettuce transplants can be set out in nice, neat rows, or in blocks, or in circles, for that matter—put them almost anywhere in the garden, as most of them will have been used by the time their space is needed for other crops. (We often transplant lettuce seedlings into the asparagus border, for instance.)

Keep young plants well watered and fed. Old-fashioned liquid manure, made by soaking horse or cow manure in a barrel or tub of water, gives the plants a great boost, if used once a week or so. (Be careful of burning, however, since fresh manures can be strong—add enough water to the manure to make a weak tea-colored solution, and be sure to water the plants after applying the manure.) Fish emulsion, used according to label directions, is also great for lettuce.

HARVESTING: Pick lettuce at almost any stage, when either the leaves or the heads are large enough to eat. Pick just the outer leaves of loose-head types ('Salad Bowl,' 'Oakleaf,' 'Salad Trim,' 'Ruby,' 'Black-seeded Simpson,' etc.) as you require them—the plants will continue to grow and produce new leaves. Harvest the heading types as they "head" and before the centers begin to elongate to produce flower stalks—lettuce becomes bitter at this stage.

If you grow endive or curly endive for a fall or winter crop, it must be blanched to whiten the hearts and prevent bitterness. Tie the outer leaves together over their centers for about three weeks just before harvesting. These two are especially cold-hardy and will withstand autumn frosts and early winter if weather is not too severe. As winter progresses, the plants can be dug and replanted, close together, in a coldframe for protection.

PITFALLS: Slugs can chew big hunks out of lettuce, especially in spring and fall. Buy a commercial slug bait, available at garden centers, and use it carefully according to directions; or else try the beer-in-a-saucer method. We have yet to decide whether the slugs succumb to alcohol or just drown. In either case, sink the saucer into the soil far enough to make it easy for the slugs to guzzle (or drown in) the brew.

Muskmelons

Thought of as a fruit, this is a "dessert vegetable" from a vine that requires a lot of space and a long, hot season (about 75 to 95 days) with ample moisture. If you can supply these conditions, by all means plant a melon patch (see also "Watermelons"), preferably at one end of the garden where the vines can wander at will—and they will!—and won't be trodden upon every time you go into the garden. Experts suggest three vines for each person. (Note: The Gurney Seed & Nursery Company offers a 'Bush Muskmelon' (60 days) which bears 4- to 5-inch fruits and which is featured as a space-saver for small gardens.) People in mild climates can grow the elegant honeydew, casaba, and Cranshaw melons, which require even longer and warmer growing seasons. Elsewhere, gardeners should stick to the muskmelon or cantaloupe. Study catalogues for variety choices.

Growing Suggestions for Muskmelons

EXPOSURE AND SOIL: Full sun. Very rich soil, full of humus. Sandy soils that have been improved with ample organic matter, such as compost or rotted manure, are best, because they become warm earlier in the season than heavier soils.

WHEN TO PLANT: After soil and weather warm, in late spring. Or sow seeds indoors in Jiffy-7 or peat pots, two seeds to a pot, about four weeks before the normal frost-free date in your region. Pinch off the weaker seedling after a week or two of growth. For additional warmth and protection after setting out, cover the plants with Hotkaps (page 88).

SOWING AND PLANTING: When sowing indoors, seeds *must* go into peat pots or similar containers so there will be no disturbance of roots when the plants are set in the garden. Outdoors, sow seeds about ½ inch deep and 6 inches apart in rows spaced about 48 inches apart. Thin the seedlings to 18 inches apart. Apply a mulch. Some space can be saved by training the vines on a trellis, but usually some sort of sling must be provided to support the heavy fruits when melons are growing vertically. We have used the plastic net bags in which supermarket lemons are sold.

HARVESTING: Pick only when the stem of the fruit is easily slipped from the vine. Refrigerate or process melons for freezing at once, as muskmelons (unlike honeydew melons) do not continue to ripen after they are removed from the vines.

Okra

Okra is a decorative plant—not so surprising, since it is a kind of hibiscus—and a 15-foot row of plants in flower and pod (the edible portion) make a handsome hedge from 3 to 5 feet high. Since we don't have space for a proper okra planting, we grow several plants as a background among annual-flowering plants—a method that supplies enough pods to add to soups or to stew with peppers and tomatoes. Okra is a favorite in the South, where it performs especially well, because it is a tropical plant that needs all the warmth it can get.

Growing Suggestions for Okra

EXPOSURE AND SOIL: Sun. Well-drained, humus-rich soil that has been fertilized with a complete fertilizer, such as 5-10-5, at the rate of about 1 to 1½ pounds per 50 square feet.

WHEN TO PLANT: After the soil and weather have warmed in spring.

SOWING AND PLANTING: Sow seeds ½ to 1 inch deep, about 3 to 4 inches apart. Thin seedlings to 15 to 24 inches apart in the row.

HARVESTING: Pick the pods when they are only 2 to 3 inches long, or they will be too tough to use. During warm weather, daily picking is necessary so pod production won't stop. Pick with a length of stem so the pods won't lose their gelatinous juice.

PITFALLS: Letting the pods grow too large.

Onions

The most convenient way for the bona-fide vegetable gardener to obtain a supply of bona-fide onions is to plant "sets" in early spring. Sets are simply baby onions or bulblets that were grown from seed the previous year. Sets are sold in bags or by the pound in most local garden outlets and by mail-order companies. (Even supermarkets now offer bags of sets, so obtaining them is no problem.) The sets are planted in furrows like large seeds, quite close together. Proper spacing for development of large onions, about 2 to 4 inches, results when you pull some of the young green onions as scallions for use in salads.

Onions can also be grown in the home garden from seed. (Some authorities say your own seed-grown onions are superior in flavor to those grown from sets.) Onions from seed require a long growing season—100 days or so, depending on variety—to reach typical market size. However, the immature onions and thinnings of the rows can be harvested from early summer on. Young onion plants, sold in bunches by seed companies and nurseries, offer another growing method. These seedlings are slower to mature than sets, but are usually faster than your own seed-grown onions.

Growing Suggestions for Onions

EXPOSURE AND SOIL: Sun. Well-drained soil that retains moisture. Mix 5-10-5 fertilizer at the rate of 5 pounds per 100 square feet into the soil before planting.

WHEN TO PLANT: Early spring.

SOWING AND PLANTING: Plant onion sets in furrows 2 inches deep; thin young plants to 2 to 4 inches apart. Sow seed in 1/2-inch furrows, allowing about 10 to 15 seeds per foot; thin to 2 to 4 inches apart. Set seedlings or transplants about 2 inches deep, thinning as above. Allow about 12 to 18 inches between rows.

HARVESTING: There's wide latitude here, and don't forget that even onion foliage can be snipped for fresh flavoring. Most onion bulbs are usable when 1/4 to 1/2 inch in diameter, but for successful storage of the bulbs, the tops or foliage of the plants must have died down before the bulbs are harvested. This process starts naturally toward the end of summer; if some tops are brown and others are lagging behind, bend down the foliage of the slowpokes by hand, or with a hoe, to speed the ripening process. Then pull—or better, carefully dig—the bulbs, and spread them out (a wire screen makes a good surface) in a dry place to continue ripening. In most climates, this means under cover, as in a garage or attic. The bulbs should be kept from rain or dew. After a week or so, or when the skin of the bulbs seems perfectly dry, the tops can be removed, or left on and braided to make decorative bunches for hanging. Store onions in a dry, cool place safe from freezing.

PITFALLS: Not many, but when growing onions from seeds, patience is needed in the early stages, as it is for leeks, a close relative.

Parsnips

For a sensational taste discovery, serve home-grown parsnips in late fall or winter. The roots have a sweetness and flavor that makes them different from any other vegetable. Unfortunately for those with space limitations, the parsnip requires a long season to reach maturity (about 105 days), but the gardener with ample space who doesn't grow them is simply missing one of the best of all vegetable treats. The parsnip can be stored in place through the winter and dug as needed; or store them in a cool cellar, covered with damp sand. Authorities seem to differ on whether freezing temperatures that occur while the parsnip is in the soil improve its flavor—grow it and make your own judgment.

Growing Suggestions for Parsnips

EXPOSURE AND SOIL: Sun. Deeply prepared, fertile soil without rocks. Mix 3 to 5 pounds of 5-10-5 fertilizer into each 100 feet of row before sowing.

WHEN TO PLANT: Early spring.

SOWING AND PLANTING: Sow seeds in furrows $1/2$ inch deep, and thin seedlings to about 4 inches apart. Allow 20 to 24 inches between rows. Mix radish seeds with the parsnip seeds, which are very slow to germinate. The radish seedlings mark the rows, and the radishes can soon be pulled without harming the parsnip seedlings.

HARVESTING: Parsnip roots can grow quite long—up to 10 or 12 inches—but harvesting can begin when they are half grown, and of course can continue as they continue to grow. Roots still in the ground by spring are edible, but the plants will soon go to seed, toughening the roots.

PITFALLS: Forked roots are usually the result of stony or poorly prepared soil (digging to the depth of a foot is not a wasted operation with this vegetable). Seeds that don't germinate at all are probably old seeds. Always buy new parsnip seeds.

Peas and Edible-podded Peas

Peas are a superb vegetable for the home garden. Never mind whether you have space for only a few short rows—the dining pleasure they give will be memorable, and just as pleasurable each time and each season you repeat it. Peas are produced on bushy, tendril-equipped vines that are 8 to 48 inches tall, according to variety. Vines under 24 inches or so rarely need support, but taller varieties will need to cling to netting, chicken wire, or "pea brush" (sturdy, twiggy branches, usually cut for the purpose from wood-lots—easy for the country dweller, not so feasible for the city or suburban gardener), set between two rows of peas.

Peas are cool-season vegetables and at their best in Northern gardens, where they are planted in early spring (Southerners and other mild-climate gardeners sow them in the fall). They mature about 65 to 70 days later. This frees their garden space for use by summer vegetables. One variety, 'Wando,' is now recommended for autumn harvest in the North, as its vines are heat-resistant. Sow 'Wando' about July 1 for an autumn harvest.

One way to stretch the pea harvest during the spring or early summer season is to plant two or three different varieties with different maturing dates at the same time. Three such varieties might include 'Freezonian' (62 days), 'Little Marvel' (64 days), and 'Wando' (70 days).

Other combinations are possible. Or you can simply make succession sowings every five to ten days of the same or of different varieties, making sure that the last variety planted will mature well before the advent of really hot weather. Consult seed catalogues for suggestions and descriptions of varieties.

For the small garden there are several possibilities: 'Little

Marvel' (64 days), 18-inch vines; 'Sweet Green' (62 days), 11-inch vines; 'Tiny Tim' (60 days), 6 inches; 'Mighty Midget' (60 days), 6 inches.

Being legumes, peas are nutritious—and delicious—whether dried, frozen, canned, or fresh, or when consumed in the pod, an act, of course, that must include the pod. Tender, edible-podded peas—snow peas, or *pois mange-tout*—popular in Oriental cuisines, are done when just barely cooked. These peas, of which 'Dwarf Gray Sugar' (68 days), is the variety most often listed in catalogues, appeal to the lazy but epicurean gardener because no shelling is required. They are also quick and easy to freeze.

Growing Suggestions for Peas

SOIL AND EXPOSURE: Sun. Humus-rich soil, deeply prepared.

WHEN TO PLANT: Early spring and spring in the North; fall in mild-climate regions.

SOWING AND PLANTING: Treat seed with Legume-Aid, which increases the yield (this preparation is available from seed houses). Seeds are large and easy to sow at proper depth and distance, about 2 inches deep and 3 inches apart, in double rows about 6 inches apart, with support placed between two rows (see above). Mulch alongside the rows. Separate double rows by 3 feet for easy harvesting.

HARVESTING: Pick peas for shelling as soon as the pods are well filled and bright green. Yellow pods are aged and filled with starchy rather than sugary peas. Pick edible-podded peas while they are still small and tender, just as peas begin to form. Eat or process peas as soon as possible after picking; or refrigerate them at once if they must be kept.

PITFALLS: Avoid overfeeding the vines with a fertilizer high in nitrogen; this can result in healthy, lush plants but few pods. If possible, rotate the planting location of your peas from year to year to thwart wilt diseases. Don't try to grow peas in hot weather (see comments on 'Wando' above).

Sweet and Hot Peppers

The pepper is a tropical plant, as are its two close relatives the eggplant and the tomato. It requires the same kind of growing weather—warm, sunny days. The gardener-cook will want to grow one or two varieties of sweet (non-hot) peppers—sometimes called "bell peppers"—such as the standard 'Early California Wonder' and 'Yolo Wonder,' which are both bell-shaped. For frying and salads, there are varieties like 'Sweet Hungarian' (also known as 'Yellow Banana'), which is long and tapered in shape. 'Earliest Red Sweet' (55 days) is recommended for growing in tubs or containers because it bears its red fruit early on small plants.

A plant or two of a favorite hot pepper can be grown in a spot away from the others, the fruits to be dried as a spice or pickled in vinegar or wine. Remember—hot peppers can look much like sweet peppers, and they, too, begin as green or yellow fruits before they change to red at maturity. Fortunately, if you mistake hot peppers in the green or yellow stage for sweet, they are often less fiery than when fully ripe. But don't count on it. Better to keep track of which plants are which—the best way is to tie a label to a stake beside the plant.

Growing Suggestions for Peppers

SOIL AND EXPOSURE: Sun. Soil prepared and fertilized as for eggplant and tomato.

WHEN TO PLANT: Sow seeds indoors at the same time as for eggplant. Or buy plants and set them out when days and nights are warm, about the end of May in the North.

SOWING AND PLANTING: As for eggplant and tomato.

HARVESTING: As needed, but hot peppers are hottest when fully red. Sweet peppers are more digestible raw when fully ripe (the red stage). They also contain more vitamin C then.

PITFALLS: Setting the plants out too early—while night temperatures are still falling below 60° F. Curiously, these tropical plants are affected adversely by stretches of very hot days, above 85° F.—blossoms may drop in such periods.

Potatoes

When you consider the space that potatoes use, their soil and fertilizer needs, and the number of bugs and blights they attract, it hardly seems worthwhile for the home gardener to grow them. Yet catalogues continue to offer seed potatoes—actually pieces of cut-up tubers, each with an "eye" or sprout which will become the potato plant above ground—of many different varieties; so some gardeners besides potato farmers must be growing them. And home gardeners often become curious about growing various vegetables—especially the ones they are warned against. (Our own efforts have been a total failure—pine mice eat the tubers, and the Colorado potato beetles devour the plants.)

If you wish to grow potatoes, here is a description of R. Milton Carleton's "lazy man's potato patch," reprinted with his and his publisher's kind permission from his *Vegetables for Today's Gardens* (D. Van Nostrand Company, 1967). This is a good way to have tiny new potatoes to go with your fresh peas—a delectable treat.

By this method potatoes can be grown so all that is needed to pick them is to lift off a foot of straw. Soil is prepared as for an ordinary garden, with the surface pulverized and raked smooth. Pieces of seed potato are then set uniformly over the entire surface of the area, about a foot apart each way. Next, instead of being covered with soil, they are buried in 18 inches of straw.

The straw is kept well dampened. If planted about May 1, the lazy man's potato patch should be ready for harvest about mid-July. To harvest, simply lift the straw covering with a fork; the small potatoes will be found right on the surface of the ground where the seed pieces were placed. To protect any unused part of the crop, simply cover with straw again.

Radishes

Growing the lovable, lowly radish is supposed to be simplicity itself, yet success with radishes isn't always automatic. The radish is a cool-season vegetable with a short growing season (24 to 40 days), and it requires, in addition to cool weather, a well-prepared, humusy soil that retains moisture. Radish seeds always germinate, but sometimes the roots disappoint the gardener.

Growing Suggestions for Radishes

EXPOSURE AND SOIL: Sun, but a few hours of light shade daily won't hurt. The best harvests come from fertilized, humus-rich soil that does not dry out. Mix 5-10-5 or a similar complete fertilizer into the soil at the rate of 1 to 2 pounds per 100 square feet.

WHEN TO PLANT: In early spring and every ten days or so thereafter, depending on how many radishes you want and how much you like them. For a switch, try the winter radish varieties, such as 'Long Black Spanish' (60 days) and 'White Chinese' (60 days), sowing them in midsummer for fall and early winter harvest and storage.

SOWING AND PLANTING: Soak the seeds overnight in a saucer of water before planting. Plant in furrows 1/4 inch deep with about 15 inches between rows, and thin seedlings to 1 inch apart. In smaller gardens, it's feasible to plant short rows closer together. Spring radishes mature so quickly they can be sown almost anywhere in the garden without tying up space you'll need for later crops.

HARVESTING: Pull radishes as you need them, as soon as they are large enough to eat.

PITFALLS: Too much top growth at the expense of root development can mean the seeds were sown too late in spring, or growth was checked by lack of water or nutrients. Wormy roots are caused by the cabbage maggot, which appears mostly in early-sown plants. If you sow seeds every ten days or so, the maggot problem decreases and is hardly evident in later sowings or among fall varieties. A remedy for this pest is to sprinkle the chemical diazinon over the row after seeding.

Raspberries

Gathering red raspberries from your garden is more possible than you might think. In fact, it's just about the only way to enjoy these fragile fruits in the fresh state, as they are much too perishable for shipping and handling in most markets. Since the bushes bear bountifully, there are usually surplus berries for freezing—a process that raspberries survive very well.

The everbearing raspberry, of which several varieties are listed in catalogues, is the best choice for home growing. It yields two separate harvests, a long one lasting for about four weeks in early summer, and a second harvest beginning in late summer and often lasting until it is ended by heavy frosts in late autumn. Although the experts recommend that rows of raspberries be set 5 to 8 feet apart, this is a luxurious use of space that few homeowners today can afford. So plant a single row or "hedge" of plants that can be reached from both sides. Our 20-foot row of bushes separates the vegetable garden from a lawn, and bears more than enough berries for ourselves, our friends, and the birds.

Growing Suggestions for Raspberries

EXPOSURE AND SOIL: Full sun is to be preferred, but raspberries will tolerate a few hours of shade daily. Give raspberries well-drained garden soil to which has been added compost, rotted manure, peat moss, and a complete fertilizer, such as 5-10-5, at the rate of 1 pound to 10 feet of row at planting time. Thereafter an annual feeding of a 10-10-10 or 10-6-4 fertilizer at the same rate can be given in early spring.

WHEN TO PLANT: Spring or fall.

PLANTING: Buy 1-year canes, which should be set out about $2\frac{1}{2}$ feet apart. As the canes become established, each one forms several suckers, and eventually a single row will become 3 to 4 feet wide. Pull up wandering suckers to keep the row within its limits, and remove any thin, weak stems when they emerge. Otherwise your row will become an unmanageable patch in which it is difficult to reach the inner berries and to prune the canes.

Pruning everbearers is easy—once you get the hang of it and accept the fact that once-a-year pruning, plus cutting back in spring, is required. Cut off at ground level the canes that have borne the first (or early summer) harvest soon after the last berries are picked. (You can easily see which these are—they look tired.) The new canes growing alongside them will produce berries in the fall and again in the following early summer. In early spring, shorten these tall canes by about a third, before they leaf out.

Supports are not required for everbearing raspberry plants, but a single line of stout cord or wire is sometimes run along each side of the row to keep the outer canes upright—especially when they are loaded with fruit. A constant mulch of very well-rotted manure or compost or leafmold, or what is available, helps retain soil moisture and prevents the soil from splashing the berries during rainstorms.

HARVESTING: Pick raspberries as soon as they slip easily from their stems; if you have to tug, they're not ready. Do not wash unless essential. Fresh, ripe raspberries will keep only a day or so at the most. Refrigerate them at once. They can be frozen without syrup or sugar.

PITFALLS: Few pests bother raspberries. Japanese beetles will feed on the foliage but, unless they appear in great hordes, they can be hand-picked and dropped into a can of kerosene. If birds are a problem use light-weight netting stretched over a frame to cover the row. Consult your friendly County Agent if unusual trouble develops in your raspberry patch. Chances are very good that none will.

Rhubarb

One of the spring season's treats from the home garden when stewed or used to make chutney or preserves or to fill pies, rhubarb is an ornamental plant that need not be confined to the vegetable garden. In fact, a few clumps have traditionally been planted near the kitchen entrance, where they are handsome as well as handy for the cook. About four to six clumps should fill the needs of most families for fresh rhubarb desserts, with an ample surplus for freezing or canning. Rhubarb is a long-lived perennial—the same plants, or divisions of them, can supply several generations.

Growing Suggestions for Rhubarb

EXPOSURE AND SOIL: Sun or partial shade. Since the plants will occupy their garden space for many years, give them a good start by preparing the soil deeply and supplying it with a lot of organic matter (partially decayed manure, compost, peat moss, etc.). Mix a complete fertilizer such as 5-10-5 at the rate of $1/4$ to $1/2$ pound per plant into the planting holes. Fertilize rhubarb again at the same rate early in succeeding springs.

TIME TO PLANT: In spring or fall.

PLANTING: Buy roots from mail-order seedsmen or local nurseries or garden centers. Set the roots so the top buds will be about 2 to 3 inches below the surface when the holes are filled, and 3 to 4 feet apart each way. Plants can remain in place for 10 years or so before they begin to deteriorate. When symptoms of decline appear, divide and replant the clumps, using the most vigorous portions.

HARVESTING: Wait until the second spring after planting to harvest stalks. To harvest, grasp each stalk near its base and free with a slight twist; never cut stalks with a knife. After the second year harvesting can continue for six weeks or so, but only if stalks remain chunky. Never decimate the plants when harvesting—leave at least half of the stalks to carry on growth. (More will appear.)

PITFALLS: Never eat the foliage of rhubarb, as it contains oxalic acid.

Roquette

The young leaves of roquette (also called rocket, rocket salad, rocket cress, rugula, rucola, ruchetta, ruca, and arugula) can be the distinctive mystery ingredient in a tossed salad, adding a welcome peppery flavor quite different from that of the various cresses and mustards to which it is related. Roquette has come here from the Mediterranean countries, but it is still unknown to many discriminating gardeners. It fetches a premium price at greengrocers in high-rent districts, and an equally high price in salads served in fine restaurants.

Growing Suggestions for Roquette

EXPOSURE AND SOIL: Sun or partial shade. The same soil as cresses and other leafy vegetables—meaning there should be plenty of organic matter in the soil.

WHEN TO PLANT: Early spring, at the same time as lettuce, spinach, and radishes; sow again from late summer to early fall.

SOWING AND PLANTING: Sow seeds in shallow furrows in short rows—2 or 3 feet long or so; or sow a patch of a few square feet, scattering the seeds and covering them lightly with soil. Make small succession plantings to stretch out the harvest.

HARVESTING: About four weeks after sowing, cut off young leaves as needed to use in salads or sandwiches (or to cook—see the recipe section). Young leaves are narrow and pointed and are best at this stage. As the plants mature and weather warms, the leaves become compound in their growth habit and are somewhat tough, as well as too peppery for the tastes of some. Cutting back unusable leaves will sometimes cause the plant to produce new young ones. Where summers remain moist and cool, leaves can be cut most of the summer.

PITFALLS: Sow only a small patch at first to be sure you like the taste of roquette—some people don't.

Sorrel

It's fun to experiment with an uncommon vegetable each year, if only to find out whether it deserves its "uncommon" rating. Sorrel is one such vegetable, but is not an unusual one in France, or to those who are familiar with French cuisine. It is a perennial, with large, light-green pointed leaves, which are cooked as greens, like spinach, or used to make a sauce or purée to accompany fish, or a hot or cold creamed soup. The flavor is acid, quite similar to that of the related edible wild plant called red sorrel. Since sorrel is a perennial, living through winter and reappearing the following spring, it should be planted where annual garden-digging won't disturb the plants. It can be grown successfully in containers, too.

Growing Suggestions for Sorrel

EXPOSURE AND SOIL: Sun or partial shade. Humus-rich soil—add plenty of organic matter, such as peat moss, compost, or rotted manure to the soil before planting.

WHEN TO PLANT: In early spring.

SOWING AND PLANTING: Sow seeds about ½ inch deep and thin the seedlings to 8 to 12 inches apart. Space rows from 15 to 24 inches apart.

HARVESTING: Cut leaves at the base of the plant as needed, beginning 60 days or so after sowing. Always remove seed stalks as soon as they start to develop.

In the spring of the second year and thereafter, apply a sprinkling of 5-10-5 complete fertilizer around or alongside the plants, and gently cultivate it into the soil.

PITFALLS: Sorrel contains an acid salt that is not the best substance for daily dining, but that is perfectly harmless in moderate amounts. Those who find the flavor too acid may enjoy sorrel cooked half-and-half with spinach.

Spinach and New Zealand-Spinach

Spinach is another vegetable that must have cool temperatures for success. It matures fast (in about 40 days), meaning that its space will soon be available for such summer producers as snap beans or Swiss chard. If you like spinach and want some for freezing, too, you can sow several rows without sacrificing valuable space for summer use. Even if your garden is limited to a few window or patio boxes, you can sow spinach to enjoy raw in salads.

New Zealand-spinach, not a true spinach, has small, fleshy leaves on large, sprawling plants, and is used as greens. While it is enjoyable when cooked like spinach, it doesn't taste very good raw. Its flavor is more earthy than that of spinach and lacks that essence-of-spring goodness of true spinach—perhaps simply because it is a summer producer! Once you sow New Zealand-spinach, you'll have it forever, as it self-sows prolifically, with volunteer plants appearing on the compost pile, among asparagus plants, and elsewhere in the garden. Since it's a sprawling plant, it needs space, and a few plants are enough for most families.

Growing Suggestions for Spinach and New Zealand-Spinach

EXPOSURE AND SUN: Sun or partial shade. A humus-rich soil for spinach. Mix a high-nitrogen fertilizer such as 10-6-4 at the rate of 1 pound per 100 square feet into the soil before sowing. Spinach responds to applications of liquid fertilizer, such as fish emulsion, applied after the plants have been thinned. New Zealand-spinach does well in average garden soil with no special attention.

WHEN TO PLANT: Early spring for both vegetables.

SOWING AND PLANTING: Sow true spinach seeds ½ inch deep in rows about 12 to 15 inches apart. Thin seedlings to about 3 to 6 inches apart (use the thinnings in salads). Germination of New Zealand-spinach can be slow, but the seedlings will show up eventually. Thin seedlings to about 1 foot apart all around.

HARVESTING: Harvest entire plants of spinach in about 40 days, or pick individual leaves as you need them from the outside of the clumps. New Zealand-spinach endures all summer, making new growth as the tender tips are cut. Remove the hard green seeds in the leaf axils before cooking.

PITFALLS: Trying to grow true spinach in warm regions or warm weather—it struggles, then quickly goes to seed. Sow seed *early*.

Summer and Winter Squash

There is something for everyone in the vast squash clan. These vegetables are unexcelled for providing nutritious fresh food, for canning, freezing, winter storage, and even for pickling and preserving. The standard winter squash fruits are produced on vigorous vines that need lots of space and a long growing season (80 to 120 days, according to variety). The fruits of some summer squash can appear with astonishing quickness after sowing—in as little as 40 days. The summer squash, a bush rather than a vining plant, can be confined to 3 to 6 square feet per plant, so the smallest garden has space for two or three plants—which will provide a whale of a harvest.

Zucchini is a summer squash, too, and it's probably now the most popular squash of all. Another kind of summer squash is the patty-pan or bush scallop, which bears gracefully shaped white fruits in 75 days from seed. Home gardeners can pick these when they are tiny and more delicate in flavor than the giants sold in markets. Among the most sought-after of all winter squash varieties is 'Butternut,' which is also one of the most prolific. There are now a few varieties of winter squash produced on bushes rather than vining plants. Burpee's 'Bush Table Queen or Acorn' squash (80 days) is one of these prolific producers in less space; 'Bush Acorn Table King' is even earlier (75 days); 'Emerald' is a Buttercup type on bush plants that can be spaced 2 to 3 feet apart. Consult seed catalogues for more complete descriptions of these and many other kinds.

Growing Suggestions for Squash

EXPOSURE AND SOIL: Sun. Well-drained soil enriched with compost, rotted manure, or other organic matter.

WHEN TO PLANT: Outdoors in mid- to late spring, after soil and weather have warmed. Seeds can be sown indoors in peat or Jiffy-7 pots about three or four weeks before it will be warm enough to plant the seedlings in the open ground. As with melons and cucumbers, squash seedlings can be set out under Hotkaps (page 88) for additional warmth and frost protection in spring.

SOWING AND PLANTING: Sow seeds about 1 to 1½ inches deep, 2 to 3 inches apart, either in rows or in groups of 6 seeds. Space groups about 3 to 4 feet apart each way. In rows, thin the seedlings to 18 inches apart. Plant winter vining varieties at one end of the garden in groups of 6 seeds, 2 to 3 inches apart, with 6 to 8 feet between groups.

HARVESTING: Pick summer squash fruits when small, at their most tender stage—when only an inch or so thick. The maturity dates for summer squash usually reflect their ultimate development, not when the fruits can be picked young for table use.

Winter squash varieties are quite different—their nutlike flavor is most pronounced when the fruits are fully ripe, so here the maturity dates have real meaning. And, too, these fruits will not store properly unless they are vine-ripened. Before the squash are picked, the rinds should be bone-hard and the colors should reflect those shown in catalogues or on seed packets. Butternut types should be fully beige or light tan, rather than showing greenish tints.

You can store winter squash in a dry cellar at a temperature of about 50°–60° F. Use any bruised fruits first, as under storage conditions they begin to spoil. All winter squash fruits—ready or not—should be picked before heavy frosts.

PITFALLS: The squash vine borer attacks bush and running varieties alike and is hard to control. Remedies include mulching around the stem area with aluminum foil; dusting or spraying plants with methoxychlor or Sevin at 10-day intervals beginning about June 25 in most Northern gardens. (Check the container instructions pertaining to dusts and sprays and note how close to time of harvesting the material can be used.) Butternut types are fairly resistant to borers. Many squash plants go on merrily producing even as the borers work. At the end of summer, if borers are in the fruit, they can be cut out and most of the fruit salvaged.

Strawberries

The flavor and aroma of the strawberry are the essence of summer. Yet the strawberry has a life far beyond its fresh state: it's one of the best fruits for freezing and preserving. If you have the space, you'll want to have several rows of the plants. If space is limited, grow them as a border around the vegetable garden or along each side of a path. Since one strawberry plant should bear about a pint of fruit in one season, you can even experiment with strawberries in containers. There's always the time-honored "strawberry barrel"—any large container with 2-inch round holes at the sides (as well as the usual top opening) in which to insert plants.

Everbearing varieties are recommended for home gardens because with them you can enjoy two seasons of harvest—the first and most bountiful in early summer, the second in late summer and through the fall. However, if space is available (see the suggestions below), growing a mixture of both the June-bearing type and the everbearers is recommended. Planting several named varieties, selected from both types, will considerably extend the harvesting season at both ends. Catalogue descriptions will help you choose among early and midseason-to-late varieties. Some varieties do better in one region than another. This is the sort of local information you can get from your County Agent. However, there are three everbearing varieties that appear to do well over most of the country—they are 'Geneva,' 'Ozark Beauty,' and 'Ogallala.'

Growing Suggestions for Strawberries

EXPOSURE AND SOIL: Full sun. Slightly acid soil (pH 5.5 to 6.5), well drained and well supplied with organic matter—the more the better. Add compost, rotted leaves, and/or peat moss or any other good organic materials available locally, such as seaweed. Then mix in a complete fertilizer, such as 5-10-5, at the rate of 4 pounds to 100 square feet. A second application of fertilizer in midsummer is recommended for very sandy soils. No fertilizer beyond the initial application made at planting time should be given in future springs. Too much fertilizing is known to cause soft berries and contribute to rot, especially in very rainy seasons.

WHEN TO PLANT: Early spring, except in the South and in mild-climate regions, where fall is best.

SPACING: Directions for growing strawberries often seem vague and confusing—they often seem to be intended for the commercial grower or farmer who works with acres rather than a small patch. The following suggestions are for those who want a generous harvest of berries in the space that is available. (Your County Agent and state agricultural experiment station can give you more detailed instructions on orthodox strawberry culture.)

>   Single rows of strawberries: Set plants from 12 to 18
>   inches apart.
>   Double, triple, or other multiple rows: Set the plants 12
>   to 18 inches apart in the rows; allow 18 to 36 inches

between the rows, according to the space available. (Remember that you must move in this space to pick the berries.)

The above spacing leaves no room for "runners," the shoots that fan out from established plants to root and form new plants. Instead, in this system, you cut off all runners as they appear—everbearers tend to be shy with runner production anyway. The original plants bear the berries, and they will bear more than they would if runner plants were allowed to survive. Plantings managed in this fashion should bear well for three or more years before the plants become exhausted and need to be replaced.

PLANTING: Keep young strawberry plants moist while planting. Do not crowd the roots in the planting hole. Spread them out, but point them down rather than letting them lie in a horizontal position close to the surface. Keep the center crown level with the soil surface—neither above nor below. Tramp around each plant so roots and soil are in firm contact. Water well at once, and thereafter as needed. Always mulch strawberries, no matter how or where you grow them. In cold climates, strawberry plants are usually covered with straw or hay in early winter. In the spring, this material is spread as a mulch between the rows and plants. Cut off the flowers that appear the first summer after planting, but permit the later flowers of everbearing varieties to form fruits for a fall harvest.

HARVESTING: Pick your home-grown berries when they are fully red and ripe. Do not squeeze or bruise them. If the plants are mulched and the berries not soil-splashed, you can skip washing. Freeze or process as soon as possible.

PITFALLS: Experts warn against planting strawberry plants in soil that has previously grown black raspberries, tomatoes, potatoes, eggplants, or peppers to avoid soil-borne diseases these plants are all afflicted by. Buy plants from a reliable source that certifies they are disease-free. A light-weight netting can be thrown over small strawberry patches to discourage birds.

Tomatoes

A lot can be said—and has been said—about growing tomatoes. Yet the tomato is one of the most obliging of all vegetables, rewarding the first-time or casual gardener and the experienced grower alike with generous harvests of delicious and beautiful fruits. And this can be in spite of careless culture, unfavorable weather conditions, or a score of pests and diseases that may plague the plants. Of course caring for the plants pays off, but the fact is that anyone can grow tomatoes that will be superior to those hard and tasteless ones shipped to supermarkets after being gassed to produce a spurious look of ripeness.

There are many varieties of tomatoes. If you elect to grow your own seedlings rather than buying transplants, you will want to study catalogue descriptions and choose the ones that meet your family's tastes and requirements. For instance, 'Roma' (76 days) is a small egg-shaped variety to grow for tomato paste and to thicken tomato juice; 'Beefsteak' (80 days) bears a glamorous, giant fruit ideal for slicing; 'Early Girl' (54 days) is outstanding because it bears good-sized fruits very early; 'Pixie,' 'Small Fry,' and other small varieties with small, rounded fruits produce abundantly when grown in pots or other containers, and they are early as well (52 days). That is a small sample of what is available.

If you choose to buy plants, you have less choice, but most garden centers and greenhouses offer a choice among several labeled varieties, so it still pays to study catalogue descriptions—then you'll know something about the varieities you're offered. Six plants are sufficient for most families, if you just want a supply for table use. Double or triple the number if you have the space, plus an ambition to can your crop.

Growing Suggestions for Tomatoes

EXPOSURE AND SOIL: Sun. Well-drained, humus-rich soil. Before planting, mix 2 pounds of 5-10-5 fertilizer into each 100 square feet of soil. There are several special tomato fertilizers on the market. Follow their label directions carefully, as they are highly concentrated.

WHEN TO PLANT: Spring. Do not set out tomatoes in the garden until the weather has warmed and frost danger is over. In very cold climates where spring comes late, some time is gained by setting out the plants under Hotkaps, little wax-paper "tents" that protect tender plants from frosts. As the plants reach the peak of the Hotkaps and the weather warms, tear a hole in the paper to permit free growth.

SOWING AND PLANTING: Indoors, sow seeds about 6 to 8 weeks before the last severe frost can be expected. Sow seeds about $1/2$ inch deep in containers or flats of sterilized soil or in one of the soilless growing mediums, such as Jiffy-Mix. Or sow two seeds each in Jiffy-7 peat pots, later pinching off the weaker of the two seedlings. After sowing and watering, slip each flat or pot into a plastic bag—remove the bag after germination. Transplant seedlings from flats, after two pairs of leaves have formed, into 3-inch peat pots filled with a soilless mix. Seedlings that are in Jiffy-7 pots can usually remain in them until it is time for outdoor planting. While indoors the seedlings need as much sun or light as they can get, about 12 hours daily for good, chunky growth. A sunny window is necessary, and its light will probably need to be supplemented by fluorescent lights. A hardening-off process of about a week (see page 35) in a fairly sheltered spot is necessary before indoor-grown seedlings can be permanently set in the garden. During this time be sure pots receive ample watering. When setting tomato transplants in their holes, bury nearly half of the stem above the root ball to ensure the plant's having a firm foundation for its later fruit burdens. Roots will form along the buried stem.

Even with this careful launching, some sort of staking is recommended, although some gardeners choose to let their tomato plants sprawl. The big advantage to supports or stakes for tomatoes is that staked plants use less space—important in the limited garden. Even if you are growing only three or four plants among flowers, you will want to stake them, if only for the sake of neatness in such a setting. Staking also keeps the fruits off the ground and out of reach of slugs, turtles, and mice. Plants to be staked should be

18 inches apart, with 24 inches between rows. If you have room to spare, you can space your tomatoes from 5 to 6 feet apart each way and omit the stakes. Mulch your plants, whether you stake them or not, using either black plastic or a 2- to 3-inch layer of straw, hay, compost, or other good mulch.

A single stout stake can be used to support plants that are to be pruned—use soft twine or strips of cloth that won't cut into the stems to hold the plants to the stake; loop the twine loosely around the stem, cross the ends, then tie them to the stake with a firm knot. Retain two or three stems to a plant—the original main stem and one or two that develop below it as the plant grows. Remove all the side shoots—or suckers—that grow out from the leaf axils (the axil is the point where the leaf is attached to the main stem).

There are other methods for supporting tomato plants. Perhaps the easiest is to enclose the plants within hoop-like wire peony supports that are available at garden centers. A currently popular method of support is to enclose the plants in a 5-foot cylinder made from construction wire with a 6-inch mesh. No pruning is recommended for plants grown within such "cages."

HARVESTING: Pick your tomatoes when they are fully ripe—the bright, natural color is the indicator, rather than the size of the fruits. (Not so with store tomatoes, which may have been sprayed with ethylene gas to turn them red before they have ripened.) Late in the fall, when frosts threaten, is the time to gather partially ripened or green fruits, both good for frying or preserving or pickling. Left on a shelf out of the sun, green tomatoes will ripen in time.

PITFALLS: Overfeeding with nitrogen causes lush growth at the expense of fruit development. Avoid this by doing the initial fertilizing at planting time (see above), and then feeding again only after fruits have started to form.

Dusting or spraying at ten-day intervals with mixtures especially recommended for tomatoes helps check most pest and disease problems. Many omit this precaution without dire consequences.

Tomato plants that suddenly appear to be stripped of some of their foliage are probably being attacked by the tomato hornworm.

Look for a large, green worm, exactly the color of tomato foliage, with a prominent "horn." These worms have several natural enemies, including a wasp that lays its eggs on the back of the worm. If your hornworm appears to be covered with small white cocoons, its days are numbered and you can let it be (but remove it from the tomato plant), allowing the natural-enemy cycle to continue. Otherwise, finish off the worm.

Turnips and Rutabagas

Two cool-season vegetables grown for their edible roots are the turnip and the rutabaga, the latter often called yellow turnip (incorrectly, say some experts). If you have the space—and the will—you can sow rutabaga seeds in most Northern areas from early- to midsummer and harvest the roots in late fall to store for winter use and serve at Thanksgiving. The main rutabaga variety is 'American Purple Top,' which takes about 90 days from seeds to harvest.

The roots of the white turnips are smaller and mature much faster than rutabagas, making them a better choice for small gardens. A recently introduced turnip, 'Tokyo Cross,' requires only 35 days to produce round white turnips that can be used like radishes. Another modern turnip is 'Just Right,' but it needs 60 days to mature. Both rutabagas and turnips can be stored in damp sand in a "root cellar" or cool basement. Immature turnip tops are often used as greens and can be canned or frozen, following the directions for "Greens" in Part Three.

Growing Suggestions for Turnips and Rutabagas

EXPOSURE AND SOIL: Sun. Average garden soil, free from stones and rocks.

WHEN TO PLANT: Rutabaga seeds, in late spring to early summer for autumn and winter use. Turnip seeds, early spring and again in midsummer.

SOWING AND PLANTING: Sow turnip seeds about ½ inch deep in furrows 15 to 18 inches apart; thin seedlings to 3 inches apart. Rutabaga seeds can be interplanted among such short-term vegetables as lettuce and cabbage. Sow seeds ¾ inch deep in rows 20 to 24 inches apart. Thin to 4 to 6 inches apart. Water during droughts.

HARVESTING: To avoid the oversized, sometimes tough roots found in supermarkets, begin to harvest turnips when they are under 4 inches in diameter; pull or dig rutabagas when they are about 4 or 5 inches in diameter. Lift before freezing weather arrives.

PITFALLS: If grown too long during hot, dry weather, the roots will be woody and maggot-ridden. See "Cabbage" and "Broccoli" for treatments for cabbage worm, which can be a turnip pest, too. Try to rotate planting areas each year for turnips and rutabagas, as well as for other cabbage family members, to avoid soil-borne problems.

Watermelons

Just about everything—good and bad—about growing muskmelons in the home garden can be said about watermelons. There is an encouraging exception, though. In recent years several varieties of watermelon have been introduced that are of special interest to backyard gardeners. These have more compact vining habits, a shorter growing season, and fruits of "ice-box" rather than "ice-house" size. If you plan to have a melon patch (see "Muskmelons") and live in Northern regions, stick to these small varieties. Mild-climate gardeners can grow the standard-sized watermelons, but even they will find these smaller varieties practical. A few are 'Golden Midget' (65 days), whose rind turns golden when ripe, a valuable attribute; 'Yellow Baby Hybrid' (70–75 days); and 'New Hampshire Midget' (65 days). Consult catalogues for descriptions of these and others.

Growing Suggestions for Watermelons

EXPOSURE AND SOIL: Full sun. Rich, sandy soil. Add generous amounts of organic matter—compost, rotted manure, etc.—and about ½ pound of 5-10-5 fertilizer to each plant grouping or "hill." (There is no need to mound up or raise the soil level before sowing seeds in "hills." The term is simply used to indicate a grouping of plants rather than a row of them.)

WHEN TO PLANT: Outdoors, in warm weather after all frost danger. Or sow seeds indoors in late spring in Jiffy-7 pellets.

SOWING AND PLANTING: Sow seed ½ inch deep, 2 to 3 inches apart, in groups about 4 feet apart. Thin seedlings to leave 3 plants in each group or hill. Or sow in rows as described for muskmelons. Indoor-started plants can be set in the garden under Hotkaps (page 88), if the weather remains cold and wet late in the spring. Black plastic mulch may help provide the warm soil the vines require.

HARVESTING: Watermelons are usually reliably ripe for picking when the underbelly is decidedly yellow rather than pale yellow or white. Watermelons do not continue to ripen after they are removed from the vine.

Herbs

Since you are growing your own vegetables, you will want to include a few plants of the major culinary herbs in your garden. Fortunately for most of us, herbs require very little growing space.

A patch near the kitchen entrance is convenient, or you can add herb plants to your flower gardens or to your rock garden, or grow them in front of shrubs in foundation plantings. In the vegetable garden, group herbs on either side of a path, or make an edging of several kinds along the path. Another handy place is in the section devoted to salad "makings"—along with lettuce and other greens include a row of parsley, chervil, basil, dill, and sweet marjoram. The perennial herbs—the ones that last for several years, such as chives, thyme, tarragon, oregano, sage, and the mints—should be planted in a location where they are not disturbed by annual garden cultivation.

Herbs make great pot or container subjects—grow them in tubs, window boxes, or planters, or in smaller pots that can be placed under fluorescent lights indoors in the winter, or in a cool, sunny window. One of the easiest ways to enjoy herbs is to buy several small plants and grow them all together in a squatty clay pot or container on a terrace or a deck.

Herbs prefer a place in the sun, but you can grow them quite successfully in partial light shade. They will grow in the same quality of soil in which you grow flowers or vegetables.

Cut the leaves to use fresh as you need them, and by all means preserve them for later use, too. While it's picturesque (and effective) to dry herbs for winter use in bunches suspended from rafters indoors, or even near a hot-air vent or a slow-burning fire, the drying methods described under "Herbs" in Part Three are preferable.

It's possible to freeze most culinary herbs for future use—again, see the discussion of methods under "Herbs" in Part Three. Frozen herbs are about equal to fresh herbs in strength; dried herbs are about twice as strong as fresh—the intensity of flavor depends somewhat on the condition of the leaves when dried, the care used in drying, and storing conditions.

The herbs listed below are among the ones most valuable in the kitchen.

Basil

Basil, an annual, forms an ornamental plant, from several inches to 2 feet tall, depending upon the species or variety, with fresh green leaves that are highly fragrant. A few plants are sufficient; grow in full sun, from seeds sown in the garden about the time you sow snap beans, or buy transplants when the weather is warm. Basil is important in most tomato recipes, but is also delicious with other vegetables, such as summer squash, zucchini, eggplant, and even lima beans.

Chervil

An annual plant with fine, fernlike foliage, chervil has a mild, sweet aniselike flavor. It grows about a foot tall. Fresh-cut leaves are often sprinkled on fish fillets or added to omelettes, and chervil is one of the classic *fines herbes* of French cuisine. Sow seeds in spring and again in midsummer. Chervil does not transplant well, but it tolerates partial shade. It often seeds itself if a few seed heads are left on the plants.

Chives

A very hardy onion relative, with clumps of grassy foliage that can be cut as needed throughout the growing season. Although chives are often potted for indoor use in winter, the plants soon languish and die under overheated, dry conditions. A better way to provide for winter supplies is to freeze the blades, finely cut crosswise, in small jars or plastic bags during the active growing season. (No blanching is necessary.) Start your chive planting by buying a few clumps from local or mail-order sources (seeds are too slow for any but the most patient gardener). Then divide the clumps by gently pulling apart the individual plants, which look like miniature scallions, and replant them in small bunches about an inch in diameter. This way you will have a supply of chives forever; the clumps can be divided again whenever they grow too large. Grow chives in sun or part shade. Cut leaves close to the base when you harvest them, and remove the attractive lavender-blue flowers after they fade.

Dill

If you grow cucumbers, you will want a fresh supply of dill foliage—"dill weed"—to sprinkle over the cut slices. Or you can let the dill plants form seed heads, and harvest them when half-ripe for pickle making. (If your cucumbers aren't ready, freeze the whole seed heads in screw-top jars.) For dried seeds, cut the heads as they begin to turn brown and drop them into a paper bag to finish drying so the seeds won't fall and be lost in the garden as they ripen. Dill is a fairly fast-growing annual to grow from seeds sowed in the spring. Sow it again in midsummer so the supply of fresh foliage will continue until late fall.

Mint

There is more to mint than the so-refreshing but familiar spearmint—there are peppermint, orange mint, and apple mint, to name only three other kinds—and there are other uses for it than garnishing iced tea or combining with bourbon for a julep. Mint leaves are important in many Mediterranean and Near Eastern recipes and, of course, they are a standby in mint sauce and mint jelly. Mints are perennials; once you introduce them to your garden you should have plants for life. Plant mints in rich, moist soil (but they will survive in almost any situation) and in partial shade, preferably where they can spread without encroaching on less robust plants. Yank out any stray plants that appear at the tips of underground runners in the spring.

Oregano

This herb is essential for many Italian and Mediterranean recipes. It is also called wild marjoram, but its flavor is quite different from that of sweet marjoram, *Majorana hortensis;* botanically, oregano is *Origanum vulgare.* Oregano is a sturdy, upright perennial up to 2 or 3 feet tall, with pretty pink flowers in midsummer. Buy plants (or grow oregano from seeds in the spring), and give this herb full sun and an average garden soil. The plants are perfectly winter-hardy and produce attractive blooms.

Parsley

Since fresh parsley is about the most universally called-for herb in recipes, it should head the list of herbs for home growing. There are two main types—the familiar curly-leaved parsley and the taller and more flavorful flat-leaved or Italian kind. Parsley is very hardy and its foliage remains green through early winter. Parsley plants are almost always available from local garden centers in early spring, if you don't want to sow seeds. If you grow it from seeds, sow it mixed with radish seeds, as germination is slow.

Rosemary

A tender shrub from the Mediterranean region, with aromatic needle-shaped leaves that are evergreen. Seeds are available, but it's more convenient to buy plants. Rosemary makes a handsome pot or tub subject for the terrace or deck, but in cold climates it must be brought indoors over winter. Be sure not to let the plants dry out, whether in the ground or in pots; but avoid drowning them, too.

Sage

One or two plants of this gray-leaved perennial should be sufficient. The plant grows about 3 feet tall, unless you order a dwarf variety.

Summer Savory

A low-growing, sprawling annual to grow from seeds sowed in spring. Harvest as soon as the tiny pinkish flowers open along the stems. A related plant is winter savory, a perennial that is somewhat less delicate in flavor. They are used interchangeably.

Sweet Marjoram

An attractive, delicate herb with small gray-green velvet-textured round leaves and clusters of small white flowers. Sweet marjoram (botanically *Majorana hortensis*) is a perennial, but it is not winter-hardy except in mild climates. Elsewhere treat it as an annual, sowing seeds each spring in carefully prepared soil that doesn't dry out. Or buy seedlings. It needs full sun.

Tarragon

Buy plants of this classic culinary herb. The seeds you see offered in packets are not of the true tarragon, a plant that does not set seed and so must be increased by root propagation. The true tarragon has a strong licorice flavor in its foliage. Established clumps are often 2½ feet tall. Give it soil with very good drainage, and divide the clumps every three years or so.

Thyme

This low-growing shrub with aromatic leaves so important to the cook rarely grows above 12 inches. Seeds are available, but it's quicker to buy plants in the spring from local garden centers. Frequent harvesting of the foliage helps keep the plants compact rather than leggy. If they become straggly and some of the stems die, cut the entire plant off close to the crown to force new growth. Thyme is a hardy perennial. Give it as much sun as possible.

Mail-Order Sources of Seeds, Supplies, and Plants

Burgess Seed and Plant Company, Box 218, Galesburg, Michigan 49053.

W. Atlee Burpee Company, Box 6929, Philadelphia, Pennsylvania 19132; Box B-2001, Clinton, Iowa 52732; Box 748, Riverside, California 92502.

DeGiorgi Company, Council Bluffs, Iowa 51501. (Catalogue, 25¢)

Farmer Seed and Nursery Company, Faribault, Minnesota 55021.

Henry Field Seed & Nursery Company, Shenandoah, Iowa 51601.

Gurney Seed & Nursery Company, Yankton, South Dakota 57078.

Joseph Harris Seed Company, Moreton Farm, Rochester, New York 14624.

Le Jardin du Gourmet, West Danville, Vermont 05873.

Nichols Garden Nursery, 1190 N. Pacific Highway, Albany, Oregon 97321.

George W. Park Seed Company, Greenwood, South Carolina 29646.

R.H. Shumway, Seedsman, Rockford, Illinois 61101.

Stokes Seeds, Inc., Box 548, Buffalo, New York 14240; also Box 10, St. Catherines, Ontario, Canada.

Part Two
Putting Up Food

According to the old rural saying, "You eat what you can, and what you can't, you can." Actually, to the old-timers canning was not merely an expedient to avoid waste: they planned their gardens in order to have plenty of vegetables and fruits to put up for eating during the winter months. In the days of horse-drawn transportation, when many households were far from retail markets, and grocery stores were even farther from the places where foods were grown on a commercial scale, putting up—"canning"—fruits and vegetables in jars was the only practical way for most families to enjoy the garden bounty of warm weather when snow was on the ground.

Many of today's gardens are also planned with a surplus in mind—a surplus to be put up by canning or, for many, by freezing. This is for economy, of course, but it is also because home-canned and home-frozen vegetables and fruits and homemade pickles, jams, jellies, and other preserves are so satisfying and delicious.

Home gardeners, fortunately, can process small amounts at a time. All vegetables and berries and other fruits are best when picked at their peak of perfection and canned or frozen as soon thereafter as possible. Equipment for day-by-day canning of small batches is less expensive than the large items of equipment needed for large-scale putting up of foods, and when this day-by-day system is followed, there is little of the stress and mess of struggling with massive quantities.

Planning for Putting Up Food

Planning for canning, freezing, and making preserves and pickles starts when you lay out your garden. When you plan, three decisions are basic: First, decide which vegetables and fruits your family enjoys the most when they are served fresh, and, second, which vegetables, fruits, pickles, relishes, jams, jellies, and preserves your family enjoys the most when they are taken from the pantry or the grocer's shelves. Third, how much of each kind of food can your family use? Your planting plans and your seed and plant orders will be based on your answers to these questions. (See Part One, "Growing Your Own.")

Planning Your Equipment

Your needs for equipment will also depend on what you and your family like most. If, for example, you are going to limit your canning to tomatoes (an acid food), you don't need to rush out to buy a large pressure canner (which is *not* the same as a pressure saucepan), but you *must* have a pressure canner for putting up all other vegetables, as well as meats, poultry, or other miscellaneous foods outside the scope of this book, if you should decide to go into those areas of canning.

If you expect to can mainly fruits (technically including tomatoes) and rhubarb (technically a vegetable, but an acid one) and to make any preserves and pickles that are to be processed in their jars, your essential canning utensil is a large kettle deep enough to allow boiling water to cover the tops of jars, when they are set on a rack, by at least a full inch—better 2 inches, or even 3. You may buy a regular canning kettle, or you may already have a stock pot or other large pot that will serve the purpose when equipped with a rack. This kettle must have a cover, too.

If you plan to freeze your garden crops, relate your plans for planting to available freezer space. Here the freezer itself is the main item of equipment to consider—it must be a true freezer, capable of maintaining a temperature of zero degrees F. or lower—it can't be just the frozen-food section of a refrigerator, which isn't cold enough for long-term storage or satisfactory initial freezing.

Most kitchens are already equipped with pots, spoons, funnels, a colander, and so on, items that are suitable for use in making jams, jellies, and pickles as well as in canning and freezing. The utensils you'll need for each process will be listed in detail farther along; the most important item will be a preserving pan, a flat-bottomed pot holding 8 to 10 quarts, made of stainless steel or of enameled or porcelain-coated steel. It should not be made of aluminum, if aluminum is avoidable—that metal interacts with certain acids and certain foods, sometimes causing food discoloration (harmless), and the acids and salt used in pickling can damage the surface of aluminum. Your preserving pan can double as a kettle for the preliminary cooking of foods to be canned by the hot-pack method and can also be used for pickling if it is enameled or made of stainless steel.

How Foods Are Preserved

Preserving methods for home use are designed to destroy or inactivate the organisms that cause spoilage or the actual production of poison in foods. In the case of freezing, the process prevents the continued action of enzymes—natural substances found in all vegetables and fruits—that cause undesirable changes in flavor, color, and texture during frozen storage of improperly processed foods or those stored at too high a temperature.

Various bacteria, molds, and yeasts, among other microorganisms, thrive in the water, soil, and air as well as in fresh foods. In foods they exist in infinitesimal quantities that are not at all harmful so long as the food is edibly fresh. If, however, the food is put up and these organisms are not destroyed, or their growth is not arrested, in the preserving process—or if the processed food is not properly sealed to exclude air—organisms can multiply in the food. This can cause, at the very least, spoilage, which can be harmless, as in the case of a film of mold on jelly; or in the destruction of the food, as in spoilage caused by yeasts; or in extremely dangerous, even fatal, contamination, such as when the toxin causing botulism is produced in food that has not been heated sufficiently during processing to kill the toxin-producing spores of *Clostridium botulinum*, a heat-resistant kind of bacteria that can thrive in the absence of oxygen. The botulinus toxin can be present in improperly canned foods that look, smell, and taste normal. Most other organisms cause obvious signs of spoilage.

THE SIGNIFICANCE OF FOOD ACIDITY.   You will have noted that we make a distinction between the kind of processing to be given acid foods and those that are nonacid. Without a lengthy discussion of the technical factors involved, we can say that the degree of acidity of a food has a direct relation to the length and temperature of the processing needed to kill or to control the growth of spoilage organisms. Acidity is a help in preserving the food, whether it is natural acidity, as in fresh tomatoes and rhubarb, or when it is added, as when vegetables are pickled in vinegar, or when it is formed by benign fermentation, as in sauerkraut.

For safe canning, *never* disregard reputable (that means up-to-date, among other things) instructions to pressure-can a food, and never risk underprocessing by skimping on the time given in the instructions. *Water-bath canning is not a safe alternative to pressure canning for low-acid or nonacid foods,* no matter what you may have been told or may have read in an outdated publication.

A CAUTION.   You should never taste any home-canned food that has a doubtful appearance or smell, or that comes from a leaking jar. Such food—or any other that you suspect—should be destroyed in a way that prevents pets or wild creatures from eating it.

Experts on canning often advise that all home-canned non-acid foods be boiled, covered, for 10 to 15 minutes (20 minutes for spinach and corn) before being tasted or eaten. This boiling will destroy even botulinus toxin, if it is present, and the heating will make off-odors apparent, too. However, those who take extreme care in every step of the canning process, using the correct high temperature in a pressure canner that functions as it should, can look forward with confidence to enjoying the fruits of their work without undue concern.

ENZYMES AND THE FREEZER.   Freezing, when done correctly, will prevent the deterioration in quality caused by the action of enzymes in foods. The process of spoilage is stopped in its tracks, or considerably slowed, by the proper preliminary preparation of food (especially scalding or blanching) and by storing at a sufficiently low temperature (zero degrees F. or lower).

VINEGAR AND SUGAR.   Pickles are preserved, in general, by the acidity of the vinegar (or by their own acid developed by fermentation); preservation is also helped by the salt used in pickling, and sometimes by heat processing. Sweet preserves are kept from spoilage in part by sugar, although heat has the primary role in killing undesirable organisms in nearly all preserves.

Other Methods of Preserving

Our emphasis in this book is on preserving foods by the most commonly used and convenient methods—freezing, canning, pickling, and preserving, including jam and jelly making. There are, of course, other ways to keep food.

DRYING.   The drying of foods, with the exception of herbs (see the herb-drying directions in Part Three, "Recipes"), is an intricate subject mainly of interest to those with large amounts of food to put up. We leave drying to specialized books—see the Bibliography for some titles.

ROOT-CELLARING.   What about root-cellaring, as cool underground winter storage of fresh vegetables and fruits is sometimes called? This, again, is a large subject; and, although occasional suggestions for short-term cellar storage are made in Part One, "Growing Your Own," this method is of most interest to those who have a root cellar, or space for one, and fairly large crops to fill it. If you are interested in this way of keeping fresh food, see the Bibliography for the titles of some helpful books.

Canning Vegetables and Fruits

Despite the popularity of freezing, canning still remains the mainstay of many home gardeners who put up a good deal of their own food. It is less costly than freezing in terms of equipment; and, once canned, the food requires no expenditure of electricity to keep it in fine condition.

We begin discussing canning, therefore, with canning by the

pressure-canning method—the *only* safe way to put up nearly all vegetables (the exception: tomatoes, actually a fruit), and absolutely all other foods except fruits. *Do not even consider* the boiling-water-bath method for processing any foods except fruits, including tomatoes; rhubarb (a vegetable that we treat as a fruit, and highly acid); certain pickled vegetables (follow your recipes); and certain preserves—again, heed your recipes as to the need for water-bath processing. Experimenting with boiling-water canning of plain, unpickled or unfermented vegetables is an invitation to the botulinus toxin, which can only be destroyed by heat far above that of boiling water (212° F.)—heat that can be produced for canning in your home kitchen *only* in a pressure canner that has reached 10 pounds of pressure and held it long enough to produce in the food an internal temperature of at least 240° F.

WHAT ABOUT TIN CANS?

A few home canners prefer to process their food in tin cans, but nearly all home canning is done in jars, the method we are discussing here. Jars are simpler to process and generally less expensive to use than cans. With proper care, jars and their metal screw bands (or glass or porcelain-lined lids) can be reused for a long time. Processing in cans requires buying a can sealer, and different kinds of cans, with various sorts of linings, are required for different foods. Glass jars, on the other hand, are simply sealed by hand and can be used for all kinds of vegetables, fruits, pickles, jellies, and whatnot—and, if they are of the right shape (sloped, without a shoulder), they're fine for the freezer, too.

Canning in cans is generally practical only for the home processor who puts up 300 or more cans of food a year—considerably more than most of us produce. Rows of glass jars filled with the luscious goodness of home-processed foods are both pleasing to the eye and easier to select among than cans when you're choosing items for meals.

Some Methods to Avoid

OVEN CANNING. Now and then an adventurous type—or a novice who has come across an interesting old cookbook—will try oven canning, which was once considered the latest wrinkle. (And, unfortunately, there are still cookbooks being sold that advocate this method.) Not only is oven canning a flirtation with spoilage—because the heating of jars in an oven is likely to be incomplete or uneven—but it also involves the risk of jars exploding or failing to seal. Oven canning is unsafe: ignore any advice, no matter whose, to try it.

STEAM CANNING.   Another unsafe but once common method is steamer canning or steam canning—not to be confused with pressure canning, often called steam pressure canning, in which the steam is superheated in the pressure canner. Steam canning involves processing the filled jars in a covered pot equipped with a rack. The jars are heated only by the steam produced by a fairly small amount of boiling water, so clearly you can't rely upon this system to produce a sufficiently high temperature to permit it to be substituted for water-bath canning, much less for pressure-canner processing. Nevertheless, descriptions of this old method still survive in out-of-date canning directions in old cookbooks, and in new reprints of some old books.

Please ignore advice to follow these methods, and please disregard (but enjoy reading) any wonderful old publications you come across that tell you how our forebears canned everything—even a moose, on occasion—by the boiling-water-bath method. They had no other means of canning food, including meat, and those who used this method for nonacid foods and survived were fortunate. Perhaps there were fewer dangerous microorganisms in their less crowded environment.

Open-Kettle Canning

This subject deserves a brief discussion to itself. There are still people who put up all their fruit, and even tomatoes, by this method, which involves cooking the food completely in a kettle on top of the stove, then sealing it into sterilized glass jars, using sterile lids. It is a method that has worked, albeit with some spoilage, for generations. But we know now that processing fruits, including tomatoes, in a boiling-water bath gives better results, and the food keeps better, especially in warm climates.

We still use open-kettle canning for pickles and some relishes, as you'll notice in the recipes, and of course for jellies and jams. Some other relishes, preserves, conserves, and the like are cooked in a pot until done, then finished in a boiling-water bath to insure sterility and a good seal. Pickles, jellies, and jams, in which the vinegar and the sugar respectively are the principal preservatives, can be put up by the open-kettle method with confidence, whenever your up-to-date recipe so directs. In general, though, we recommend a final heat processing for foods formerly done entirely in this way.

Pressure Canning

As we have emphasized, pressure canning is *the only safe method* to use for canning all vegetables except tomatoes and rhubarb. (In a subsequent section we'll cover the foods it's safe to can by the boiling-water-bath method.)

Your steam-pressure canner *must* have an accurate gauge: it is only by being absolutely certain of the pressure inside the canner that you can be certain that your food reaches and holds the temperature (240° F., attained at 10 pounds of pressure) necessary for safe processing. An occasional recipe will direct the use of 5 pounds of pressure for processing, or perhaps of 15 pounds—but those pressures aren't often used, and recipes calling for them should be followed carefully.

CHECKING YOUR GAUGE

How can you find out if your gauge is accurate? Ask your dealer how to have it checked, or write to the manufacturer of the canner, or consult your county or regional office of the Federal Extension Service (often called the Agricultural Extension Service)—see your telephone book. A canner gauge is usable if it is not inaccurate by more than 4 pounds in the pressure it registers; if it is off by 5 pounds or more, get a new one.

Your gauge should be checked before each canning season, and several times during the season if you are canning on a large scale. When your gauge is checked, you are told of any variation it shows from the master gauge (the standard). According to your gauge's variation, if it has one, process your food as follows:

Pressures to Use When Canner Gauge Shows Variation from Standard

High Variation		Low Variation	
Amount	*Process At*	*Amount*	*Process At*
1 pound	11 pounds	1 pound	9 pounds
2 pounds	12 pounds	2 pounds	8 pounds
3 pounds	13 pounds	3 pounds	7 pounds
4 pounds	14 pounds	4 pounds	6 pounds

Processing pressure is calculated at sea level. At altitudes above 2,000 feet, processing in a pressure canner requires that you use a higher pressure to bring the internal temperature up to the necessary 240° F. (You do *not* increase the processing time—that is the method of compensating for high altitudes used when canning in a boiling-water bath.) Below are the pressure adjustments for high altitudes recommended by the United States Department of Agriculture:

Processing Pressures to Use at High Altitudes

Altitude	*Processing Pressure to Be Used*
2,000 feet	11 pounds
4,000 feet	12 pounds
6,000 feet	13 pounds
8,000 feet	14 pounds
10,000 feet	15 pounds

TIMING PRESSURE CANNING

Processing times are stated precisely in the directions given for each food in this book (and in other publications on the subject). These times must be followed exactly: successful canning depends on exact timing as well as on correct pressure (hence correct temperature).

CAPACITY OF CANNERS

Rather misleading, the capacity of canners is usually stated in quarts. However, this is a statement of the pot's capacity for liquid, not of the number of quart jars that can be accommodated. The table below indicates the working capacity of canners of various sizes.

Designated Size of Canner	*Actual Capacity (Jars)*
4 quarts	4 pint jars
8 quarts	7 pint jars or 4 quart jars
16 quarts	9 pint jars or 7 quart jars
21 quarts	18 pint jars (stacked 2 deep) or 7 quart jars

ADDITIONAL EQUIPMENT FOR PRESSURE CANNING

Besides your pressure canner, equipped with a rack and an accurate gauge, and a preserving pot or other suitable large kettle for precooking food to be packed hot, you will need:

Glass jars intended for home canning—"Mason jars," as they are often called—not commercial mayonnaise jars and the like

Lids, most often the two-piece kind—"dome lids"—consisting of a reusable screw-band or rim and a separate liner, for one-time use, which has a sealing compound around the edges. There are also one-piece metal lids that seal jars in the same fashion, and older types of lids (see below) are also still in use.

A jar lifter, strong tongs, or sturdy pot holders to lift filled jars

A timer or an alarm clock

A sturdy rack or a thick towel on which to set jars for cooling

Labels

A wide-mouthed jar-filling funnel

A ladle and a slotted spoon

A colander

A wire basket to hold foods being washed or scalded.

You will also find that household scales and a food mill or another sieving or puréeing device will be helpful. You'll need the usual measuring cups and measuring spoons.

CHECKING YOUR EQUIPMENT

With all your equipment on hand, the next step is to check it. Make sure all your jars are the tempered-glass kind made especially

for canning. Do not use for canning any jars saved from purchased foods—however, such jars are fine for jams or other preserves that need not undergo heat processing in the jar. Plastic containers are never used for home canning. Inspect jars for cracks, or for chips or nicks in the sealing edge. Discard, or use for storing dry foods, any jars that are so damaged.

Be certain that you have the right kind of lids to fit your jars, and enough of them. If you are using jars with glass lids held in place with wire bails or clamps, or zinc lids lined with porcelain, provide fresh rubber rings for either kind. Rings should be used once only, and manufacturer's instructions should be followed carefully when using these older types of lids.

Read, or reread, the manufacturer's instructions for using your canner and be sure you understand all details.

PREPARING EQUIPMENT FOR USE

Wash all equipment, jars, and lids thoroughly with soap and hot water—but never immerse the cover of your pressure canner in water. If you are using rubber rings, make sure they are new and wash and rinse them; don't test them by stretching.

Keep jars and lids in hot water, if you will be using them promptly, or reheat them just before use, either in hot water or in your oven, heated to 150° F. Some metal dome lids are to be put into simmering-hot water for a few moments before they are used—follow the manufacturer's instructions on this point. Keep rubber rings wet until they are needed.

PREPARING THE FOOD

Before you can your vegetables and fruits you must prepare them by selecting, washing, trimming, and carrying out other steps that are detailed farther along in this section. But it will be easier to understand the entire process of canning if all procedures are outlined before we specify methods of preliminary preparation and give precise directions for processing times and so on. At this point, therefore, we'll go on, on the assumption that your food is washed and otherwise prepared, to how to pack food.

PACKING METHODS

Packing the food—not to be confused with the actual canning or processing—is simply the filling of your jars. You can pack your prepared vegetables and fruits raw and cold (raw pack, or cold pack), or you can heat or partially cook them and fill the jars while the food is hot (hot pack). Some fruits—applesauce, for example—should always be packed hot. For many fruits and vegetables, you can suit yourself as to whether to use hot or cold pack.

For both hot pack and raw pack there should be liquid in the jar, usually to a level near the top of the jar—but see the specific directions for each food farther along for the correct headspace allowances, and for the occasional exceptions to the inclusion of liquid. For hot pack, the liquid is usually that in which the food was heated. For raw pack, boiling water is the usual liquid, unless otherwise specified in a recipe. Raw or cold pack eliminates the need to time the preliminary cooking that is required by hot-packed foods (but it does not eliminate timing the actual processing). It is perhaps a little simpler than hot pack for that reason.

PROS AND CONS: HOT PACK AND RAW PACK.   Vegetables and fruits with a high water content, such as tomatoes, are more attractive when packed raw, as they are then less likely to lose their shape. Hot-packed foods make a more solid pack, however, as they shrink less during processing. Fruits in syrup are packed hot. The alphabetically arranged individual directions farther along state whether cold pack or hot pack is to be preferred for each food, or whether either of the two methods is satisfactory.

RAW (COLD) PACK.   The prepared food is placed in the jars as compactly as possible (unless the directions specify a loose pack), and liquid, usually boiling water, is added to the correct level. You then slip a narrow spatula or a long knife blade around the inside of the jar to eliminate any air spaces or bubbles. Wipe the jar edge with a clean, damp cloth and add the lid.

   If you are using metal dome lids with a rim of sealing compound, tighten them firmly—they are not to be tightened further after processing. When using glass lids with rubber rings and wire clamps or bails, fasten the cap down over the ring by putting in place over the top the longer of the two clamps, leaving the short one in "up" position. It will be pushed down to complete the seal after processing. When using zinc lids lined with porcelain and resting on a rubber ring on the jar shoulder, tighten the lid firmly over the ring, then loosen it by turning it back one-fourth of an inch. It will be tightened again after processing.

HOT PACK.   Proceed exactly as for raw or cold pack, but the food you place in the jars will first have been heated or partly cooked, as directed in the individual instructions farther along. Place food in jars, add boiling-hot liquid, remove air bubbles, and put on lids as described above.

PROCESSING PROCEDURE FOR PRESSURE CANNING

Once your food has been packed and the lids added—and be sure you have packed only enough jars to make one load for the canner—place the rack in the canner. Set the canner over the stove burner and pour in about 2 inches of boiling water (for hot-packed jars) or 2 inches of hot water (for cold-packed foods); use a little more water if the canner tends to leak steam after the petcock or vent is closed.

Set the filled, covered jars on the rack, allowing enough space between them and between the jars and the sides of the pot to let steam flow freely. Clamp the lid on securely, but leave the petcock open, with the canner over high heat, until steam has escaped for 10 minutes. At the end of that time, close the petcock and let the pressure rise to 10 pounds (or to the pressure reading your recipe calls for; or to the pressure reading that compensates for an inaccurate gauge—see page 108.

Start your clock timer, or make a note of the time at which processing at full pressure has begun. Keep the heat adjusted so that the pressure remains constant—this means keeping an eye on the pressure gauge.

WHEN PROCESSING IS COMPLETED. At the end of the processing time, immediately remove the canner from the heat, or turn off the heat. Do not try to open or to adjust the cover in any way until the pressure has dropped to zero. Be patient. Never put a pressure canner in cold water, or pour water over it to hasten the pressure drop. (These two techniques are acceptable when using a small pressure saucepan for preparing food for the table, but even then they should be used only according to the manufacturer's recommendations.)

A minute or two after the pressure gauge has registered zero, open the petcock, but do this very slowly. After unfastening the cover, lift it by tilting it away from you so that the steam doesn't blow into your face or scald your hands.

Using a jar lifter, tongs, or thick pot holders, remove the jars from the canner and set them to cool, spaced well apart, on a thick towel or on a rack, in a spot free from drafts.

COMPLETING THE SEAL. If you are using two-piece or one-piece metal dome lids rimmed with sealing compound, the seal is now complete—do not try to tighten the lids further, or you might break the seal instead. If yours are all-glass or porcelain-lined zinc lids with rubber rings, you complete the seal at this point: For the all-glass lids, you will have already clamped the longer bail over the lid to hold it in place during processing. To complete the seal, snap down the shorter bail (or clamp) onto the shoulder of the jar.

For porcelain-lined zinc lids with rubber rings, tighten the lids manually, reversing the quarter-inch turn by which you loosened them before processing began.

Let the jars cool for 12 hours before checking seals.

CHECKING THE SEAL. When the jars have cooled for 12 hours, the metal dome lids will usually be slightly depressed in the center and will "ping" clearly when tapped with the bowl of a teaspoon. If the center of any lid is not already depressed, press it with your finger: if it stays down, the seal is complete. You can also test further by tilting the jar sharply to see whether there is any leakage.

If you wish, screw bands may be removed at this point and saved for reuse. If they tend to stick, loosen them by covering them for a moment with a damp cloth.

If you have used jar lids with rubber rings, test the seal by lifting the jar and tilting it sharply this way and that. If the contents bubble, or leaks appear around the ring, the seal is incomplete.

SALVAGING UNSEALED JARS

Should you find a poor seal, refrigerate and use the food as soon as possible. (Throw it away if the jar has been sitting more than 24 hours before the leak is found.) Or you can empty the jar or jars and can the food again, following exactly the same steps as for fresh food and using a fresh metal lid liner or rubber ring, as the case may be. Cool, and check the seal of the recanned food as described above.

Because such food has been processed twice, it will be of somewhat lesser quality than the rest of the batch—you may wish to label it accordingly.

LABELING AND STORING

Wipe each jar clean with a damp cloth and label it with the date and its contents. If you can more than one batch of the same food in a day, you may want to put the batch number on the label.

Store your jars in a dark, cool cupboard or basement—light in the storage area causes the color of some foods to fade. Avoid storing in places with freezing or near freezing temperatures, or dampness, or excessive heat: all these conditions affect the quality of the canned food.

Canning in a Boiling-Water Bath

As we have said, canning in jars immersed in a deep bath of boiling water is a safe way of putting up fruits, certain preserves and pickles, and tomatoes, but *no vegetables,* unless they are pickled in a strong vinegar solution or have been fermented, or are included

---

Points to Remember When Canning

- Garden goodness in canned vegetables and fruits depends on the quality of the fresh food you process. Vegetables should be young and tender and free of blemishes. Fruits should be ripe but firm, free of any spoilage or severe bruising.
- Can vegetables and fruits as soon as possible after harvesting. If there is unavoidable delay, store them in a cool, airy place, or in your refrigerator.
- For raw pack, no preliminary cooking is necessary. The prepared food is packed as compactly as possible in jars, then boiling water or boiling syrup is added before processing.
- For hot pack, the canning liquid for vegetables is either the liquid in which they have been briefly cooked, or boiling water. For fruits that have been briefly cooked in syrup, the syrup is used; or, if sweetening is omitted, boiling water is used.
- Vegetables may be packed without salt, or with 1/2 teaspoon salt per pint.
- Leave headspace in jars as directed in the canning directions for specific vegetables and fruits.
- When packing is completed, jars should be sealed and processed immediately. Do not pack more jars at a time than you can process in one canner load.

in a relish that contains sufficient added acid and/or sugar to aid in the preservation of the food.

EQUIPMENT

The large kettle described under "Planning Your Equipment" near the beginning of this section is the main item of equipment you will need. The other utensils listed for pressure canning (see page 110) are equally useful when you use the boiling-water method.

If you have a large pot otherwise suitable for canning but without a rack, try using a very sturdy stainless-steel cake-cooling rack (a shop selling professional restaurant supplies would have this), or make a wooden rack out of slats or odds and ends of wood. Some canners even fold a towel several times to make a pad that prevents the jars from resting directly on the bottom of the pot.

You can use your pressure canner for water-bath canning, too—be sure to use the rack, do not fasten down the cover, and leave the petcock open to prevent the buildup of steam pressure. It will work fine.

Check and prepare your jars, lids, and other items of equipment exactly as described for pressure canning. You need not sterilize jars and lids, as they will be adequately sterilized at the temperature of boiling water (212° F.).

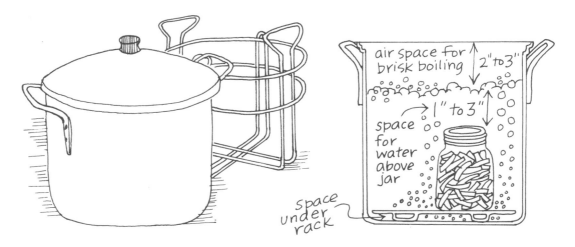

PACKING THE FOOD

Proceed exactly as for pressure canning, taking care not to fill more jars at a time than you can process in one load. Use either hot or cold pack, depending on the food—see the alphabetically listed directions for specific foods to determine which pack is preferable for the food you're canning, or consult your own preference when the directions indicate that either hot or cold pack will be satisfactory.

PROCESSING PROCEDURE FOR A BOILING-WATER BATH

For cold-packed foods, fill the canner half full of water, set it over the heat, and have the water hot, but not boiling, when you add the jars. For hot-packed foods, have the water in the canner boiling. Needless to say, the rack will be in place for either method.

Place your filled and covered jars (directions for using lids are the same as for pressure canning) on the rack, being sure that they do not touch one another or the sides of the pot and are far enough apart for the water to circulate freely.

Next, add enough boiling water (for either raw or hot pack) to bring the level of the water to at least 1 inch above the tops of the jars—better yet, the jars should be covered by 2 or even 3 inches. Don't pour the boiling water directly onto the jars—pour it down along the side of the canner.

Bring the water in the canner to a rolling boil, put on the cover, and set your timer (or make a note of the time at which processing started). Begin counting when a full boil begins. Processing continues at a steady, gentle boil with few exceptions—exceptions which will be specified in certain recipes. Occasionally, a food, such as a fruit juice, is processed at a lower temperature than that of boiling water. This is "hot-water-bath" processing—quite a different thing from the boiling-water process we're describing here.

If the water level drops to even a fraction under the allowance of 1 inch or more above the jar tops, add boiling water to maintain the proper depth. Keep an eye on the clock or on your timer: underprocessing can cause spoilage, overprocessing means overdone, sometimes mushy and strong-flavored food.

PROCESSING-TIME ADJUSTMENTS. When you process food by this method at an elevation above 1,000 feet, the lower atmospheric pressure must be compensated for by a longer processing time. Add 1 minute for each 1,000 feet of altitude above sea level if the sea-level processing time is 20 minutes or less. If the sea-level processing time is more than 20 minutes, add 2 minutes for each 1,000 feet above sea level.

Thus at 2,000 feet you would add 2 minutes to the processing time for a food requiring 20 minutes or less at sea level, but you'd add 4 minutes if the sea-level processing time were more than 20 minutes. Further examples: At 3,000 feet, add 3 minutes or 6 minutes, as the case may be; at 4,000 feet, add 4 minutes or 8 minutes, and so on.

These timing adjustments apply only to boiling-water processing. When you use a pressure canner, the adjustment for a higher altitude is made in the processing pressure—see page 109.

WHEN PROCESSING IS COMPLETED. As soon as the processing time is up, remove the jars from the canner with your jar lifter, tongs, or pot holders. Set the jars, with ample space between them, on a thick towel or a rack on the kitchen counter. They should be in a place free from drafts where they can remain undisturbed for at least 12 hours.

If you are using lids that require this step (see "Completing the Seal" in the discussion of pressure canning), complete the seal.

When the jars are thoroughly cool, 12 hours or so after processing, check the seals just as described for pressure-canned jars. Any jars with incomplete seals may be reprocessed in a boiling-water bath, using a new metal lid or a new rubber ring—see the directions under "Salvaging Unsealed Jars," above.

Store your jars exactly as if they had been pressure canned.

Preparing Food for Canning

Now that the two methods for home-canning fruits and vegetables have been outlined in detail, we turn to the preliminaries of preparing foods, then go on to the specific directions for canning every home-garden food in this book.

Fruits selected for canning should be firm-ripe, fresh, and free from blemishes and any sign of spoilage. Select tender, young vegetables without serious bruises or other discolorations and without signs of spoilage. The more nearly perfect your vegetables and fruits are before processing, the greater your later enjoyment of them will be.

Sort vegetables and fruits for close-to-uniform ripeness and for size, for the best results.

WASHING

Whether or not the vegetables or fruits are to be pared or peeled, be sure to wash them thoroughly beforehand. Wash a few pieces at a time in a bowl set under running cold water, rubbing or scrubbing if necessary to remove all soil particles (which can contain some of the bacteria hardest to eliminate in processing), and also to get rid of any residue of chemical sprays or dusts. Avoid bruising during washing, and remove the food promptly from the water—when vegetables or fruits are left to soak, there is a loss of flavor and food value.

PACKING

The processing directions for vegetables and fruits that follow in alphabetical order indicate whether to use raw (cold) pack or hot pack, or when either one is satisfactory, according to your preference. Raw or cold-packed foods should fill the jars fairly tightly, to compensate for shrinkage during processing. But there are exceptions: peas, lima beans, soy beans, broad beans, and corn expand during processing, so they should be packed loosely. Cold-packed jars are filled with boiling-hot liquid (usually water) before the lids are added. The specific directions that follow give the headspace allowance for each food.

For hot-packed foods, fairly loose packing is to be preferred. The food should be put into the jars when close to boiling hot, and the jars are filled with boiling-hot liquid—usually that in which the food was precooked—before the lids are put on.

Shake jars gently after packing and before capping, and run

a narrow knife or spatula blade around the inside of the jar to make sure that liquid fills all the spaces between the pieces of food. Be sure that the liquid covers the food.

Canning Fruits in Syrup or Without Sweetening

The addition of sugar helps produce canned fruits that have better color, texture, and flavor than fruits canned without sweetening. But if for dietary reasons you wish to can fruits in water only, or in fruit juice only, use hot pack and proceed exactly as if you had used syrup.

Syrup for canning fruit may be made with water or with fruit juice, or with a combination of water and juice. Mild-flavored honey or light corn syrup may be substituted for half of the white sugar called for in the syrup formulas given below.

MAKING CANNING SYRUPS

Directions for canning fruits (and sometimes for freezing them) may call for light (or thin), medium, or heavy syrup, and may call for syrup whose sweetness is expressed in terms of percentages (see also the formulas for syrups to be used in freezing fruits, page 162).

SYRUP FORMULAS FOR CANNING FRUIT. To make three of the most commonly used syrups, combine 4 cups water, or water combined with fruit juice, with the correct quantity of sugar as given in the table below, and heat until sugar dissolves. Skim off any scum.

Syrup Consistency	Amount of Sugar	Yield
Light or thin (30%)	2 cups	5 cups
Medium (40%)	3 cups	5 1/2 cups
Heavy (50%)	4 3/4 cups	6 1/2 cups

Preventing Discoloration in Canned Food

Eventual darkening of food due to oxidation may be limited by adding ½ teaspoon ascorbic-acid powder to each quart jar of food before adding liquid. Pure ascorbic acid is vitamin C and may be bought at drugstores. Ascorbic-acid preparations for use in home canning and freezing are sold in grocery stores. When using one of these, follow the manufacturer's directions.

Citric acid also prevents darkening of food, but you need to use a fairly large amount, which can affect the flavor of food; so ascorbic acid is to be preferred.

Discoloration of food can also be caused by overprocessing and, in some localities, by a heavy concentration of any of various minerals, such as iron or copper, in the water. The remedy is obvious in the first case: watch your timing. In the second, using soft water, if possible, will solve the problem.

Light in your storage space will cause red fruits, berries, and juices to lose color.

Leaving excess headroom, or putting too little liquid in the jar, will cause food to darken at the top of the jar.

The Matter of Spoilage

For generations Americans have canned their home-grown food with great safety, using methods such as those we describe. But there has always been the likelihood that at least some of their home-canned food might spoil. For the sake of safety, be aware of these signs of spoilage in jars of canned foods—vegetables in particular—and discard, *without tasting,* any doubtful food. (Recall what we said, at the beginning of this section, about the ways foods are preserved, and the importance of impeccable canning procedures.)

Signs of spoilage: Leaking jars, or jars that spurt liquid when they are opened; bulging lids; gas bubbles inside the jar; bad odor or color; mold, slime, mushiness of the food, or abnormal cloudiness of the liquid. If in doubt, destroy the food (don't discard it where animals can eat it), discard the metal lid or rubber ring, and wash and sterilize the jar and the reusable section of the lid.

If food at the top of a soundly sealed jar has darkened because of a low liquid level, the darkening is not, in this instance, a sign of spoilage. A little mold on the top of jelly, jam, or sweetened fruit is harmless—simply scrape it off. Don't use heavily molded canned fruit, however.

An Alphabet of Canning Instructions for Vegetables and Fruits

The detailed directions that follow cover all the cannable foods in this book. Each entry tells you the type of pack and the method and length of processing to use. The details of adding liquid, sealing jars, and carrying out the processing have been covered in the preceding text.

SALT FOR CANNED VEGETABLES. If you wish to add salt to vegetables, do so before adding the hot liquid to the jars. The usual amount is 1/2 teaspoon per pint, 1 teaspoon per quart. The salt is for flavoring only—it has no effect on keeping quality in such small amounts.

Artichokes—Globe Artichokes (Whole)

PREPARATION FOR CANNING: Wash, trim stems short, remove damaged outer leaves, and cut off prickly tips of leaves. Boil 3 minutes in water to cover.

PACKING: Pack hot, leaving 1-inch headspace. Or pack raw, with the same headspace. Add hot liquid. Put on lids.

PROCESSING: Pressure canning only, at 10 pounds. Pints, 25 minutes; quarts, 30 minutes.

Artichokes—Globe Artichokes (Hearts or Bottoms)

PREPARATION FOR CANNING: Trim off stems and remove all but very tender yellow or white leaves at the heart. Snip remaining leaves to 1 inch. Separate leaves and scrape out chokes with spoon. Pack and process as for whole artichokes, above.

Asparagus

PREPARATION FOR CANNING: Wash, trim off woody bases, cut into jar lengths or 1-inch pieces. Boil 3 minutes in water to cover.

PACKING: Pack hot, leaving ½-inch headspace. Or pack raw, with the same headspace. Add hot liquid. Put on lids.

PROCESSING: Pressure canning only, at 10 pounds. Pints, 25 minutes; quarts, 30 minutes.

Beans—Broad or Fava Beans

PREPARATION FOR CANNING: Shell, wash. If beans are still green but large, peel outer skin off each bean. Boil 1 minute in water to cover.

PACKING: Pack hot, leaving ¾-inch headspace for pints, 1¼ inches for quarts. Or pack raw, leaving same headspace. Pack loosely. Add hot liquid. Put on lids.

PROCESSING: Pressure canning only, at 10 pounds. Pints, 40 minutes; quarts, 50 minutes.

Beans—Lima (Green)

PREPARATION FOR CANNING: Shell, wash.

PACKING: Boil 1 minute in water to cover and pack hot, leaving ³/₄-inch headspace for pints, 1¼ inches for quarts. Or pack raw, leaving same headspace. Pack loosely. Add hot liquid. Put on lids.

PROCESSING: Pressure canning only, at 10 pounds. Pints, 40 minutes; quarts, 50 minutes.

Beans—Snap Beans; also Wax Beans and Italian or 'Romano' Beans

PREPARATION FOR CANNING: Wash, trim ends. Leave whole, cut into lengths, or slice lengthwise (French-cut). Boil 5 minutes in water to cover.

PACKING: Pack hot, leaving ½-inch headspace. Or pack raw, with same headspace. Add hot liquid. Put on lids.

PROCESSING: Pressure canning only, at 10 pounds. Pints, 20 minutes; quarts, 25 minutes.

Beans—Soy Beans

PREPARATION FOR CANNING: Choose young beans with bright-green pods. Wash; boil in pods for 5 minutes, cool in running water, shell.

PACKING: Reheat 1 minute in boiling water to cover and pack hot; or pack cold, leaving ³/₄-inch headspace for pints, 1¹/₄-inch headspace for quarts. Pack loosely. Add hot liquid. Put on lids.

PROCESSING: Pressure canning only, at 10 pounds. Pints, 55 minutes; quarts, 65 minutes.

Beets

PREPARATION FOR CANNING: Trim off tops, leaving 2-inch stubs; leave roots. Sort and wash. Boil in water to cover 15 to 25 minutes, until skins and stems will slip off. Cool, peel, and trim off roots. Leave small beets whole. Slice, cut into julienne, or dice larger beets.

PACKING: Pack hot (that is, technically "hot"—it's not necessary to reheat). Allow ¹/₂-inch headspace. Add hot cooking liquid. Put on lids.

PROCESSING: Pressure canning only, at 10 pounds. Pints, 30 minutes; quarts, 35 minutes.

Beet Greens

See directions under "Greens," below.

Blueberries

PREPARATION FOR CANNING: Sort; discard broken or over-soft berries, and wash. If to be packed raw, put 2 or 3 quarts of berries at a time in a large single-layer square of cheesecloth. Bring a large pot of water to a boil and, holding cloth by corners, dip berries very briefly into water, just until juice spots appear on cloth—no more than 30 seconds. Dip at once into large bowl of cold water and drain. For hot pack: Measure sorted and washed berries. Put into kettle, adding ¼ to ½ cup sugar per quart of berries. Let stand 2 hours, then set over moderate heat until sugar dissolves and berries are boiling hot.

PACKING: For hot pack, ladle berries into hot jars with syrup from the kettle, plus added boiling water, if needed; leave ½-inch headspace. For raw pack, pack drained berries in hot jars, leaving ½-inch headspace. Add no liquid or sugar. Put on lids.

PROCESSING: In boiling-water bath. Pints, 15 minutes for raw pack, 10 minutes for hot pack; quarts, 20 minutes for raw pack, 15 minutes for hot pack.

Broccoli

NOTE: Broccoli and most other members of the cabbage family (Brussels sprouts, cabbage, cauliflower, etc.) are at their best when fresh or frozen, rather than canned.

PREPARATION FOR CANNING: Trim off leaves and any woody skin. Split large stalks to pieces of uniform thickness. If necessary, soak in salted cold water (4 teaspoons salt per gallon) for ½ hour to remove insects. Cook 3 minutes in boiling water to cover.

PACKING: Hot pack, with 1-inch headspace. Add hot liquid. Put on lids.

PROCESSING: Pressure canning only, at 10 pounds. Pints, 30 minutes; quarts, 35 minutes.

Brussels Sprouts

NOTE: If possible, freeze this vegetable instead of canning it.

PREPARATION FOR CANNING: Trim bases and remove blemished leaves. If there are insects, soak and drain as for broccoli, above. Boil 3 minutes in water to cover.

PACKING: Hot pack, with 1-inch headspace. Add hot liquid. Put on lids.

PROCESSING: Pressure canning only, at 10 pounds. Pints, 30 minutes; quarts, 35 minutes.

Cabbage

NOTE: See what we say under "Broccoli," above, about the undesirability of canning cabbage and its relatives. Freeze cabbage, or store the heads in a cool cellar, or make them into sauerkraut (index).

PREPARATION FOR CANNING: Trim off any blemished outer leaves. Wash and shred, or cut into wedges, each attached to a piece of core. Boil 3 minutes in water to cover.

PACKING: Hot pack, with 1-inch headspace. Add hot liquid. Put on lids.

PROCESSING: Pressure canning only, at 10 pounds. Pints, 30 minutes; quarts, 35 minutes.

Cabbage—Chinese Cabbage or Celery Cabbage

Not suitable for canning.

Carrots

PREPARATION FOR CANNING: Wash, scrape or pare, rinse. Slice, dice, cut into strips, or leave whole if small (baby carrots).

PACKING: Pack raw; or boil in water to cover 2 minutes. Pack, add hot liquid, allowing ½-inch headspace. Put on lids.

PROCESSING: Pressure canning only, at 10 pounds. Pints, 25 minutes; quarts, 30 minutes.

Cauliflower

NOTE: Like broccoli, cabbage, and their kin, cauliflower is a vegetable that tastes much better when frozen than canned.

PREPARATION FOR CANNING: Wash. Separate flowerets, rinse, drain. If necessary, soak in salted cold water (4 teaspoons salt per gallon) for ½ hour to remove insects. Drain. Boil 3 minutes in water to cover.

PACKING: Hot pack, with 1-inch headspace. Add hot liquid, put on lids.

PROCESSING: Pressure canning only, at 10 pounds. Pints, 30 minutes; quarts, 35 minutes.

Celeriac—Knob Celery or Celery Root

PREPARATION FOR CANNING: Wash and pare. Cut into thin slices, julienne, or dice.

PACKING: For hot pack, boil 3 minutes in water to cover; pack with 1-inch headspace; add hot liquid. For raw pack, allow 1½ inches headspace; add hot liquid. Put on lids.

PROCESSING: Pressure canning only, at 10 pounds. Pints, 20 minutes; quarts, 25 minutes.

Celery

PREPARATION FOR CANNING: Cut off base of bunch, separate ribs, wash well. Slice in 1- or 2-inch pieces. Boil in water to cover for 3 minutes.

PACKING: Hot pack. Add hot liquid, allowing 1-inch headspace. Put on lids.

PROCESSING: Pressure canning only, at 10 pounds. Pints, 30 minutes; quarts, 35 minutes.

Chard—Swiss Chard

See directions under "Greens," below.

Collards

See directions under "Greens," below.

Corn—Whole-Kernel Style

PREPARATION FOR CANNING: Husk, remove silk, wash. Cut kernels from cobs at two-thirds their depth. Do not scrape. To pack hot, add 1 pint boiling water to each quart of corn and heat together in a kettle to boiling.

PACKING: For hot pack, pack corn loosely with its heating liquid, boiling hot, leaving 1-inch headspace. For raw pack, pack corn loosely and add boiling water, leaving 1-inch headspace. Put on lids.

PROCESSING: Pressure canning only, at 10 pounds. Pints, 55 minutes; quarts, 85 minutes.

Corn—Cream-Style

PREPARATION FOR CANNING: Husk, remove silk, wash. Cut kernels from cobs at one-half their depth. Scrape milk and hearts of kernels from cobs and add to cut corn. For hot pack, place corn in saucepan, add boiling water to cover, and return to full boil.

PACKING: For hot pack, pack corn in pint jars with heating liquid, leaving 1-inch headspace; pack loosely. For raw pack, put corn loosely into pint jars, leaving 1½-inch headspace. Fill with boiling water to ½ inch from top. Put on lids.

PROCESSING: Pints, 95 minutes. Canning in quarts is not recommended.

Cresses

Not suitable for canning.

Cucumbers

Not suitable for canning unless pickled (see Part Three, "Recipes").

Eggplant

PREPARATION FOR CANNING: Wash, pare, and slice or cut into cubes. Soak in salted cold water (1 tablespoon salt per quart) for 45 minutes. Drain. Boil 5 minutes in water to cover.

PACKING: Pack hot, with 1-inch headspace. Add boiling water and put on lids.

PROCESSING: Pressure canning only, at 10 pounds. Pints, 30 minutes; quarts, 40 minutes.

Greens: Beet Greens, Chard, Collards, Kale, New Zealand-Spinach, Spinach, Turnip Greens

PREPARATION FOR CANNING: Remove tough stems and damaged leaves. Wash thoroughly through several waters; drain. Steam or boil, turning the mass of leaves several times, until wilted, and heated thoroughly.

PACKING: For hot pack, pack loosely, with the liquid produced in heating, and additional boiling water if needed; leave 1-inch headspace. Put on lids.

PROCESSING: Pressure canning only, at 10 pounds. Pints, 70 minutes; quarts, 90 minutes.

Kale

See directions under "Greens," above.

Kohlrabi

NOTE: Freezing is preferable to canning for this vegetable.

PREPARATION FOR CANNING: Peel, wash, and slice or dice. If to be packed hot, boil 3 minutes in water to cover.

PACKING: For hot pack, pack with heating liquid, with 1-inch headspace. For raw pack, fill jars, add hot liquid, leaving 1-inch headspace. Put on lids.

PROCESSING: Pressure canning only, at 10 pounds. Pints, 20 minutes; quarts, 25 minutes.

Leeks

Not suitable for canning.

Lettuce, Romaine, and Endive

Not suitable for canning.

Muskmelons—also Cantaloupes, Casabas, Cranshaws, Honeydews, Persian Melons

Not suitable for canning unless made into preserves or pickles.

New Zealand-Spinach

See directions under "Greens," above

Okra

PREPARATION FOR CANNING: Choose small pods only. Wash well and trim stems, taking care not to cut into pods. Boil 1 to 2 minutes in water to cover. Reserve liquid. If sliced okra is desired, slice after boiling.

PACKING: Hot pack, with hot cooking liquid; add boiling water if necessary. Leave 1-inch headspace. Put on lids.

PROCESSING: Pressure canning only, at 10 pounds. Pints, 25 minutes; quarts, 40 minutes.

Onions

NOTE: Onions are less successful when canned than most vegetables; they tend to darken.

PREPARATION FOR CANNING: Select small, uniformly sized white onions. Wash and peel. Boil 5 minutes in water to cover.

PACKING: Pack hot with heating liquid, allowing ¹/₂-inch headspace. Put on lids.

PROCESSING: Pressure canning only, at 10 pounds. Pints or quarts, 40 minutes.

Parsnips

NOTE: For early-spring use, parsnips are better when left in the ground through winter. They can be frozen successfully, too.

PREPARATION FOR CANNING: Wash. Peel and cut into slices or dice, or into sticks if preferred. If to be packed hot, boil 3 minutes in water to cover.

PACKING: Hot pack: Pack parsnips with heating liquid, allowing 1-inch headspace. For raw pack, allow 1¹/₂ inches of headspace, then fill with hot liquid to within 1 inch of top. Put on lids.

PROCESSING: Pressure canning only, at 10 pounds. Pints, 20 minutes; quarts, 25 minutes.

Peas—Green Peas

PREPARATION FOR CANNING: Shell, wash, drain. Sort by size if desired. If to be packed hot, boil in water to cover for 2 minutes.

PACKING: For hot pack, pack loosely, adding hot cooking liquid and leaving 1-inch headspace. For raw pack, pack loosely, allow same headspace, and fill jars with boiling water. Put on lids.

PROCESSING: Pressure canning only, at 10 pounds. Pints or quarts, 40 minutes.

Peas—Snow Peas or Edible-podded Peas

Not suitable for canning; freeze them instead.

Peppers—Sweet Peppers, Either Red or Green

PREPARATION FOR CANNING: Wash. Remove stem ends, cores, and seeds. Cut into pieces or strips. Boil 3 minutes in water to cover. To peel, chill pieces in cold water until skin will strip off.

PACKING: Hot pack. Flatten pepper pieces in hot jars, leaving 1-inch headspace. Add 1 tablespoon vinegar and 1/2 teaspoon salt per pint, twice the amount of each per quart. Add boiling water, leaving 1-inch headspace. Put on lids.

PROCESSING: Pressure canning only, at 10 pounds. Pints, 35 minutes; quarts, 45 minutes.

Peppers—Hot Peppers

These are generally more suitable for putting up in other ways. See some of the suggestions in Part Three, "Recipes."

Peppers—Pimientos or Pimiento Peppers

PREPARATION FOR CANNING: Boil 5 minutes in water to cover, then cool quickly in cold water. Strip off skin. Remove stems, cores, and seeds.

PACKING: Flatten into hot half-pint or pint jars, leaving headspace of ½ inch. Add 1 tablespoon vinegar and 1 teaspoon salt per pint (half as much for a half-pint), if desired. Do not add water or oil. Put on lids.

PROCESSING: Pressure canning only, at 10 pounds. For pints or half-pints, 20 minutes.

Potatoes

PREPARATION FOR CANNING: Wash and scrape skins from small new potatoes. For packing hot, boil in water to cover 3 minutes; reserve liquid.

PACKING: For hot pack, fill jars, adding hot parboiling liquid and leaving 1-inch headspace. For raw pack, allow the same headspace and fill jars with boiling water. Put on lids.

PROCESSING: Pressure canning only, at 10 pounds. For pints or quarts, 40 minutes.

Radishes

Not suitable for canning.

Raspberries

NOTE: Raspberries are better when frozen than when canned.

PREPARATION FOR CANNING: Sort, wash gently, drain well. Make light syrup (see formula, page 122) and have it boiling hot.

PACKING: Raw pack. Pour 1/2 cup boiling-hot syrup into each hot jar. Add berries and shake jars lightly to settle them. Allow 1/2-inch headspace. Add more syrup to headspace line, if necessary. Put on lids.

PROCESSING: Boiling-water bath. Pints, 10 minutes; quarts, 15 minutes.

Rhubarb

PREPARATION FOR CANNING: Cut off leaves well below their bases. Trim bases of stalks. Wash. Cut stalks into 1/2- to 1-inch lengths. Put into enameled or stainless-steel kettle with 1/2 to 1 cup sugar for each quart of rhubarb. Cover; let stand 3 hours. Stir, then bring slowly to a boil over moderate heat.

PACKING: Hot pack, with the hot syrup. Leave 1/2-inch headspace. Put on lids.

PROCESSING: Boiling-water bath. Pints or quarts, 10 minutes.

Roquette

Not suitable for canning.

Rutabagas

See directions under "Turnips," below.

Sorrel

Not suitable for canning.

Spinach and New Zealand-Spinach

See directions under "Greens," above.

Squash—Summer Squash, Including Zucchini

PREPARATION FOR CANNING: Wash, scrubbing if gritty. Trim ends, but do not pare unless skin is not tender. Cut into ½-inch slices, halving or quartering slices if you wish. If to be packed hot, cover squash with water and bring to a boil. Drain, reserving hot liquid.

PACKING: For hot pack, put squash loosely into jars, leaving ½-inch headspace. Fill to headspace line with cooking liquid. For raw pack, leave 1-inch headspace. Fill with boiling water to same headspace line. Put on lids.

PROCESSING: Pressure canning only, at 10 pounds. Pints, 25 minutes for raw pack, 30 minutes for hot pack; quarts, 30 minutes for raw pack, 40 minutes for hot pack.

Squash—Winter Squash

PREPARATION FOR CANNING: Wash, peel, remove seeds. Cut

into 1-inch cubes. Bring to boil in barely enough water to cover, then pack. Or continue cooking until tender and sieve pulp and juice together.

PACKING: Hot pack. For cubes, pack with hot cooking liquid, leaving ½-inch headspace. If sieved, reheat squash until boiling and pack without added liquid; allow ½-inch headspace. Put on lids.

PROCESSING: Pressure canning only, at 10 pounds. Cubes: Pints, 65 minutes; quarts 90 minutes. Sieved squash: Pints, 65 minutes; quarts, 80 minutes.

Strawberries

PREPARATION FOR CANNING: Select firm, fully ripe berries. Sort, hull, wash, drain. Place in enamel or stainless-steel kettle with alternate layers of sugar—¾ cup sugar per quart of berries. Cover and let stand 2 hours. Heat slowly to simmering, over moderate heat.

PACKING: Hot pack, with the syrup from the kettle. Shake down to pack closely. If additional syrup is needed, heat and add light syrup (see syrup formulas, page 122). Leave ½-inch headspace. Put on lids.

PROCESSING: Boiling-water bath. Pints, 10 minutes; quarts, 15 minutes.

Tomatoes

PREPARATION FOR CANNING: Wash firm-ripe tomatoes. Dip into boiling water for ½ minute, then dip quickly into cold water. Strip off peel and cut out stem end. Leave whole, or cut into halves or quarters. If to be packed hot, bring quartered tomatoes to a boil, stirring.

PACKING: For raw pack, press down firmly into jars to fill all spaces; add no liquid; allow ½-inch headspace. For hot pack, fill jars with tomatoes, then add hot juice from the kettle. Leave ½-inch headspace. Put on lids.

NOTE: Tomatoes—technically a fruit, and high in acid—are the one exception to the rule that the foods we consider vegetables *must* be processed by pressure canning. Experts say that canning in a boiling-water bath is safe even for those newer tomato varieties described by seedsmen as "low-acid" or "sub-acid." However, a few home canners prefer to take the precaution of adding acid when canning such varieties. If your tomatoes are on the sweet side, or you have grown a sub-acid variety, add 1 teaspoon of fresh lemon juice per pint before processing.

PROCESSING: Boiling-water bath. Pints, 35 minutes; quarts, 45 minutes.

Turnips—White Turnips

NOTE: Turnips are among the vegetables that tend to darken and become strong in flavor when canned. Freezing is preferable.

PREPARATION FOR CANNING: Wash, trim tops and roots, pare. Slice or dice. Boil 3 minutes in water to cover.

PACKING: Hot pack, with cooking liquid. Allow 1-inch headspace. Put on lids.

PROCESSING: Pressure canning only, at 10 pounds. Pints, 30 minutes; quarts, 35 minutes.

Turnips—Yellow Turnips or Rutabagas

NOTE: These have the same characteristics when canned as

white turnips—they darken and become strong in flavor. If you wish to can them, follow the directions for white turnips, above.

Turnip Greens

See directions under "Greens," above.

Watermelons

Not suitable for canning.

Zucchini

See "Squash—Summer Squash. . . ," above.

Making Jellies, Jams, and Other Sweet Preserves

Probably the most popular foods put up at home are jellies, jams, fruit preserves (which are different from jams in that the fruit is in larger pieces, even whole), conserves, fruit butters, and marmalades. Who hasn't brightened a breakfast or other meal with a spoonful or so of jelly or jam? These and other preserves have a double appeal of flavor and appearance that gives pleasure whenever they are served. They are great as toppings for ice cream and puddings, or as fillings for cakes and tartlets, and are delicious ingredients for use in many cooked desserts.

Unlike canned vegetables and fruits, jellies, jams, and most sweet preserves are completely prepared before being ladled into their jars or glasses. They must be sealed at once, while very hot, with rare exceptions that will be described in recipes.

Certain preserves with a fairly low sugar content (sugar in sufficient concentration is a preservative) should be processed in a boiling-water bath, but these preserves are exceptions. Recipes state the need, if any, for processing. Otherwise, the direction "seal" means to use either a covering of paraffin (as for jellies) or sterilized canning lids, put onto the jars as quickly as they are filled.

Ingredients for Jellies and Jams

Making jellies, jams, and other sweet spreads is an excellent way to use fruit that may be unsuited for canning or freezing due to being overmature, or blemished but not spoiled.

The jellied consistency of both jelly and jam depends upon the presence of pectin, a natural substance found to some degree in all fruit, plus sugar and a sufficient amount of fruit acid or added acid, such as lemon juice. Some fruits have more pectin than others, some have so little, especially when very ripe, that liquid or powdered pectin (such as Certo or Sure-Jell) must be used if the jelly or jam is to have the right consistency. Use the type of pectin called for in a given recipe, as the liquid and powdered types are not interchangeable without making adjustments in the cooking method and the quantities of ingredients.

Because of the variation in the amount of natural pectin in berries and fruits, it may be necessary to adjust your formula after the first batch to achieve a softer or a firmer product. (But remember that jams and jellies tend to "firm up" for two weeks or so after being made.)

For recipes with added pectin, to make a softer consistency, use ¼ to ½ cup more fruit or juice per batch; for a firmer jell, use ¼ to ½ cup less fruit or juice. For recipes without added pectin, shorten the cooking time for a softer consistency (or use a lower reading on your jelly thermometer); or lengthen the cooking time (or use a higher thermometer reading, by a degree or two) for a firmer texture.

EQUIPMENT FOR MAKING JELLY

A preserving pan—a large kettle, preferably holding 8 to 10 quarts, with a flat bottom. It should be made of stainless steel, or be enameled, with no cracks or chips inside.

Jelly bag, either purchased or made from several layers of cheesecloth or a piece of muslin

Colander

Large bowl

Wide-mouthed jar-filling funnel

Ladle and large metal spoon, plus a slotted spoon or a skimmer

Jars or jelly glasses (recycled commercial jars may be used for preserves that receive no further heat processing in the jar)

Jar lids (canning lids) for screw-top canning jars; or other lids for covering the contents of jars sealed with paraffin

Tongs for handling hot jars and lids

Paraffin for sealing, unless you are using canning jars and canning lids

Clock with a second hand (for accurate timing), or a very accurate clock timer.

If you plan to make jelly without added pectin, a jelly or candy thermometer will be a help. Use it to make sure the boiling jelly has reached the jellying point (220° F. at sea level, or 8° higher

than the boiling point of water; if, for example, you live at an elevation of 1,000 feet, you'd add 8° to the boiling point in your locality).

PREPARING JARS OR GLASSES. Check jars or glasses for cracks or chipped edges. Wash containers and lids in hot soapy water and rinse in hot water. Place jars and glasses in a kettle, cover with water, and boil for 10 minutes. Leave in the hot water until you are ready to use them.

LIDS. If you are using self-sealing (dome) lids, do *not* boil them; simply pour boiling water over them and let them stand in the hot water until they are needed; or follow the manufacturer's directions.

EXTRACTING THE JUICE

Wash berries or fruit. It is not necessary to remove pits and skins of fruit. Very juicy berries may be crushed, if you wish, and the juice pressed out without heating. Put fruit in a kettle and crush it with a potato masher. Add a small amount of water—just enough to prevent sticking—and heat the fruit over low heat to soften it and release the juice, about 10 minutes for berries, longer for firm fruits. Stir occasionally. Small batches give the best results.

STRAINING THE JUICE. Suspend a dampened jelly bag in its stand, or line a colander with 2 or 3 layers of dampened cheesecloth, and place over a bowl. Pour in the fruit and its juice and let the juice drip through. Fruit should not be squeezed vigorously, as this causes cloudy jelly. However, the fruit may be pressed lightly with the back of a spoon for better juice flow.

MAKING THE JELLY

Measure the fruit juice and follow the recipe for the jelly being made. Do not deviate from the proportions or directions of the recipe, as the balance of pectin, acid, and sugar is crucial, as are the directions for timing and when to add the sugar.

THE JELLY TESTS.   When jelly is made with commercial pectin, following the package directions exactly will insure success. If you are relying on the natural pectin in the fruit, you can't use timing in order to determine when your jelly is done. The boiling time will vary from batch to batch, but there are at least two reliable ways to tell when the jellying point has been reached:

The first way is to use a candy or jelly thermometer. It will have a marking indicating the sea-level jellying point—220° F. If you live at a higher altitude, adjust the reading as we describe above. (That is, add 8° to the reading for the temperature of boiling water at your altitude.)

sheeting

Your other choice is the time-honored sheet (or sheeting) test. Dip a cold, dry metal spoon into the boiling jelly, then hold it over the pan, bowl held on edge, and let the jelly run from it. When the jelly is done, two or three drops will run together, instead of dropping separately, and will shear away from the edge of the spoon in a sheet.

SEALING THE JELLY. While the jelly is being prepared, put paraffin, if you are using it, to melt over low heat. Never melt paraffin over direct heat. If you don't want to use your double boiler, set a small pan containing the wax inside a larger one holding an inch or two of water, and heat until the wax has melted.

As soon as the jelly is done, remove the kettle from the heat. Skim off any foam quickly and fill the jars or glasses immediately, using a wide-mouthed canning funnel and a ladle.

If you are using canning jars, fill them to within 1/8 inch of the top. As each jar is filled, wipe the edge with a clean, damp cloth and seal it at once with a lid, removed at the moment of use (use tongs) from its pan of hot water and fastened in place with a screw band.

Glasses to be sealed with paraffin should be filled to within 1/2 inch of the top. If any drips appear on the inside of the glass above the surface of the jelly, wipe them away carefully with a fold of paper toweling dipped into hot water. At once pour an 1/8-inch layer of melted paraffin over the hot jelly, making sure that the wax touches the glass all around. If any air bubbles appear in the wax, prick them before the wax hardens.

LABELING AND STORING JELLY. After the paraffin has hardened, cover the glasses with metal lids or heavy foil, or use parchment-type paper securely fastened with tape, a twist of wire, or string.

Label the cooled jars or glasses with the contents and the date and store them in a dark place that is cool and dry.

EQUIPMENT FOR MAKING JAM

You will need the same equipment as for making jelly, except that no jelly bag is required. If you are preparing a large quantity of fruit, a food grinder is useful for any but the softest fruits—those can be mashed by hand.

The jars or glasses and the lids or paraffin are prepared exactly as for jelly.

PREPARING THE FRUIT

Preparing fruit for jam is similar to the process we have just described for jelly, but you don't heat the fruit or strain off the juice—the jam is made with all of the fruit except pits and, sometimes, the skins—peaches, for instance, are peeled before being cut up or crushed.

After a thorough washing, in several changes of cold water, if necessary, berries or fruit for jam are drained well, then chopped, grated, or crushed, according to the consistency of the fruit and your recipe directions. Again, you'll have the greatest success when you make jams in small batches.

MAKING THE JAM

Cook the jam according to your recipe directions. If you use commercial pectin, follow the label instructions precisely—this will make it certain that your jam will jell. Jam made without added pectin usually is done when the boiling mixture registers a temperature 9° F. above the boiling point of water at a given altitude—the "done" reading would thus be 221° F. at sea level.

As jam thickens while cooking, stir it frequently to prevent sticking and scorching. If you do not have a jelly or candy thermometer, you can judge when the jam has reached its correct stage of doneness when it will begin to hold its shape in a chilled spoon; or when a small amount, put on a chilled plate, congeals when set in the refrigerator, and wrinkles without running much when the plate is tipped sharply. (If you use this test, set the pot off the heat meanwhile, or you may overcook the jam.)

SEALING THE JAM. When your jam is done, remove the kettle from the heat and ladle the jam immediately into the hot, sterilized jars. Leave the same headspace as for jelly—1/8 inch for jars to be sealed with lids and screw bands, 1/2 inch for jars or glasses to be sealed with paraffin. Add wax, or cover with lids, exactly as for jelly.

LABELING AND STORING JAM: Exactly as for jelly.

Fruit Preserves, Butters, Marmalades, and Conserves

The equipment you will need for making these preserves is the same as for jam, except that you will need a food mill or a sieve for making fruit butters. No thermometer is needed.

PRESERVES

Preparing fruit for preserves is somewhat different from preparing it for jam, if you accept the general definition of "preserve"—a jam in which the pieces of fruit are large—or in which some fruits, such as berries, are whole. In general, be guided by your recipe as to the size of the pieces.

Most authorities suggest processing preserves in their jars for 10 to 20 minutes in a boiling-water bath, exactly as described for canned fruits. For preserves to be so processed, canning jars rather than jelly glasses must be used, as must canning lids.

FRUIT BUTTERS

Fruit butters are made from the pulp of fruit, sometimes partially cooked, sometimes not, which has been pressed through a food mill or a sieve. The pulp is cooked slowly with sugar and often spices until it is thick enough to be spread when cool.

Fruit butters are processed for 10 minutes or so (always follow your recipe) in a boiling-water bath, so you'll need canning jars and lids for them. These butters are a pleasant change from jelly and jam.

MARMALADES

For marmalades, prepare the fruit according to the recipe directions—there are innumerable versions of orange marmalade alone (see Part Three, "Recipes," for a marmalade we have chosen). Cooking methods vary, too, but in general you cook marmalades slowly at first, then rapidly, with constant stirring, until the clear portion has thickened to its jelling point, as with jam. Either pour hot marmalade into jars, seal them, and process them in a boiling-water bath if your recipe so directs, or ladle the marmalade into sterile, hot glasses or jars and seal them with paraffin or lids, as directed for jelly.

CONSERVES
Somewhat like preserves, somewhat like jam, but richer, conserves are often spiced and have such added ingredients as nuts or dried fruits (see Part Three).

Making Pickles and Relishes

Pickles add piquant interest to sandwich lunches and to simple suppers, as well as pleasant contrasts of color and flavor to sophisticated foods. They are the dieter's delight—except for those with added sweetening, pickles are low in calories. Pickle flavors are enhanced by storage on your shelves for several weeks.

The array of pickles you can enjoy from your home garden includes relishes, brined or fermented pickles such as the familiar dill pickles, fresh-pack pickles, and fruit pickles. In Part Three, "Recipes," as well as in your general cookbooks, you will find recipes for pickles in each of these groups.

EQUIPMENT FOR PICKLING
The same jars, kettles, lids, and other items listed for canning are needed for pickling. The household scales suggested as a convenience for canning are required when you make sauerkraut (see our recipes), and they are handy when making other pickles, too. You will need an enamel-lined pan (no chips in the lining), or one of the other types of preserving pans we have described. You will also need a large stoneware jar or crock, or a large glass jar or ceramic or glass bowl or casserole, for brining, plus a glass lid or a plate that fits snugly inside the brining container and a heavy weight to be set upon the lid to keep the food below the brine. You can use a glass jar, or a heavyweight plastic bag, filled with water, for the weight.

A CAUTION. Although you may take pride in your copper saucepans, or in an heirloom iron kettle, never use such pots as these for cooking, heating, or brining of pickles or for heating pickling liquids. Avoid all unlined copper or brass or galvanized or iron utensils when pickling; acids and salts in the pickling liquid may react with these metals to form undesirable compounds. Use pots of enamelware, completely free of any chipped areas on the inside, or use vessels of stainless steel or glass for heating pickling liquids.

Brining or fermenting should be carried out in unchipped enamelware, a crock, or a stoneware jar. You could also use a large casserole of suitable material, a glass jar, or a bowl.

INGREDIENTS USED IN PICKLING

Besides the raw materials—cucumbers, eggplants, green beans, okra, fruit, and any number of other home-garden foods—pickling calls for certain ingredients about which the home canner needs some basic information. Among them are salt, vinegar, sugar, and spices.

SALT.   Salt for pickling with a clear brine should be pure granulated salt—the kind called pickling salt, if available, or dairy salt, or the coarse salt in packages marked "kosher salt." If ordinary table salt, noniodized, is used, the brine may become cloudy from additives which prevent the salt from caking. Iodized salt should not be

153

Part Two: Putting Up Food

used—the iodine darkens pickles. However, in nonbrined pickle or relish mixtures where the salt is a seasoning only, table salt, preferably noniodized, may be used.

The 10 percent brine solution called for in many pickle recipes is made by dissolving 1½ cups of pure salt per gallon of water.

VINEGAR. For successful pickling it is essential to know the approximate acidity of the vinegar, so for this reason it isn't desirable to use homemade vinegar—save that for salads. The vinegar for pickling should be of from 4 percent to 6 percent acidity (40 to 60 grain); usually the acidity is indicated on the label of the bottle. This degree of acidity is necessary to prevent spoilage of pickles. You should use a high-quality cider vinegar or a white distilled vinegar. White vinegar is preferable for light-colored pickles, but many prefer the flavor of cider vinegar despite its tendency to darken light-colored pickles.

To decrease the tartness of a pickle, more sugar may be added, but do *not* dilute the vinegar to reduce sourness—the correct acidity is essential to help preserve the food. Never dilute vinegar except as specified in the recipe.

SUGAR. Unless your recipe calls for brown sugar, use white granulated sugar. If brown sugar is called for, pack it firmly in the cup when measuring, and use either light or dark brown sugar, as you prefer. The dark sugar has more of a tinge of molasses in its flavor, and seems less sweet.

SPICES. Use the freshest spices you can obtain. Old and shelf-weary spices, whether they have been on your shelf or the grocer's, will never give you the full measure of flavor for your pickles. Sniff your spices and weed out the feeble ones.

OTHER INGREDIENTS. When unusual ingredients are called for in some of our recipes—alum, spice oils, pickling lime, and rare Indian spices, for instance—we have suggested sources when the grocery story isn't likely to carry what you need.

MAKING THE PICKLES

Select vegetables and fruit of uniform size—tender vegetables and firm but ripe fruit. Use as soon as possible after gathering from the garden. Wash a few pieces at a time, thoroughly, with a brush, either under running cold water or in several changes of cold water in a container from which the food is lifted out of the water after each washing. Remove any blossoms from cucumbers.

IF YOU HAVE HARD WATER. If your water supply is classified as hard, boil a supply for 15 minutes the day before pickling—this is for use in making brine. Let the boiled brining water stand for 24 hours, then remove scum from the top and carefully ladle out the water, leaving behind any sediment. Before using boiled water for brining, add 1 tablespoon of vinegar per gallon.

THE ROLE OF HEAT. Organisms that cause spoilage in pickled foods are destroyed by the heat of boiling-water processing. Imperfections in color, texture, or flavor may be the result of continuing enzyme action in pickles. This cause of pickle problems is eliminated by proper heat treatment.

Despite the preservative effect of a properly made brine, or of fermentation, there is always danger of spoilage in the jar, even with the most careful sealing of sterilized lids on sterilized jars. Heat processing by the boiling-water-bath method already described is therefore recommended in most pickle recipes. The method is exactly the same as for canned fruits and tomatoes.

Relishes and Chutneys

Relishes and chutneys are cooked condiments in the pickle group, prepared from chopped, seasoned, spiced, and vinegared vegetables and fruits. Deservedly popular, they provide flavorsome ways to use small amounts of such vegetables as corn and cauliflower and the late-season green tomatoes. Some vegetables and fruits for relishes and similar condiments are brined for a rather short period before spices and other ingredients are added and the mixture is cooked, then ladled into jars for heat processing.

Fresh-Pack Pickles

Like relishes, fresh-pack, or quick-process, pickles are brined for only a few hours, or overnight at most, before they are covered (and sometimes briefly cooked) with a solution of boiling-hot spiced and seasoned vinegar, then heat-processed in their jars. These easily prepared pickles are delicious and tender, usually with a tart-pungent flavor which is improved by ripening for a few weeks in a cool, dark storage area that is dry and safe from freezing. Examples of pickles of this type, among the recipes in Part Three, are Bread and Butter Pickles, Mustard Pickles, and Pickled Brussels Sprouts (see Index).

Fruit Pickles

One of the most popular of all pickles made from home-garden raw material is pickled or preserved watermelon rind. This, like other fruit pickles, after being cooked in spicy and often vinegared syrup, is placed in jars, sealed, and processed in a boiling-water bath.

Brined Pickles

Properly brined pickles, including sauerkraut and the many kinds of dilled cucumbers, go through a fermentation process in the brine solution, then are packed into jars with their own strained and heated brine, or fresh boiling-hot brine. Water-bath processing is often recommended if brined pickles are to be kept in storage for more than a fairly short time. See our recipes for two kinds of sauerkraut and for Polish Dill Pickles (Part Three).

Freezing Vegetables and Fruits

You can enjoy almost all the fresh vegetables you have grown, plus fresh home-garden fruits, even after the ground has been covered with snow for weeks or even months. Freezing is the answer.

Nutritive qualities, flavor, and natural color are kept better in most foods by freezing than by other methods of preservation. Most vegetables and fruits suitable for canning are also suitable for freezing, and frozen foods are more like freshly gathered foods than those that have been canned. Furthermore, preparing vegetables and fruits for freezing is quick and relatively simple—it's not very different from preparing them for immediate serving at a meal.

Vegetables and fruits can be frozen in quantities that would be too small to justify the time and work involved in putting them up in jars by canning. Putting up only a pint or two by freezing is perfectly feasible, but canning such a small quantity would be uneconomical.

The Freezer

For successful freezing, you must have a true freezer—not just an ice-cube compartment in a refrigerator. The freezer must be capable of maintaining a temperature of zero degrees F., or below, for effective initial freezing and safe storage. The colder, the better—the freezer life of frozen vegetables and fruits kept at zero degrees F. or below is from 8 to 12 months, but is much shorter if the freezer temperature is only a few degrees higher.

If you don't own a freezer and are thinking of buying one, there are points to consider beyond the initial cost of the unit. Although it costs nothing to store canned foods, frozen foods require the continuing use of electric power for the freezer, with the greatest expense incurred by the so-called self-defrosting and frost-free units.

If you live in an area where power failures occur fairly often, you should also consider the availability of dry ice near by, or whether there is access to a freezer-locker concern that will take temporary locker tenants during power-failure emergencies.

Equipment and Supplies for Freezing

For preparing vegetables and fruits no special equipment is necessary beyond some of the items we have already discussed for canning. Mainly you'll need a large pot for blanching or scalding. You can use a preserving pan or a pot made of any material, but it's convenient to have a pot with a perforated basket insert; or provide

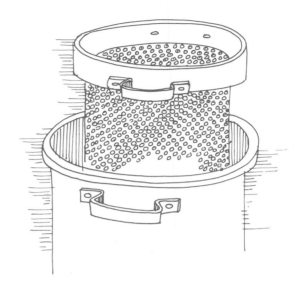

yourself with a large frying basket or a colander that will fit inside your scalding or blanching pot, which should hold 2 gallons or so. You'll also need a large bowl or pot for cooling the food in cold water after blanching, and a colander for draining it after cooling. Household scales are helpful.

PACKAGING SUPPLIES.   For packaging, you can choose among many possibilities. You can use slope-sided (not shouldered) dual-purpose freezing and canning jars sealed with screw-band lids; or rigid freezer containers and lids of plastic (the most usual material) or aluminum. Or, if you prefer not to use containers, food can be put into plastic freezer bags, either the plain kind for storage or the heavy, heat-sealed plastic kind that allows the food to be finally cooked for the table still in the same bag ("boil-in bags"). Food for freezing can be folded into freezer-weight aluminum foil and sealed with freezer tape; or wrapped in plastic freezer film and sealed; or wrapped in heavily waxed or plastic-coated freezer paper or other odor-free, odor-proof, moisture-proof, and vapor-proof wrappings manufactured especially for use in freezing.

The size of your containers will depend upon the size of your family and the kinds of foods you will be freezing. Pint and quart

containers are the most common sizes, but bags come in many sizes and a small amount of food can be wrapped in a packet, or frozen in a small screw-top jar—baby-food jars, or jars in which spices have been sold, are especially good for storing frozen chopped herbs and the like.

SEALING AND LABELING

Wrapped freezer packages, whether the wrapping is foil, plastic, or coated paper, should be closely sealed with freezer tape,

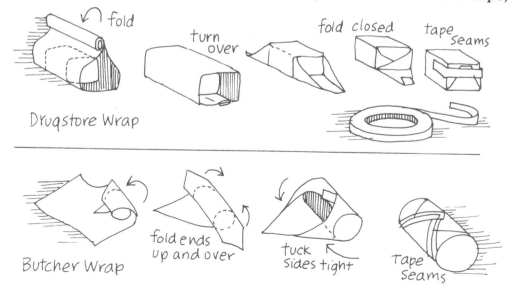

which resembles masking tape. The tape can also serve as a label—write the contents and the date on it, using a china-marking pencil or a waterproof felt-tip marker.

Jars and freezer containers and all types of freezer bags should be sealed according to the manufacturer's directions. (Don't forget to label these, too.) The keys to quality frozen foods are high-quality foods to begin with, correct processing, and, finally, good wrapping—which means packaging that excludes air.

KEEPING AN INVENTORY

Frozen food should be used before it reaches the limit of its storage time, if you want to eat it at its best. To assure this, keep an inventory. List the number of packages of each batch of vegetables or fruits put into the freezer, with the date of freezing. When removing foods for use, take those with the earliest dates. And don't forget to change your inventory to reflect what you have taken out.

STORAGE LIFE IN THE FREEZER. The storage life of correctly frozen fruits and vegetables, kept at zero degrees F. or lower, is at least 8 months; 10 to 12 months is a reasonable period during which you can expect quality to remain high, so long as the freezer temperature remains low.

Freezing Vegetables

Vegetables for freezing should be garden-fresh and at the perfect stage for table use. Soft spots or discolored or blemished areas should be cut out. Do not freeze overmature vegetables or fruit.

PRELIMINARY PREPARATION

Thoroughly wash vegetables, scrubbing with a brush if necessary, either in a container set under cold running water or in several changes of clear water, from which you lift the food after each washing.

Prepare the vegetables as for canning or for cooking for the table, trimming or paring as necessary. Cut them up or leave them whole, according to their size or your preference. Prepare only at one time the amount of food that your freezer can freeze completely hard within a 24-hour period. A good amount to prepare is about 2 or 3 pounds per cubic foot of available freezer space.

SCALDING OR BLANCHING

Nearly all vegetables must be scalded or blanched before being frozen, in order to discourage the continuing action of enzymes, which, if not impeded first by heat and then by cold, will impair both quality and flavor during frozen storage.

The simplest and most commonly used scalding or blanching method is to place 1 pound of prepared vegetables in your perforated pot insert or a wire basket and immerse the vegetables in a large kettle holding at least 1 gallon—better 2 gallons—of rapidly boiling water. Blanching time varies with the kind of vegetable and the size of the pieces, as you will see in the detailed directions that follow. The water should return to the boil almost at once. Cover the pot and start counting the blanching time when you add the food.

COOLING THE SCALDED FOOD. As soon as the blanching time is up, remove the vegetables from the kettle and cool them immediately in a large container of ice water, or in a big bowl of cold water set under cold running water. (The water in the pot may be reused for subsequent batches.) Hold the vegetables in the cold water for at least the length of time they were scalded. Feel a piece or two—the vegetables should be cold, even chilled. Drain thoroughly.

SCALDING AT HIGH ALTITUDES. Add 1 minute to the specified scalding or blanching time for any vegetable if you live at an elevation of 5,000 feet or more.

PACKING

Pack vegetables without delay. Include no liquid beyond that clinging to the pieces, and when using rigid containers be sure to allow the correct amount of headspace for the kind of food, as specified in the detailed directions that follow. Seal the packages or containers and place the vegetables in the coldest part of the freezer, allowing space for the cold air to circulate around the packages. (Some freezers have special quick-freezing sections or extra-cold surfaces—if your freezer has one of these, be sure to use it).

A NOTE ON HEADSPACE. Foods packed in rigid containers require varying amounts of headspace, or space between the top surface of the food and the top of the container, to allow for expansion. Liquids and dense purées generally require the most headspace, while food in large pieces—broccoli, cauliflower, or asparagus, for instance—needs no actual headspace, as there is enough expansion room between the pieces.

Headspace allowances are given in the detailed instructions farther along for freezing vegetables and fruits.

Freezing Home-Garden Fruits

Certain fruits retain better flavor and color when sweetened and treated with an antioxidant, such as ascorbic acid, before being frozen. Among the home-garden fruits we include in this book, this is true of muskmelons or cantaloupes in particular. Sweetening may be with sugar syrup—this is called wet pack—or with dry sugar plus the juice the sugar draws from the fruit, called dry pack—more accurately, perhaps, this should be "damp pack," as a considerable amount of syrup is formed by certain fruits packed this way.

Other wet-pack possibilities are fruits packed in fruit juice, or in a solution of an artificial sweetener. If one of the synthetic sweeteners is used, follow the manufacturer's instructions. Another dry pack—this one actually dryer than the other—is the method of layering berries in the freezer container with dry sugar, ³/₄ cup sugar per quart of berries.

A number of fruits are ideal for freezing without sweetening. Strawberries are fine when done this way, although most people prefer to sweeten them for use as a dessert fruit. But most of the garden fruits we discuss—strawberries, raspberries, blueberries, and rhubarb (which is of course a vegetable) are fine when simply frozen in what is called "unsweetened pack." Melons are better when done in syrup, as we have noted.

PREPARING THE FRUIT

Wash fruit or berries gently but thoroughly after sorting out overmature, broken, or badly blemished specimens. Drain. Most fruits are not blanched or scalded (exceptions: fruits such as peaches, dipped briefly into boiling water to aid the removal of skins), but rhubarb, among the fruits we're considering, may be blanched if you wish, although it's not essential for good results. Pare melons and remove seeds. Cut up fruit as you wish, leaving berries and small fruits whole. The fruit is now ready to be packed in the fashion you prefer.

FREEZING FRUITS IN A SYRUP PACK

Directions for freezing fruits in a syrup pack often state the sugar content, or sweetness, of the syrup in terms of percentages. Sometimes, however, the terms "light," "medium," and "heavy" are used, as for canning syrups.

For most fruits a 40 percent syrup (medium) is recommended. Very tart fruits may need a heavier syrup, but lighter syrups are desirable for some mild-flavored fruits, such as melons.

For dessert use, fruits packed in syrup are usually preferred. Fruits packed in dry sugar, or packed unsweetened, are more satisfactory for most cooking purposes, as they have less liquid than wet-packed fruits.

SYRUP FORMULAS FOR FREEZING FRUITS. To prepare syrup for freezing fruits, dissolve granulated white sugar in either cold or hot water, in the proportions given in the table below. Light corn syrup may be substituted for up to one-fourth of the sugar called for, or fruit juice may be partly or entirely substituted for the water. Cool hot syrup completely before using. Syrup may be made the day before freeze-packing and kept in the refrigerator in a covered container.

Syrup Consistency	*Amount of Sugar Per 4 Cups of Water*	*Yield*
30% syrup (light syrup)	2 cups	5 cups
35% syrup	$2^1/_2$ cups	$5^1/_3$ cups
40% syrup (medium syrup)	3 cups	$5^1/_2$ cups
50% syrup (heavy syrup)	$4^3/_4$ cups	$6^1/_2$ cups
60% syrup	7 cups	$7^3/_4$ cups
65% syrup	$8^3/_4$ cups	$8^2/_3$ cups

PACKING THE FRUIT. The syrup must cover the top of the fruit in the freezing container, so jars or rigid containers are preferable to bags. Settle fruit in the container by jarring it gently before and after adding the syrup. Allow the headspace indicated in the directions for the fruit you're packing. Crumple a piece of freezer paper or waxed paper and place on top of the fruit to hold it under the syrup when the lid is put in place.

THE DRY-SUGAR PACK

The dry-sugar pack is accomplished by gently mixing the fruit with dry sugar, turning it over several times and letting it stand for 10 minutes or so, or until the sugar is dissolved, before packing. This method is often preferred for soft, juicy fruits, such as strawberries packed in halves or in slices. Sometimes the fruit and sugar are placed in alternate layers in containers.

The proportion of sugar to fruit in this pack will be stated in the detailed directions that follow. The sugar draws out some of the fruit juice and dissolves the sugar; an alternative is to layer the fruit with dry sugar, as suggested above. As with the wet pack, it's a good idea to top fruit stirred with sugar with a wad of crumpled freezer paper or waxed paper, to hold it under the juice, before sealing with the lid.

THE UNSWEETENED PACK

The quality of some fruits, such as raspberries, whole strawberries, gooseberries, currants, cranberries, and blueberries, as well as of that fruity vegetable rhubarb, is as good when they are frozen perfectly plain and unsweetened as when they are frozen with syrup or sugar. For this pack, the washed, well-drained, and cut-up (in the case of rhubarb) fruit is simply sealed into containers, labeled, and placed in the freezer. The unsweetened pack requires little or no headspace.

FREEZER PRESERVES

As has been pointed out in the Introduction, freezing has remarkable possibilities beyond preserving our basic fruits and vegetables. Certain fruits lend themselves to use in uncooked jams and jellies which can be stored for a short period in the refrigerator, or frozen for longer storage. The best source of information on these remarkable sweets is the booklet accompanying bottled liquid pectin. Among the fruits suitable for use in uncooked jelly or jam are strawberries, blackberries, raspberries, grapes, peaches, rhubarb, and cherries.

An Alphabet of Freezing Instructions for Vegetables and Fruits

The detailed directions that follow cover all the freezable foods that this book includes. When you have a choice as to preparation or pack, it has been given. All vegetables are packed without liquid. The entries for fruits indicate the possibilities: unsweetened pack, dry pack, wet pack, and so forth. When headspace is given it is for rigid containers—there is, of course, no "headspace" when food is put into freezer bags.

Artichokes—Globe Artichokes (Whole)

PREPARATION FOR FREEZING: Remove any blemished outer leaves and trim off stems. Cut off tips of remaining leaves and trim artichokes, if you wish, to a cone shape. Wash in cold water acidulated with lemon juice. Scald, cool, drain, pack.

SCALDING TIME: 7 minutes for small to medium artichokes.

PACKING: Wrap individually, or pack in bags. If packed in containers, leave no headspace.

Artichokes—Globe Artichokes (Hearts or Bottoms)

PREPARATION FOR FREEZING: Remove and discard all but the very tender yellow or white leaves at the heart. Trim off stems. Snip tips of remaining leaves to 1 inch. Separate leaves and scrape out chokes with a spoon. Rinse in water acidulated with lemon juice. Scald, cool, drain, pack.

SCALDING TIME: 4 to 6 minutes, depending on size.

PACKING: In bags or rigid containers (no headspace).

Asparagus

PREPARATION FOR FREEZING: Sort according to thickness; remove woody bases; wash thoroughly. Leave whole, or cut to desired length. Blanch, cool, drain, pack.

SCALDING TIME: Thin stalks, 2 minutes; medium stalks, 3 minutes; large stalks (1 inch thick or more), 4 minutes. Slant cut (1/4 inch thick), 1 minute.

PACKING: No headspace for whole stalks; pack tips and stem ends alternately. Freeze cut or slant-cut asparagus in containers with 1/2-inch headspace, or freeze loose, then pack (see directions in Part Three.)

Beans—Broad or Fava Beans

PREPARATION FOR FREEZING: Wash and shell; rinse. If very young, proceed to blanch them. If still green but more mature, skin each bean, then scald, cool, drain, and pack.

SCALDING TIME: Small and young beans, 2 minutes; larger beans, 3 minutes.

PACKING: 1/2-inch headspace.

Beans—Lima Beans (Green)

PREPARATION FOR FREEZING: Shell and sort for size. Wash scald, cool, drain, and pack.

SCALDING TIME: Small, 2 minutes; medium, 3 minutes; large, 4 minutes.

PACKING: ½-inch headspace.

Beans—Snap Beans; also Wax Beans and Italian or 'Romano' Beans

PREPARATION FOR FREEZING: Wash; remove ends. Cut lengthwise (French-cut) or cut into the lengths you prefer. Scald, cool, drain, pack.

SCALDING TIME: 3 minutes.

PACKING   ½-inch headspace.

Beans—Soy Beans (Green)

PREPARATION FOR FREEZING: Choose young, bright-green beans. Boil in their pods in water to cover for 5 minutes. Cool under running water, shell, rinse, drain, pack.

SCALDING TIME: No further scalding is needed after initial preparation.

PACKING: ½-inch headspace.

Beets

PREPARATION FOR FREEZING: Select young beets 2 inches or less in diameter. Trim tops to 1 or 2 inches. Sort for size. Wash, scrubbing if necessary. Boil in water to cover until tender. Cool, slip off skins, trim roots. Cut into slices or cubes, or leave whole if tiny.

SCALDING TIME: None—beets are cooked until done during the preparation step.

PACKING: ½-inch headspace.

Beet Greens

See directions under "Greens," below.

Blueberries

PREPARATION FOR FREEZING: Sort, wash, drain.

SCALDING: None.

PACKING: Pack dry, unsweetened, or mixed with ¾ cup sugar per quart. Or use wet pack, with 40 or 50 percent syrup (page 162) for berries to be served as a dessert.

Broccoli

PREPARATION FOR FREEZING: Wash. Peel and trim stalks. If necessary to remove insects, soak ½ hour in solution of 4 teaspoons salt per gallon of cold water. Divide flowerets by splitting stalks so that no floweret is more than 1 or 1½ inches across. (See also suggestions in Part Three, "Recipes," for freezing slant-cut stems and making broccoli purée.) Scald, cool, drain, pack.

SCALDING TIME: For 1½-inch flowerets with stalks attached, 3 minutes. For smaller flowerets, 2 minutes. For slant-cut stems (peeled), 1 minute.

PACKING: No headspace.

Brussels Sprouts

PREPARATION FOR FREEZING: Remove coarse outer leaves and trim bases. Sort (and process) according to size. Wash thoroughly; if necessary to remove insects, soak ½ hour in solution of 4 teaspoons salt per gallon of cold water. Scald, chill, drain, pack.

SCALDING TIME: Small, 3 minutes; medium, 4 minutes; large, 5 minutes.

PACKING: No headspace.

Cabbage

NOTE: Frozen cabbage and frozen Chinese cabbage (below) are not suitable for use in cole slaw or salads.

PREPARATION FOR FREEZING: Remove coarse outer leaves. Wash thoroughly. Shred leaves, or cut into 1-inch wedges, each attached to part of core. Scald, chill, drain, pack.

SCALDING TIME: Wedges, 3 minutes; shreds, 1½ minutes.

PACKING: No headspace for wedges; ½-inch headspace for shreds.

Cabbage—Chinese Cabbage or Celery Cabbage

PREPARATION FOR FREEZING: Cut off root end, separate ribs, wash thoroughly. Trim any blemished leaves. If desired, separate ribs and the leafy parts and freeze separately; or cut crosswise in 1-inch slices, ribs and leaves together. Scald, cool, drain, pack.

SCALDING TIME: 1 minute.

PACKING: 1/2-inch headspace.

Carrots

PREPARATION FOR FREEZING: Cut off tops, wash, and pare or scrape off skin. Leave small carrots whole; cut larger carrots into 1/4-inch cubes or into slices or strips. Scald, cool, drain, pack.

SCALDING TIME: Whole (small), 5 minutes; cubes or slices or strips, 3 minutes.

PACKING: 1/2-inch headspace.

Cauliflower

PREPARATION FOR FREEZING: Trim stem, break head into flowerets about 1 inch across. Wash well. If necessary to remove insects, soak 1/2 hour in solution of 4 teaspoons salt per gallon of water. Scald, cool, drain, and pack.

SCALDING TIME: 3 minutes.

PACKING: No headspace.

Celeriac—Knob Celery, Celery Root

PREPARATION FOR FREEZING: This vegetable is seldom frozen, but it's feasible to do so. Pare, cut into julienne strips, wash. Add 6 tablespoons lemon juice to each 4 quarts of scalding water. Scald, cool, drain, and pack as described below.

SCALDING TIME: 1 minute.

PACKING: Spread on baking sheet covered with waxed paper. Freeze until solid, then pack in plastic bags or rigid containers (no headspace).

Celery

PREPARATION FOR FREEZING: Cut off base, separate ribs, and remove coarse strings from outer ribs, if desired. Wash, trim, slice crosswise into 1-inch pieces. (Reserve twiggy tops for the treatment described in Part Three, "Recipes.") Scald, cool, drain, pack.

SCALDING TIME: 3 minutes.

PACKING: $1/2$-inch headspace.

Chard—Swiss Chard

PREPARATION FOR FREEZING: If you wish to separate the leaves and stalks for freezing, follow instructions for "Greens" (below) for the leaves. Choose tender stalks of chard, cut off bases, separate ribs, wash well. Separate leafy portions, or cut ribs and leaves together crosswise into 1- or $1^1/2$-inch pieces. Scald, cool, drain, pack.

SCALDING TIME: Leaves only, same as for greens. Ribs or ribs and leaves, 3 minutes.

PACKING: $1/2$-inch headspace.

Collards

See directions under "Greens," below.

Corn on the Cob

PREPARATION FOR FREEZING: Select freshly picked ears in the early milk stage. Husk, trim ends, remove silk, wash. Scald, cool, drain, pack.

SCALDING TIME: 6 minutes for ears 1½ inches in diameter; 8 minutes if 2 inches in diameter; 10 minutes if larger.

PACKING: No headspace.

Corn—Whole-Kernel Style

PREPARATION FOR FREEZING: Husk, trim, remove silk, and wash as for corn on the cob. Cut kernels from cobs at two-thirds their depth after scalding, cooling, and draining whole ears.

SCALDING TIME: 4 minutes (on the cob—see "Preparation" above).

PACKING: ½-inch headspace.

Corn—Cream-Style

PREPARATION FOR FREEZING: Exactly as for whole-kernel corn, except that the kernels are cut from the cob at about one-half their depth, then the milk and the heart of the kernels are scraped from the cob and added to the kernels before packing.

SCALDING TIME: 4 minutes (on the cob).

PACKING: ½-inch headspace.

Cresses

Cresses are generally not suitable for freezing. For an exception, see the directions for Watercress Purée in Part Three, "Recipes."

Cucumbers

Cucumbers do not freeze satisfactorily.

Eggplant

PREPARATION FOR FREEZING: Wash, peel, and slice ⅓ inch thick, preparing just enough (about a pound) for one scalding at a time. Add 4½ teaspoons of citric-acid powder or ½ cup lemon juice to 4 quarts boiling water for scalding. Scald, cool, drain, pack.

SCALDING TIME: 4 minutes.

PACKING: In freezer wrap, with 2 sheets of waxed paper or freezer paper between the stacked slices.

Greens: Beet Greens, Chard, Collards, Kale, New Zealand-Spinach, Spinach, Turnip Greens

PREPARATION FOR FREEZING: Select tender, young leaves. Remove tough or large stems. Wash thoroughly in several changes of water. During scalding, stir leaves to avoid matting and inadequate heating. Cool, drain, pack.

SCALDING TIME: Beet greens, 2 minutes; chard, 2 minutes; collards, 3 minutes; kale, 3 minutes; New Zealand-spinach, 2 minutes; spinach, 1½ minutes; turnip greens, 2 minutes.

PACKING: ½-inch headspace.

Herbs

See the section on herbs in Part Three, "Recipes."

Kale

See directions under "Greens," above.

Kohlrabi

PREPARATION FOR FREEZING: Trim tops and roots. Wash and peel. Sort for size, if to be left whole; or cut into ½-inch dice or ¼-inch slices. Scald, cool, drain, pack.

SCALDING TIME: Whole, 2 to 3 minutes, according to size. Dice or slices, 1 minute.

PACKING: No headspace, if whole; ½-inch headspace for dice or slices.

Leeks

PREPARATION FOR FREEZING: Wash thoroughly to remove sand. Slice the white part and the pale-green, tender part of tops into ⅛-inch crosswise slices. Wash again. Scald, cool, drain, pack. (See also discussion of leeks in Part Three, "Recipes," for a method of freezing leeks for use as a seasoning vegetable.)

SCALDING TIME: 1 minute.

PACKING: No headspace. Seal airtight in jars or rigid containers, with added tape, to prevent possible escape of odor into freezer.

Lettuce, Romaine, and Endive

Not suitable for freezing.

Muskmelons—also Cantaloupes, Casabas, Cranshaws, Honeydews, and Persian Melons

NOTE: See also "Watermelon," below.

PREPARATION FOR FREEZING: Wash, cut in half and remove seeds. Cut into slices, cubes, or balls. Pack with or without sweetening. For wet (syrup) pack, use 30 or 40 percent syrup (see syrup formulas, page 162), adding ½ teaspoon of ascorbic acid powder per quart of syrup.

SCALDING: None.

PACKING: Pints, ½-inch headspace; quarts, 1-inch headspace.

New Zealand-Spinach

See directions under "Greens," above.

Okra

PREPARATION FOR FREEZING: Wash. Trim stems short, but avoid cutting into pod before blanching. Scald, chill, and drain. Slice crosswise after scalding if desired; pack.

SCALDING TIME: 3 to 4 minutes, according to size.

PACKING: ½-inch headspace.

Onions

PREPARATION FOR FREEZING: Trim off tops and roots and remove dry outer skin. Slice ¼ inch thick, or cut into dice. Pack raw.

SCALDING: Not needed.

PACKING: Seal in jars with airtight lids or in rigid containers, sealed with tape, to prevent escape of onion odor into freezer; or freeze in heat-sealed heavy plastic bags.

Parsnips

PREPARATION FOR FREEZING: Pare, wash, and cut into slices, sticks, or dice. Scald, cool, drain, pack.

SCALDING TIME: 1 to 3 minutes, depending on thickness (from ¼ to ½ inch) of pieces.

PACKING: No headspace for sticks; ½-inch headspace for dice.

Peas—Green Peas

PREPARATION FOR FREEZING: Select fresh, tender peas with bright pods and process as soon as possible after harvesting. Shell and wash; scald, chill, drain, and pack.

SCALDING TIME: 1¹/₂ minutes.

PACKING: ¹/₂-inch headspace.

Peas—Snow Peas or Edible-podded Peas

PREPARATION FOR FREEZING: Select fresh, tender peas, as small as possible, with bright pods. Process promptly after picking. Leave pods whole—simply remove the tips and wash. Scald, cool, drain, and pack.

SCALDING TIME: 1 to 1¹/₂ minutes.

PACKING: ¹/₂-inch headspace.

Peppers—Sweet Peppers, Either Red or Green

NOTE: Hot peppers may also be frozen by this method. Be sure to label them HOT.

PREPARATION FOR FREEZING: Wash, remove stem ends, cores, and seeds; cut up, or cut into halves, rings, or dice, as you prefer. For use in cooking, or for pepper halves to be stuffed, scald, chill, drain, and pack. For future use in uncooked foods, freeze without scalding.

SCALDING TIME: Cut-up peppers, 2 minutes; halves, 3 minutes.

PACKING: ½-inch headspace.

Peppers—Pimientos or Pimiento Peppers

PREPARATION FOR FREEZING: Either roast in a hot oven (400° F.) until skins will rub off easily, or scald for 3 to 5 minutes in boiling water. Rinse and cool. Remove skins, stems, and cores.

SCALDING TIME: No further scalding after processing described above.

PACKING: Lay peppers flat, packing them closely. Leave ½-inch headroom.

Potatoes

PREPARATION FOR FREEZING: Select freshly harvested, smooth, small new potatoes. Wash, sort for size, peel or scrape off skin, and rinse. Scald, cool, drain, pack.

SCALDING TIME: 3 to 5 minutes, according to size.

PACKING: ½-inch headroom.

Radishes

Not suitable for freezing.

Raspberries

PREPARATION FOR FREEZING: Sort, rinse carefully, and drain.

SCALDING: None.

PACKING: Either pack unsweetened, or in a dry-sugar pack ($^3/_4$ cup sugar per quart of berries) or in a wet (syrup) pack, with 40 to 50 percent syrup, for berries to be served as a dessert. Leave $^1/_2$-inch headspace for pints, 1 inch for quarts.

Rhubarb

PREPARATION FOR FREEZING: Trim off leaf bases and root ends. Wash and cut into 1- or 2-inch lengths. May be frozen with or without scalding, cooling, and draining.

SCALDING TIME: 1 minute.

PACKING: Raw, either with or without sweetening; or raw or scalded and covered with 40 percent syrup (see syrup formulas, page 162). Leave $^1/_2$-inch headspace for pints, 1 inch for quarts when syrup is used.

Roquette

This green is not suitable for freezing for salads, but see the index for a rugula (roquette) soup to be frozen.

Rutabagas

See directions under "Turnips—Yellow Turnips or Rutabagas," below.

Sorrel

This tart, tender green is best when handled differently from other greens for freezing. See the suggestions for sorrel preparations in Part Three, "Recipes."

Spinach and New Zealand-Spinach

See directions under "Greens," above.

Squash—Summer Squash, Including Zucchini

PREPARATION FOR FREEZING: Cut off stem and blossom ends. Wash, scrubbing if gritty, and cut into $1/2$-inch slices or pencil-thick sticks. Scald, cool, drain, pack.

SCALDING TIME: 3 minutes.

PACKING: $1/2$-inch headspace.

Squash—Winter Squash

PREPARATION FOR FREEZING: Wash, cut up, and remove seeds and the stringy lining of cavity. Cook in boiling water or over steam until tender. Remove pulp from rind and mash through sieve. Set bowl of mashed squash in bowl of ice water and stir at intervals until cold. Pack.

SCALDING: None—squash is fully cooked.

PACKING: $1/2$-inch headspace.

Strawberries

PREPARATION FOR FREEZING: Sort and wash gently. Remove hulls.

SCALDING: None.

PACKING: Pack whole, unsweetened; or in dry sugar pack (6 quarts sliced berries to 1 part sugar); or in wet (syrup) pack, with 50 per cent syrup (see syrup formulas, page 162); or purée 1 pint strawberries with 1/4 cup sugar and 1 teaspoon lemon juice, pack, and freeze. For all packs allow 1/2-inch headspace for pints, 1 inch for quarts.

Tomatoes

PREPARATION FOR FREEZING: If you'd like to have a supply of ripe, frozen raw tomatoes for use in cooking, as suggested in Part Three, "Recipes," or a stock of precooked tomatoes, also frozen, select tomatoes that are fully ripe but firm. Dip into boiling water for a few seconds, then into cold water. Strip off skins. Cut out stem ends and cores. Pack whole, if being frozen raw, or cut into halves or quarters for either the raw or the cooked pack. For precooked tomatoes, cook quartered tomatoes, covered, over medium heat just until soft, then cool rapidly and pack.

SCALDING TIME: A few seconds only, to loosen skins for peeling.

PACKING: 1-inch headspace. Pack raw tomatoes down firmly to eliminate air pockets.

Turnips—White Turnips

PREPARATION FOR FREEZING: Cut off tops and roots and wash. Pare and slice, or cut into 1/2-inch dice, or leave whole, if very small. Scald, cool, drain, and pack.

SCALDING TIME: For slices or dice, 2 minutes; for small turnips (1 inch), 3 minutes.

PACKING: ½-inch headspace.

Turnips—Yellow Turnips or Rutabagas

PREPARATION FOR FREEZING: Pare deeply and cut into cubes (½ inch). Wash. Scald, cool, drain, pack. Alternatively, cook cubes over steam or in boiling water until tender; drain; mash through sieve. Cool purée quickly, stirring often. Pack.

SCALDING TIME (for cubes): 2 minutes.

PACKING: ½-inch headroom, whether cubed or mashed.

Turnip Greens

See directions under "Greens," above.

Watermelon

PREPARATION FOR FREEZING: Wash, cut in half, and remove the seeds as you cut the flesh into slices, cubes, or balls.

SCALDING: None.

PACKING: Plain, without syrup; or in 30- or 40-percent syrup (see formulas for syrups, page 162). For pints, allow ½-inch headspace; for quarts, 1 inch.

Zucchini

See "Squash—Summer Squash. . . ," above.

Part Three

300 Ways to Serve the Good Foods You Have Grown

For each of the vegetables and fruits and herbs included in this book, this section—Part Three—includes, in alphabetically arranged entries, several kinds of information about ways to enjoy your harvest.

First, each entry indicates the best way or ways to put up your food, whether by canning, or freezing, or in preserves of one kind or another, or in pickles. Second, there are general suggestions—some of them actually brief recipes—for preparing for the table your home-canned and home-frozen vegetables and fruits. Third, there are full-scale recipes by experts who include famous chefs and teachers, food editors and food writers, cookbook authors, and people whose talent in the kitchen has made them famous among their friends. These recipes are not only for pickles and preserves and such—they include a wide variety of dishes using the produce of your garden, sometimes fresh but more often after you have "put it by" in your freezer or your pantry. Even if you have not grown or preserved the fruits and vegetables discussed in the preceding pages, the following section stands by itself as an excellent fruit and vegetable cookbook.

In the entry for each vegetable or fruit, an asterisk (*) indicates the method or methods of choice for putting it up: If canning and freezing are equally good so far as the quality of the final product is concerned, both canning and freezing are starred. If freezing is better than canning for a specific food, an asterisk beside "freezing" and the absence of the same mark beside "canning" indicates that fact.

In the three hundred or more suggestions and full-scale recipes that follow for using the foods you have grown, the "mini-recipes" are descriptive enough to be used by any cook of average experience. For the less practiced cook, or for the novice, they are intended as indications of the type of detailed recipe to look for in the full-scale cookbooks that belong on the shelf of expert and novice alike. (In the Bibliography at the end of the book you will find a short list of some cookbooks that are especially good sources of ideas for using vegetables and fruits.)

The recipes our experts have contributed to this section are not meant to be an exhaustive collection, but to present instead some of the best and some of the more unusual ways to pickle, to preserve, and to prepare for the table the harvests of your garden. They are a sampler, in other words—a sampler designed to stimulate your imagination by showing you ways to enjoy better eating from your home garden, whether it is half an acre of rich soil in full sun, a few pots of herbs in the kitchen, or a window box.

Because few of us can grow everything we'd like to cook, pickle, or preserve, we have included, under "Exotica" at the end of this section, a special collection of recipes using foods that aren't commonly found in most home gardens, either because of the requirements of space or the requirements of climate. There you will find recipes for figs, for quinces, for guavas and mangoes; for berries out of the ordinary; for avocados and kumquats; for plums, pears, and peaches; for bitter oranges, and for more besides.

Artichokes (Globe Artichokes)

Especially if they are small, artichokes can be frozen* or canned whole. The hearts (including the small center tuft of leaves) and the bottoms or bases (denuded of all leaves and the "choke") can be frozen* or canned. Both hearts and bottoms are excellent when pickled* or preserved in a marinade* (see our recipes below).

Canned artichokes are usable in recipes calling for precooked artichokes. Frozen ones may or may not require cooking before use, depending upon the recipe.

Some suggestions: Defrost frozen whole artichokes, remove the choke, if this hasn't already been done, fill with your favorite stuffing mixture (Italian stuffings are especially good), and complete the cooking by steaming.

Defrost, pat dry, and halve or quarter frozen artichoke hearts, dip them in fritter batter, and either deep-fry them in hot oil or shallow-fry them in 1 inch of hot oil in a skillet (olive oil would be our choice).

Prepare canned hearts, or cooked frozen hearts, au gratin for an excellent vegetable course: Bathe them in a good sauce enriched with cream and top them in a shallow baking dish with buttered crumbs; brown well in a hot oven.

Artichoke bottoms—either canned and drained, or frozen, defrosted, cooked and drained—are among the most distinguished of garnishes for a steak when gently browned in butter on both sides. In the French cuisine especially, they are often stuffed with mixtures ranging from puréed vegetables to pâté de foie gras.

Marinated Artichoke Bottoms

PILAR TURNER

A recipe in the Spanish tradition for an artichoke delicacy that makes a distinguished appearance on the hors d'oeuvre tray.

Makes about 6 pints

24 fresh artichokes
Lemon halves, 2 or 3
6 quarts water, plus 3 cups (see directions below)
4 tablespoons salt
1 cup dry white wine
1 cup olive oil

1/2 cup strained lemon juice
6 sprigs parsley
4 cloves garlic
1/2 teaspoon saffron strands
1 teaspoon crumbled dried thyme
10 whole peppercorns

1. Trim stems of artichokes flush with their bases, then bend back and snap off each of the leaves. Rub the surface of each artichoke with a lemon half as you trim, to prevent darkening. When all the leaves have been removed, scoop out with a teaspoon the hairy central part, the "choke."

2. Meanwhile, in a large enameled or stainless-steel kettle bring 6 quarts of water to a boil with 3 tablespoons of the salt (reserve 1 tablespoon).

3. Drop artichokes into the boiling water and return to a boil. Reduce the heat and boil gently, covered, for 15 to 25 minutes, or until not quite

done when tested with the tip of a sharp knife. Remove from pot and drain.

4. While artichokes are being cooked, prepare marinade: In an enameled or stainless-steel saucepan combine 3 cups of water, 1 tablespoon salt, the white wine, olive oil, lemon juice, parsley, garlic, saffron, thyme, and peppercorns. Bring to a boil, lower heat, cover partially, and simmer for 45 minutes.

5. Pack artichoke hearts into clean, hot wide-mouthed pint canning jars. Strain marinade over artichokes, leaving 1/4-inch headspace.

6. Add lids and process in a pressure canner for 20 minutes at 10 pounds pressure.

Artichoke Hearts Amaroussion

MONOROMA PHILLIPS

"Amaroussion is a place outside of Athens where my older sister used to spend her summers away from Pakistan," writes the contributor of this recipe. "While holidaying with her, living in a pension where I never saw a tourist other than Greek visitors, I had an opportunity to learn several dishes. . . . An elderly lady accompanied by two teen-agers would come once a week and spend the day putting up these artichokes. When I tried the recipe I changed some of the ingredients, as I preferred the taste of those that I substituted.

"One of my favorite ways of serving these artichokes is to arrange them on a small plate of shredded grape leaves and top them with an avgolemono [Greek lemon] or skordalia [potato and garlic] sauce."

Makes 3 to 4 pints

12 medium-sized artichokes
2 1/2 cups wine vinegar
2 tablespoons coarse sea salt
  (kosher salt could be
  substituted)
2 cloves of garlic, peeled
2 medium-sized sweet red
  peppers

1 small lemon
1 teaspoon crushed dried
  oregano, preferably Greek
1 tablespoon crushed dried basil
1 tablespoon finely chopped
  fresh dill
2 dried bay leaves, coarsely
  broken

1. Place each artichoke on its side and with a sharp knife remove the stem. With the fingers, break off the leaves until only a small tuft of leaves is left at the center. Wash, pat dry, and place in an enameled or

stainless-steel pot containing the vinegar. Repeat until all artichokes are prepared.

2. Bring vinegar to a boil, lower heat, cover, and cook for 20 minutes.

3. In a small bowl place the salt and garlic. Gently pound the garlic with a pestle so that it is flattened but not completely crushed.

4. Seed, wash, and dry the peppers. Slice into 1/2-inch strips.

5. With a small sharp paring knife, cut a 2-inch strip of the outer peel from the lemon (include no white pith); it should be about 3/4 inch wide.

6. Remove artichokes from vinegar and cool, leaving vinegar in the pot.

7. To the vinegar add the garlic, salt, peppers, lemon peel, oregano, basil, dill, and bay leaves. Return to a simmer and continue to cook over low heat while carrying out the next step.

8. Remove central tuft of leaves from each cooled artichoke and gently scrape out and discard the hairy choke. Wipe artichoke hearts (by now they are what some cooks call bases or bottoms), and if desired cut them into quarters.

9. Return artichokes to the simmering vinegar and cook, covered, for 15 minutes. Remove lid, raise heat, bring to a boil, and cook for 2 or 3 minutes more.

10. Pack immediately in sterilized canning jars, making sure that artichoke hearts are completely covered with seasoned vinegar and that the seasonings are divided among the jars.

11. Add lids and process for 15 minutes (for pint jars) in a boiling-water bath.

NOTE: If when filling jars there is not enough liquid to reach to about 1/4 inch from the top, bring additional wine vinegar to a boil and add the required amount.

Asparagus

Frozen* asparagus is superior to home-canned, although canned asparagus is not to be despised—witness the cost of the tins on the shelves of fancy-food shops.

Canned asparagus is good in any recipe calling for the precooked vegetable. Because of the long cooking it has undergone, it has lost all its texture except tenderness, so it benefits from a creamy sauce, or one enriched with cheese, and a topping of crisp, browned bread crumbs and butter.

Try cooking unthawed, frozen asparagus spears just long enough for them to reach tenderness without mushiness. Drain and serve hot as a side dish, with a herbed vinaigrette sauce spooned over the stalks. Alternatively, cool the asparagus quickly by spreading it out in a single layer, then serve it at room temperature with the vinaigrette or another favorite dressing. Especially good as a first course.

Tips, frozen separately, are luxurious as a garnish (see suggestions below for preparing slant-cut asparagus). Either steam them briefly and serve with butter, or thaw them just until they are well separated, dip them into beaten egg, then into fine, dry bread crumbs, and deep-fry them as a garnish for Scaloppine al Limone or another favorite veal or chicken dish.

It's quite feasible to stir-fry frozen slant-cut asparagus in the Chinese manner (see recipe), and the slant-cut stalks can also go into a splendid main dish for luncheon or a first course for dinner—see Elizabeth Colchie's Asparagus-Cheese Tart.

To Freeze Slant-cut Asparagus

ELIZABETH SUSAN COLCHIE

1. Wash asparagus and sort the stalks according to thickness. Break off the woody base of each where it snaps easily.

2. If you wish to freeze the tips separately, cut them off and set them aside to be blanched, cooled, and packed according to the directions for whole asparagus in Part Two.

3. Peel the asparagus stalks (a swivel-bladed peeler works best) and cut them into long diagonal slices no more than 1/2 inch thick; 1/4 inch is preferable.

4. Drop the slices, about a pound at a time, into 4 quarts of boiling water and blanch each batch for 1 minute (for 1/4-inch slices). Lengthen or shorten the time a few seconds if asparagus has been cut in thicker or thinner slices.

5. Let cool under cold running water, or in a bowl of water and ice, for 3 minutes. Drain and spread out on a towel to lose surface moisture.

6. Spread the slices in one layer on a baking sheet and freeze at once. When frozen, pack in plastic freezer bags or rigid containers and seal.

Stir-fried Asparagus Two Ways

HELEN WITTY

Serves 4

4 cups frozen slant-cut asparagus (see freezing directions above)
2 tablespoons vegetable oil, preferably peanut
2 scallions, trimmed and cut into long slanted slices crosswise (include a little of the tender green tops)

1 slice (¹/₄ inch thick) fresh ginger, flattened
¹/₂ cup chicken broth
Optional thickening: 2 teaspoons cornstarch mixed with ¹/₄ cup chicken broth or water
Salt, to taste

1. Heat a large wok or skillet (the wok is preferable, if you have one) until a drop of water will dance about and evaporate almost instantly.

2. Add oil and spread over surface of pan very quickly. Instantly add the scallions and the ginger and toss with a spatula for a moment to coat with the oil.

3. Add the frozen asparagus slices and toss and cook over high heat, mixing with the oil and seasonings for about 2 minutes.

4. Add the chicken broth and cover. Cook for about 1 minute, then test for doneness; asparagus should be quite underdone, not mushy.

5. If thickening is being used, stir the cornstarch mixture well again and mix into the asparagus, tossing until sauce clears and thickens, 1 minute or less.

6. Taste, and add salt as needed; the amount needed will depend upon the saltiness of the chicken broth. Serve at once while still tender-crisp.

NOTE: This is a stir-fry in the Chinese tradition. It fits well into most menus, but a simpler version without the Oriental seasonings can be made by heating the pan only medium-hot and adding the frozen asparagus and 2 to 3 tablespoons butter all at once. Cook and toss over medium to medium-high heat for about 2 minutes, then add the chicken broth and cover, cooking until the vegetable is as tender as you like it. Either add the chicken broth and the thickening or not; season with salt (and pepper, if you like), and serve with wedges of lemon on the side.

Asparagus-Cheese Tart

ELIZABETH SUSAN COLCHIE

Makes a 9½-inch tart

PASTRY:
1½ cups flour
½ teaspoon salt
5 tablespoons chilled, unsalted
  butter, cut into tiny bits

3 tablespoons chilled lard
3 tablesoons ice water

FILLING:
2 tablespoons butter
¼ cup finely minced scallions
½ cup chopped, cooked ham
1 cup frozen slant-cut asparagus
  slices (see directions above)
1 cup freshly grated Parmesan
  cheese

1 egg, extra-large size
1 egg yolk
1¼ cups milk
¼ teaspoon salt
⅛ teaspoon nutmeg
⅛ teaspoon white pepper

PASTRY:
1. Measure flour and salt into a bowl; add butter and lard and cut in with a pastry blender to form tiny, even crumbs. Sprinkle in the ice water, a tablespoon at a time, blending lightly with a fork to incorporate the liquid.

2. Form dough into a ball, wrap it in plastic, and chill for 2 hours or more.

3. Lightly grease a 9½-inch, fluted, false-bottomed tart pan.

4. Roll out the dough on a floured surface to form a circle 13 inches in diameter. Lift the pastry gently into the pan, easing it into place without stretching, and folding down extra pastry to overlap the sides to make them slightly thicker than the bottom. Roll the pin across the top of the pan to cut away excess pastry. Press the pastry firmly into the flutings of the pan, using a fingertip, to raise a ¼- to ½-inch rim above the edge.

5. Line the shell with aluminum foil and half-fill it with dry beans. Place

pan on a baking sheet and bake in an oven preheated to 400° F. for 10 minutes. Remove the beans and foil and prick the bottom crust all over with a fork. Bake 15 minutes more, or until crust is pale golden. Place on a rack to cool.

FILLING:
1. Melt the butter in a frying pan and cook the scallions and ham, without browning, until the scallions are tender.

2. Add the asparagus slices and cook a few minutes more, just until the slices are well thawed. Cool to lukewarm, or cooler.

3. Sprinkle half the grated cheese into the cooled, baked shell and top with half of the asparagus-ham mixture. Sprinkle on the remaining cheese and the rest of the asparagus mixture.

4. In a bowl blend together the egg, egg yolk, milk, salt, nutmeg, and pepper. Pour custard into the tart shell.

5. Bake in a preheated 350° F. oven for 40 minutes, or until the filling is set.

6. Let cool on a rack for 10 to 20 minutes before serving.

Beans

In Part One we have learned how to grow several kinds of beans, including some that are unfamiliar to many cooks—broad or fava beans, for example. Then there are the lima beans, either small-seeded or large, and edible both when green or dried; the snap or green or "string" beans, green-, yellow-, or purple-podded, again usually eaten fresh, but producing seeds that can be dried in the pod, then sorted out and stored for winter use; and soy beans, one of the most nutritious of foods, just being discovered in the Western world as a delicious green vegetable as well as a dried legume with innumerable uses.

Recipes for all of these beans abound in good cookbooks, but we offer here a few of our favorite suggestions and recipes.

BROAD, FAVA, GREAT, OR BROAD WINDSOR BEANS. These are much used in many cuisines of Europe and in Britain, although they are unknown to most Americans. The fresh beans are at their best when very young, before they form a tough skin that must be peeled off.

Can or freeze* the young green beans. If more mature green beans are being processed, count on blanching, then skinning them before freezing or canning them. Broad beans may be allowed to ripen on the plants. Harvest the fully ripe pods, spread them out in an airy, dry place to cure, then separate the beans from the pods and the trash and store them when they are thoroughly dry. Some experts recommend further drying. They place the shelled beans in a very low oven—about 120° F.—for about 3 hours to destroy any possible insect life.

Savory is a favorite seasoning for green broad beans, whether cooked when fresh, when frozen, or when taken from a canning jar. Many Europeans season both fresh and dried broad beans lightly with bacon, salt pork, or even ham. The Dutch, especially, like the springtime combination of very young broad beans with chervil (see recipe). Dried, the beans make a fine soup (see recipe), or they may be cooked as a vegetable after overnight soaking. Pull off the skins of the soaked beans and cook the vegetables slowly in salted water. Drain and season with salt, pepper, and a little olive oil.

LIMA BEANS. The flavor of the "baby" lima beans—which are actually small-seeded varieties, not underdeveloped beans—seems to us especially delicate, but many prefer the large-seeded varieties. Limas are equally good for serving while green or for using after being dried in the fashion described for broad beans.

Can or freeze* green limas, being sure to pick them before they become mature and rather starchy. If the whole crop or a good part of it goes beyond the best stage for eating fresh, consider drying them.

Like all the members of the bean family, limas have an affinity for savory, either summer savory or the perennial (winter) savory. We like them cooked briskly (but thoroughly—they're not good when underdone) in a little salted water, buttered generously, and sprinkled with any one of several favorite herbs. Try a little chopped mint one time, basil another, and parsley, either alone or mixed with chives, another.

Limas are traditional in all-American succotash (see recipe), but they are nontraditional (and excellent) in a two-vegetable purée for which we also give a recipe.

SNAP BEANS (GREEN BEANS, STRING BEANS). Although plant breeders have virtually eliminated the stringy filaments that gave these beans the common name that was formerly most used— "string beans"—they haven't cut down on the number of kinds you can grow—quite the reverse. There are long, thin beans, wide, flat ones (Italian beans, especially the 'Romano' variety), green ones, yellow ones, and even purple-podded ones ('Royalty' variety) that turn green as they cook.

Freeze* green beans, can them (but they're better when frozen), and use them in special pickles and mixed pickles (see recipes).

Canned or freshly cooked frozen beans make a good combination salad-and-vegetable course when served hot with lemon butter or a vinaigrette sauce—especially if the sauce is seasoned with all the mixed herbs that suit your palate, not omitting parsely, chives, tarragon, chervil, and a little thyme, if you have them. Your big recipe books have innumerable recipes that include beans—hot, cold, sweet and sour, with other vegetables, or solo.

If your pole-bean crop should get ahead of the picking and the pods are suddenly lumpy with large but not hardened beans, pick them anyway instead of leaving them to dry (which would end the season's production). Shell the beans—the pods will be too tough to eat—and cook them in salted water until tender. A little bacon is a traditional and good seasoning, and don't omit the salt and pepper. And, if you like, add a pinch or two of savory, known for good reason in Europe as the "bean herb."

SOY BEANS. Only the larger home garden is likely to have space for soy beans, which is a pity, as these are among the most nutritious of all vegetables and are especially good when young and green. The fresh young beans are rarely to be found in markets, but a row or two of soy beans in the garden would afford you at least a sample. Be sure to pick them before the pods turn yellow. Can or freeze* them, but use a special preparatory technique: Blanch them *in their pods* for about 5 minutes before trying to shell them. Then cool them enough to handle, shell and rinse them, and proceed with the canning or freezing.

Once stored, cook your frozen green soy beans in the same fashion as green limas or peas, allowing enough time for them to become tender. Season them simply—salt, pepper, and butter—or try them with some of the good bean herbs we've discussed. As a special dish, cook them as directed in Grace Chu's recipe for Green Soy Beans and Ground Beef.

Young Broad Beans with Chervil

ALLIANORA ROSSE

This Dutch way of preparing broad beans is very simple. Cook the young beans (it's not necessary to thaw them first if frozen) in boiling salted water until they are tender. (They will take longer than green peas to cook.) Drain them, if any liquid remains, and season them with butter and finely chopped fresh chervil. The chervil is at its best when young, just at the time when the broad beans are ready for use. About one tablespoon of the chopped herb should be enough for six servings of broad beans.

As both young broad beans and fresh chervil freeze well, this delicate combination is one that can be enjoyed out of season as well as in.

Minestrone di Fave all'Abruzzi—Dried Fava Bean Soup Abruzzi Style†

EDWARD GIOBBI

Serves 6

2 cups (1 pound) dried fava
  beans
2 slices salt pork, about 3 inches
  long by ¼ inch thick; or 3
  tablespoons olive oil
2 cloves garlic, peeled and
  chopped
2 tablespoons chopped parsley,
  preferably the Italian kind

2 quarts water
1 bay leaf
1 medium onion, chopped, or ¾
  cup frozen chopped onion
Salt and freshly ground black
  pepper
½ cup small pasta shapes
  (tubettini, ditalini, or others)
Freshly grated Parmesan cheese

1. Soak fava beans overnight in water to cover them generously.

2. If you are using the salt pork, chop it with the garlic and parsley to make a *battuto,* using a heated knife blade to prevent the pork from sticking to the blade. Put *battuto* into a heavy-bottomed soup pot. If olive oil is used, combine it in the pot with the finely chopped garlic and parsley. Simmer either mixture over low heat until most of the fat is rendered from the salt pork, or until the vegetables in olive-oil mixture are soft but not browned.

3. Meanwhile, drain the fava beans and remove the tough outer skin from each.

4. Add to the *battuto* the beans, water, bay leaf, onion, salt, and pepper to taste. Bring to a boil, then lower heat and cover. Simmer for about 2 hours, stirring occasionally, until beans are done.

5. If you want to include the pasta, cook it separately in boiling salted water until tender but firm, *al dente.* Drain pasta and add to soup and continue to simmer for a few minutes.

6. Serve hot, with grated Parmesan cheese.

†NOTE: Adapted, with permission, from Edward Giobbi's book *Italian Family Cooking,* Random House, 1971.

A Traditional Succotash

ELIZABETH SUSAN COLCHIE

Serves 6

¼ pound slab bacon
1½ quarts boiling water
3 cups frozen green baby lima beans
1 teaspoon crumbled dried savory, or 2 to 3 teaspoons minced fresh savory

1 cup water
4 cups frozen whole-kernel corn
1 cup light cream
1 teaspoon salt
Freshly ground pepper

1. Remove rind from bacon and cut bacon into ½-inch dice.

2. Blanch the bacon pieces in the boiling water for 2 minutes. Drain bacon pieces and dry them on paper towels. Transfer them to a heavy casserole and cook over medium heat, stirring, until they are crisp. Remove the bits with a slotted spoon and reserve them. Pour out all but 2 tablespoons of the fat.

3. Add to the fat in the casserole the lima beans, savory, and ½ cup of the water. Bring to a simmer and cook, covered, for 10 minutes.

4. In a saucepan simmer together the corn and the remaining ½ cup of water for 5 minutes, covered.

5. Combine the lima beans and their liquid with the corn and its liquid. Add the salt and simmer for 5 minutes (or longer, up to half an hour or so, if you prefer the old-fashioned texture of very well-cooked succotash). Add the cream and cook, uncovered, 10 minutes longer.

6. Add the reserved bacon bits and pepper to taste, and serve hot.

NOTE: Some cooks add a small onion, minced, to the fat before the lima beans are added. If you use the onion, cook it for a few moments, until translucent, then add the limas, savory, and water.

Baby Lima Beans Puréed with Spinach and Cream

HELEN WITTY

For a family where one person doesn't care especially for spinach and another scorns limas, this purée was a happy inspiration. Light in texture and delicate in color and flavor, it tastes not exactly like either of its happily matched components. We like it as a bed for sauced scallops of veal or chicken breasts, or as a vegetable side dish with any meat or poultry course.

Serves 4 to 6

2 pints frozen baby lima beans
1 pint frozen spinach, whole or chopped
½ cup heavy cream, or to taste
3 tablespoons butter
1 teaspoon finely minced fresh basil, or ⅓ to ½ teaspoon crumbled dried basil

Pinch of freshly grated nutmeg
Salt
Pepper (optional)
Lemon juice (optional)

1. Cook the vegetables separately, steaming them or cooking them in as little water as possible until soft.

2. Drain vegetables and purée them separately. A blender or a food processor is good for the spinach, and a food mill or the processor works well for the limas.

3. Combine the vegetables in a saucepan and beat in the cream, butter,

basil, a little nutmeg, salt to taste, and a little pepper if you like it. (The basil has something of a peppery character, so the black pepper may be superfluous to some palates.) Taste, and add more cream or seasonings if needed. If the spinach is somewhat low in acid, a few drops of lemon juice will be a good addition.

4. Reheat, stirring constantly, and serve hot.

Pickled Green Beans with Dill

ELIZABETH SUSAN COLCHIE

Makes 3 pints

2 pounds tender green beans, washed and drained
3 tablespoons finely snipped dill leaves
3 tiny, peeled garlic cloves
2 tablespoons kosher salt or other coarse salt

2 cups water
2 cups white wine vinegar
1 teaspoon sugar
1/2 teaspoon white peppercorns

1. Trim the beans to lengths to fit into pint-sized canning jars with about 1 inch to spare and pack them tightly into 3 jars, with 1 tablespoon dill and 1 garlic clove in each one.

2. In a stainless-steel or enamel saucepan combine the salt, water, vinegar, sugar, and peppercorns and bring to a full boil.

3. Divide the pickling liquid among the filled jars.

4. Add the lids, and process the jars for 15 minutes in a boiling-water bath.

5. Store for at least two weeks and chill the beans before serving. Reserve the liquid for vegetable dressings and marinades.

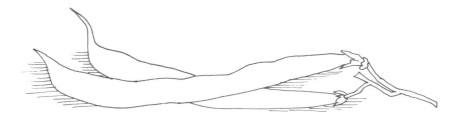

Wax Beans Pickled with Honey and Savory

ELIZABETH SUSAN COLCHIE

Makes 4 pints

1/2 cup honey
2 cups water
2 cups fine white vinegar, preferably wine vinegar
1 tablespoon dried savory

4 teaspoons salt
2 1/2 pounds wax beans, washed, drained, ends removed, and cut into 1-inch pieces
4 bay leaves

1. Combine the honey, water, vinegar, savory, and salt in a large enamel or stainless-steel saucepan and bring to a boil.

2. Add the beans and bring the mixture to a boil again.

3. Pack into 4 sterilized pint jars with a bay leaf in each. Add pickling liquid, leaving 1/4-inch headspace.

4. Cover jars with their lids and process for 15 minutes in a boiling-water bath.

5. Store for at least a week, and chill before serving as a relish.

String Beans Plymouth Style

GLENNA McGINNIS

Years ago, reports Glenna McGinnis, she happily ate some unforgettable string beans—as they were always called then—while touring Cape Cod. Later, when overwhelmed by a bumper crop of beans in the garden, she recalled the dish and worked out this recipe. These beans are equally good hot or cold, and they can be reheated without suffering. Frozen beans may be used, either "French cut" or diced.

Serves 4

1 pound fresh or frozen green or yellow snap (or "string") beans, or 1 pint frozen beans
2 tablespoons butter

2 tablespoons heavy cream
2 teaspoons sugar
Salt
Freshly ground white pepper

1. Wash fresh beans and remove the ends and any strings. Split them lengthwise or dice them (that is, cut them into pieces just as long as they are wide). If frozen beans are used, thaw before cooking.

2. Cook in as little unsalted water as possible in a covered saucepan.

3. Drain and add butter, cream, sugar, and salt and pepper to taste.

Green Soy Beans and Ground Beef

GRACE ZIA CHU

Serves 4

1 cup shelled, frozen green soy beans
½ cup canned water chestnuts, drained
2 tablespoons vegetable oil
2 slices fresh ginger root
½ teaspoon salt

½ teaspoon sugar
½ pound (1 cup) ground round steak
1 tablespoon dark soy sauce (see note)
2 tablespoons dry sherry

1. Thaw the frozen green soy beans.

2. Cut the water chestnuts into dice about the size of the soy beans.

3. Heat 1 tablespoon of the oil in a frying pan (or a wok) and add the ginger. Let ginger sizzle for a minute and discard.

4. Add soy beans and cook, stirring and tossing, for about 1 minute. Add salt and sugar and mix again. Add water chestnuts and mix. Cook over medium heat without a cover for a minute. Dish and set aside for later use.

5. In the same frying pan, add the second tablespoon of oil and heat. Using a spoon or fork, separate the meat as it cooks, to prevent its forming into a cake. Cook, stirring, for about 2 minutes, or until red color disappears. Add dark soy sauce and Sherry and mix well.

6. Return the peas and water chestnuts to the pan and mix a few more times. Serve hot.

NOTE: Dark soy sauce is available at Oriental food stores. If you use fresh soy beans, cook them, in their shells, in boiling water for 5 minutes, cool under the cold-water faucet, and then shell.

Beets

Beets are one of the few vegetables for which canning* may be recommended without reservation. Beets also freeze* very well, but not raw—they must be cooked to make it possible to slip off their skins (this is also true when they are canned). Freeze or can them whole, sliced, cut into julienne, or diced.

Beet tops—called "beet greens"—are excellent when frozen* or canned, too—directions will be found in Part Two. Too often wasted by cooks who don't realize how flavorful and nutritious they are, these tender leaves are the key ingredient in Pink Barley and Beet Greens (recipe), and are also very good cooked all by themselves, with the usual seasonings of salt and butter, plus a bit of lemon juice.

If you have a lot of beets, pickle* them or make them into relish* (recipes). Canned or frozen beets are good for quick "icebox" pickling—use any of the recipes found in standard cookbooks.

An interesting hot salad (or vegetable course) is Allianora Rosse's Pink Potatoes (recipe), and an enchanting cold soup is borscht, which comes in as many versions as there are good cooks in Central and Eastern Europe and in Russia—for this soup, look in one cookbook for one kind of borscht, in six cookbooks for six kinds.

Beet and Carrot Pickle

RUTH ELLEN CHURCH

In this mixed pickle the carrots take on the color of the beets, but keep their own flavor. The combination is very good.

Makes 3 quarts

1½ quarts young carrots, either whole or cut into diagonal slices on a ruffled cutter
1½ quarts small, young beets, with an inch or so of their stems
2 cups sugar
1 cup water

3 cups white vinegar
1 teaspoon whole cloves
1 teaspoon whole allspice
1 small stick cinnamon, broken up
1 whole lemon, sliced very thin and any seeds removed

1. Cook carrots in a small amount of water until tender-crisp; do not overcook.

2. Cook beets in their skins in water to cover until tender. Cool enough to handle, then slip off their skins. Leave them whole if carrots are whole, or slice them diagonally on a ruffled cutter if carrots have been cut in that fashion.

3. In a preserving pan bring sugar, water, vinegar, and spices to a boil. Add the vegetables and the sliced lemon and cook 5 minutes, stirring gently to make sure the mixture is boiling-hot throughout.

4. Ladle into hot, clean canning jars.

5. Add lids and process for 30 minutes, for either pints or quarts, in a boiling-water bath.

Orange Pickled Beets

FLORENCE FABRICANT

Orange peel and orange juice give a new glow to a favorite condiment, pickled beets.

Makes 6 pints

8 to 9 pounds beets, without tops
12 narrow strips orange peel, an inch or so long
3½ cups cider vinegar
3 cups sugar

1 cup orange juice, preferably freshly squeezed
1 tablespoon pickling or kosher salt

1. Wash beets, leaving an inch or so of the stems on them. Place in a large kettle, cover with water, and bring to a boil. Cover the kettle and simmer the beets until tender, about one hour, depending on their size.

2. While the beets are cooking, simmer the orange peel in water to cover for 15 minutes, then drain.

3. Combine vinegar, sugar, orange juice, and the prepared orange peel in a saucepan. Bring to a boil and boil for 5 minutes. Set aside.

4. When the beets are tender, drain them and rinse in cold water. Slip off the skins and slice the beets.

5. Fill clean, hot pint jars with hot beet slices, leaving headroom of $1/2$ inch. Add $1/2$ teaspoon salt to each jar.

6. Return the orange syrup to a boil and fill each jar to within $1/2$ inch of the top with boiling syrup. Include 2 strips of peel in each jar.

7. Adjust lids and process the jars in a boiling-water bath for 30 minutes.

Pink Potatoes—Hot Potato and Beet Salad

ALLIANORA ROSSE

This is a very old Dutch recipe that suggests a good way to use canned or frozen cooked beets in a salad that could also serve as a vegetable course. Frozen chopped onions, if you have stored part of your crop in that form, can be used, too.

Serves 6

6 large potatoes
5 or 6 medium-sized cooked beets, canned or frozen and thawed
6 strips of thick-cut bacon, cut crosswise into $1/4$-inch strips

2 large onions, peeled and chopped
Salt and pepper
Vinegar

1. Peel potatoes and boil until very well done. Drain and keep warm.

2. Separately, heat the beets (they may be sliced or diced, or whole, as they are going to be mashed anyway).

3. Meanwhile, fry the bacon until crisp and remove it from the pan. Set bacon aside and reserve the fat.

4. Fry the onions in all or part of the bacon fat (depending on taste) until lightly browned.

5. Return bacon to the pan and add the potatoes and beets. Mash all ingredients thoroughly together with a large fork.

6. Season with salt and pepper and a bit of vinegar. More fat, or some butter, can be added if you like. Serve hot. This is especially good with ham.

Pink Barley and Beet Greens

JANE MOULTON

This dish may be served either as a main course or as a vegetable. It can also be made with spinach, but without the beet stems the barley won't turn its pretty pink color. The unusually long cooking contributes to the character of the dish.

Makes 5 servings as a side dish

2 slices bacon, cut into ¼-inch pieces
1 small onion, peeled and chopped, or ¼ cup frozen chopped onion

2 tablespoons medium pearl barley
¾ cup water
1½ pints frozen beet greens
½ teaspoon salt (approximately)

1. Sauté bacon pieces in a heavy saucepan (use one that has a tight lid) until bacon is about half cooked. Add onion and barley and continue cooking until onion is translucent but not browned.

2. Add water and beet greens, still frozen. Cover and cook over medium heat, stirring occasionally to break up the greens. When greens are thawed continue to cook, covered, until barley is tender—about 30 minutes. Stir as needed and remove cover toward end of cooking to evaporate liquid, if necessary.

3. Taste and add salt near end of cooking time. Serve hot.

Beet, Cabbage, and Pepper Relish

JANE MOULTON

Beets lend their color to all the ingredients of this relish, so it comes out a delightful cranberry shade. Not too spicy and not too tart, the flavor complements cold meats of any kind.

When you make it, don't waste your beet greens—freeze them for later use (see Part Two).

Makes 6 pints

3¹⁄₃ cups cider vinegar
2 cups sugar
1 tablespoon prepared
  horseradish
1 tablespoon mustard seed
2 teaspoons salt

5 cups chopped, cooked beets
  (about 9 medium beets, or 5
  pounds of beets, weighed fresh
  with their tops)
2 quarts coarsely chopped
  cabbage (about 3 pounds)
1 cup finely diced sweet red
  peppers or pimientos

1. In a preserving kettle holding 5 quarts or more combine the vinegar, sugar, horseradish, mustard seed, and salt. Stir well and bring to a boil.

2. Add all the vegetables and mix well. Bring to a boil, cover, and simmer 5 minutes.

3. Place in clean, hot pint jars, making sure the liquid is evenly distributed among them.

4. Add lids and process jars in a boiling-water bath for 10 minutes.

Blueberries

A beautiful fruit from a beautiful plant, the blueberry is one of the most satisfactory of all home-garden fruits. If you follow our expert's advice in Part One and plant several varieties that will bear from early in the season until late, you will have an ample and well-spaced-out supply of berries.

What to do with the part of the crop you don't eat fresh is no problem. Blueberries freeze* perfectly—we prefer to freeze them without sugar, so that they may be used in many ways—in blueberry muffins, cakes, and pancakes, for instance—without having to take the sweetening into account. They are also satisfactory when canned, and they are marvelous raw material for jams, jellies, conserves, and other preserves—the excellent recipes that come with powdered or bottled pectin will supply ideas, as will your big cookbooks.

Three of our favorite recipes follow: they are for a chilled soup, a steamed pudding, and a blueberry buckle, a dish with origins far back in American history.

Cold Blueberry Soup

ELIZABETH SUSAN COLCHIE

Serves 4

4 cups frozen blueberries, defrosted
2 cups water
1/2 cup sweet vermouth
1/4 cup sugar
1/4 cup strained fresh lemon juice

1 large strip lemon peel
1 large strip orange peel
2 teaspoons arrowroot
Slivered orange peel for garnishing

1. In a saucepan combine the blueberries, water, 1/3 cup of the vermouth (reserve the rest), sugar, lemon juice, and the lemon and orange peels. Bring to a boil, lower heat, and simmer 10 minutes, covered.

2. Press the mixture through a sieve and return it to the saucepan.

3. Stir together the remaining vermouth and the arrowroot and add to the soup. Bring just to a simmer over moderately low heat, stirring; do not boil.

4. Cool the soup, then chill it.

5. Serve in cups as a first course, sprinkled with a tiny bit of very finely slivered orange peel.

Blueberry Buckle with Vanilla Sauce

ELIZABETH SUSAN COLCHIE

Serves 6

VANILLA SAUCE:

2 cups milk
Half a vanilla bean

6 egg yolks
2/3 cup sugar

BLUEBERRY BUCKLE:

2 cups frozen blueberries,
  frozen loose, without sugar
1 cup sugar
1¾ cups plus 2 tablespoons cake
  flour
5 tablespoons soft, unsalted
  butter
1 egg

2 teaspoons double-acting
  baking powder
½ teaspoon salt
¼ teaspoon ground mace
¼ teaspoon ground nutmeg
¼ teaspoon ground coriander
2/3 cup milk

VANILLA SAUCE:

1. In the top of a double boiler over boiling water scald the milk with the vanilla bean, heating it to just below simmering. Cover the pan, remove it from the heat, and let it stand for 15 minutes.

2. In the bowl of an electric mixer briefly beat the egg yolks; gradually beat in the sugar; beat until the mixture is very pale and thick.

3. Remove the vanilla bean from the milk. Slowly beat the milk into the yolk mixture. Pour the custard mixture back into the top of the double boiler.

4. Cook the sauce over barely simmering water, stirring, for about 15 minutes, or until the foam disappears and the custard thickens very slightly.

5. Strain the sauce into a bowl set in a bowl of ice water and let it cool, stirring often.

6. Chill the sauce.

BLUEBERRY BUCKLE:

1. Toss the still-frozen blueberries in a bowl with ¼ cup of the sugar and 2 tablespoons of the cake flour.

2. In the small bowl of an electric mixer beat the soft butter until it is fluffy; gradually beat in the remaining sugar; beat in the egg.

3. Sift into a bowl the remaining flour, the baking powder, salt, mace, nutmeg, and coriander.

4. Alternately add the flour mixture and the milk to the butter mixture, using a spoon or a rubber spatula and blending the batter well.

5. Spread the blueberries in a buttered 8×8×2–inch baking dish. Pour in the batter and smooth the top.

6. Bake the buckle in a preheated 375° F. oven for 40 minutes. Serve warm with the chilled Vanilla Sauce.

Steamed Blueberry Pudding with Sour-Cream Sauce

ELIZABETH SUSAN COLCHIE

Serves 6 to 8

BLUEBERRY PUDDING:

2 cups plus 2 tablespoons flour
1/4 cup sugar
2 teaspoons double-acting baking powder
1/2 teaspoon salt
1/4 teaspoon ground mace
6 tablespoons cold, unsalted butter, cut into small bits

1 egg
1/4 cup honey
1 tablespoon lemon juice
1 scant cup milk
1 1/2 cups frozen blueberries, frozen loose, without sugar
Extra butter and sugar for preparing the mold

SOUR-CREAM SAUCE

2/3 cup dairy sour cream
1/3 cup heavy cream

2 tablespoons honey
2 tablespoons lemon juice

BLUEBERRY PUDDING:

1. Sift together into a bowl 2 cups flour (reserve the rest), the sugar, 1 1/2 teaspoons of the baking powder (reserve 1/2 teaspoon), the salt, and the mace.

2. With a pastry blender cut the butter into the flour mixture to form small, even crumbs. Make a well in the center.

3. Beat together the egg, honey, and lemon juice and pour into the well in the flour. Add the milk and, using a fork, blend the flour into the liquid.

4. Toss the still-frozen blueberries in a bowl with the 2 tablespoons flour and ½ teaspoon baking powder. Shake off any surplus flour in a sieve and fold the berries lightly into the batter.

5. Butter heavily a 6-cup steamed-pudding mold and its lid, and coat the inside of the mold with sugar, shaking out any excess.

6. Turn the batter into the mold. Cover it with a piece of buttered waxed paper and clamp on the lid.

7. Place the mold on a rack in a large pot containing enough very hot water to come halfway up the mold. Bring water to a boil, then turn heat as low as possible. Cover the pot and steam the pudding for 2 hours.

8. Remove the mold from the pot and remove lid and waxed paper. Let pudding stand 30 minutes.

9. Unmold onto a serving dish and serve with the Sour-Cream Sauce.

SOUR-CREAM SAUCE:
1. Beat together the sour cream, heavy cream, honey, and lemon juice until mixture is smooth.

2. Serve cool or at room temperature.

Broccoli

Broccoli is one of the best vegetables we have for freezing,* either in the standard fashion (see Part Two) or separated into batches of flowerets and of slant-cut stems, or made into a purée—the directions are given below. Although it's possible to can broccoli, we don't recommend it—the vegetable will be dark and mushy.

When preparing frozen broccoli for serving, avoid overcooking it—remember that the preliminary blanching has already cooked it partially. Use the handsome flowerets for dishes in which appearance counts the most, and try the stir-frying recipe for a delicious way to use the stems, which taste as good as the tops, although they are less attractive in their natural shape.

Hot broccoli is a classic when served with Hollandaise sauce, and it is almost as good with lemon butter, or with a vinaigrette containing parsley, minced capers, and a few bits of chopped pimiento. Try Edward Giobbi's Broccoli con Oliva (below) for an unusual flavor combination. And, for an estimable first course, cook and chill whole stems of broccoli (again, don't overcook) and garnish them with your best mayonnaise.

Broccoli Flowerets and Stems Frozen Separately, and Frozen Broccoli Purée

FLORENCE FABRICANT

1. Cut flowerets from broccoli, leaving only the short, small stems attached. Trim off the leaves and peel the thick skin from the lower, coarse stalks. Soak flowerets and stems separately in salted cold water for 30 minutes if you suspect the presence of insects—otherwise, omit this step. Rinse well and drain.

2. Slice the stems on the diagonal into ¼-inch-thick slices. Divide the flowerets, if very large, into fairly uniform sections.

3. Blanch and cool the stems and tops separately in small batches, following the methods described in Part Two. Blanch small flowerets (about 1 inch across) 2 minutes, the sliced stems 1 minute.

4. Pack flowerets and stem slices separately in freezer containers, leaving no headroom. Seal, label, and freeze.

5. To make broccoli purée for freezing, place sliced, blanched, and cooled stems in a blender jar and purée until moderately fine. Pack in freezer containers, leaving ½-inch headroom. Seal, label, and freeze.

Stir-fried Frozen Broccoli Stems

FLORENCE FABRICANT

Florence Fabricant's way of stir-frying frozen vegetables without first thawing them requires turning normal procedure upside-down. Instead of placing the vegetable in the heated cooking oil, she first cooks the frozen vegetable alone in a hot wok (or a skillet) until the pieces separate and much of the water evaporates. Then oil and seasonings are added to finish the recipe. This is to prevent the cook and kitchen being assaulted by the spattering which would occur if the frozen food were put directly into hot oil.

4 servings

1 pint frozen sliced broccoli
  stems (see above)
1½ teaspoons salt
½ teaspoon sugar

2 tablespoons vegetable oil
2 tablespoons minced scallions,
  including some of the green
  part

1. Heat a wok or a skillet. Add the broccoli stems and stir and toss them in the wok, cooking them until the pieces separate and much of the water which collects in the pan has evaporated, about 2 minutes.

2. Add salt, sugar, and oil and stir-fry for 30 seconds, tossing the pieces constantly.

3. Add scallions, stir once or twice, and transfer to a serving dish. The broccoli may be served hot or at room temperature.

Broccoli con Oliva—Broccoli with Olives

EDWARD GIOBBI

Adapted, with permission, from Edward Giobbi's book Italian Family Cooking *(Random House, 1971), this recipe makes interesting use of frozen broccoli and, if you have them on hand, either canned or frozen tomatoes. (Fresh tomatoes may be used, too.) The dried black olives are optional, but they give a distinctive character to this dish.*

Serves 4 to 6

2 pints frozen broccoli, either
  flowerets and peeled stems or
  flowerets only, thawed just
  until pieces can be separated
3 tablespoons olive oil
1 good-sized clove garlic, peeled
  and minced
¾ cup coarsely chopped
  tomatoes, either canned, or

frozen and thawed, or peeled
  fresh tomatoes, drained of any
  surplus juice
½ to ⅔ cup dried black olives,
  pitted (optional)
Salt and freshly ground pepper,
  or salt and crushed dried red
  pepper

1. The broccoli should be in pieces of fairly uniform size; if not, divide the pieces before cooking.

2. In a skillet or saucepan that has a lid, heat the oil and cook the garlic for a moment or two without browning. Add the tomatoes and cook, uncovered, for about 5 minutes if canned tomatoes are used, 8 to 10 minutes if frozen raw tomatoes or fresh tomatoes are used.

3. Add the broccoli and olives and season with salt and pepper. Cover and simmer until broccoli is tender but not mushy. The time will depend on the size of the pieces—begin testing after 10 minutes, even sooner if the pieces are small. Serve hot.

Brussels Sprouts

From the gardener's point of view this is one of the most obliging of the autumn vegetables, as the tiny cabbages that constitute the "sprouts" remain in perfect condition on the plant for many weeks, even after freezing weather begins. You just harvest what you need, when you need it.

However, the time comes when the sprouts will become coarse or inedible if left any longer. Before that point is reached, we recommend harvesting and freezing* the remaining crop. Certainly, Brussels sprouts can be canned, but we advise against it—they will be overcooked, dark, and soggy.

What to do besides freeze them? Try pickling* them (recipe). When you open a container of your home-frozen sprouts, for a simple and good dish melt some butter in a skillet that has a lid, add the partially thawed sprouts, cover, and cook over medium heat, rolling the sprouts about in the pan from time to time, until they are just tender at the heart. Some people like to uncover them and let them brown a bit—consult your own taste. For seasoning, add salt, pepper, and a few drops of lemon juice.

Less simple—in fact, a downright elegant treatment for a member of the cabbage family—is a creamy purée of sprouts, topped with toasted hazelnuts (recipe). Delicious with meat, fowl, and especially with ham.

Pickled Brussels Sprouts

FLORENCE FABRICANT

Tiny, home-grown Brussels sprouts make a pickle with a distinctly Continental look and flavor.

Makes 3 pints

2 pounds fresh Brussels sprouts	1½ cups sugar
Cold water	1 teaspoon dill seed
Pickling or kosher salt	1 teaspoon whole peppercorns
3 cups cider vinegar	½ teaspoon whole allspice

1. Select sprouts of uniform size, the smaller the better. Trim off any brown stem ends and damaged leaves.

2. Soak the Brussels sprouts in cold water to cover, with 1 teaspoon salt added, for 30 minutes, to disperse any insects lurking within them. Rinse and drain.

3. Combine 1 quart of cold water with ½ cup pickling or kosher salt in a bowl or a stoneware crock. Add Brussels sprouts, cover with a plate which will fit down into the container, and place a weight on the plate (a jar or plastic bag filled with water will do) to keep the vegetables submerged. Set aside for 24 hours.

4. Bring a large kettle of water to a boil. Drain and rinse Brussels sprouts. Add them to the kettle and boil for 10 minutes.

5. While sprouts are boiling, combine in a saucepan the vinegar, sugar, dill seed, peppercorns, and allspice. Bring to a boil and boil for 5 minutes.

6. When Brussels sprouts are barely tender, pack them tightly into hot pint jars and ladle the pickling syrup over them, leaving ½-inch headroom.

7. Adjust the lids and process the jars in a boiling-water bath for 10 minutes.

Purée of Brussels Sprouts with Cream and Hazelnuts

HELEN WITTY

Cook part of your frozen store of Brussels sprouts this way and, instead of a collection of tiny cabbages, you'll serve a celadon-green purée with something of the texture of light mashed potatoes that is yet pleasantly grainy, with a delicate flavor. This is an especially good accompaniment for ham, or for fresh pork cooked with a sweet-sour or fruit glaze.

Serves 4 to 6

1 quart water

Salt

¼ cup raw rice

2 pints frozen Brussels sprouts,
 thawed and drained

¼ cup heavy cream, or to taste

2 tablespoons butter, or to taste

Freshly grated nutmeg
 (optional)

Few drops lemon juice

¼ cup skinned and sliced
 hazelnuts, toasted lightly

1. Bring water to a boil in a pot large enough to hold the sprouts and add a teaspoonful of salt and the rice. Stir, then boil gently until the rice is three-quarters done—still quite firm.

2. Add the Brussels sprouts and boil gently, uncovered, until the sprouts are barely tender—do not overcook them, or you'll lose their pristine flavor.

3. Drain sprouts and rice well in a colander.

4. Purée sprouts and rice, using a food mill or a food processor. If a processor is used, don't overbeat—some slight unevenness of texture should remain.

5. Beat in the cream, butter, a little nutmeg (use a light hand), more salt if needed, and a few drops of lemon juice to point up the flavor. Taste and adjust seasonings carefully: how much you'll need depends on the quality of your vegetable, and on your own taste.

6. Reheat at once and serve hot, sprinkled with the hazelnuts.

Cabbage

Cabbage is perhaps the most readily (and often cheaply) available of all vegetables in the market, and only if your garden crop is a bumper one and you have no cool storage available for the harvested heads should you consider freezing* it. Pickling* is perhaps an even better choice if you like sauerkraut. Cabbage can be canned, but the waterlogged finished product isn't worth the trouble. (However, directions are given in Part Two.)

Use some of your cabbage in mixed pickles,* too—chowchow, for instance (see recipe), and Beet, Cabbage, and Pepper Relish (see under "Beets"). The best pickle of all is sauerkraut. Making kraut is a feasible project if you have a fairly cool (65° F.) place where the kraut can ferment in its crock without being in the way, either physically or in the olfactory sense. However, it shouldn't be completely out of both sight and mind: the liquid level must be checked frequently—the brine must cover the cabbage at all times—and as much air as possible must be excluded from the surface of the brine. Further, if any scum forms, it must be skimmed off, and the plate, weight, and cloth must be thoroughly scalded or exchanged for freshly scalded replacements.

The two recipes that follow mention established ways of weighting down the kraut as it ferments. Lately, however, USDA experts have hit upon a brilliant expedient: A heavy-duty plastic bag filled with just enough water will expand over the surface of the kraut in the crock, weighting it down and at the same time excluding all air. If you want to try this and doubt the sturdiness of your bag, use two bags, one inside the other.

And, for stuffed-cabbage aficionados, a tip from Florence Fabricant, one of our contributors: The night before a stuffed-cabbage feast, put your head of cabbage in the freezer. When it has thawed, the leaves will have been softened enough so that no blanching will be needed before you proceed with the stuffing.

Red-Cabbage Sauerkraut

ALLIANORA ROSSE

From the cuisine of Holland comes this beautifully colored pink-purple sauerkraut, unusual both for its appearance and the method of its making—buttermilk is among the ingredients. Allianora Rosse points out that you'll need a two-gallon earthenware crock or glass container to make it in, and she recommends that you keep your crock on a moderately cool porch or in a cellar during fermentation—it can emit a very pungent aroma before the kraut is ready to use.

Makes about 6 to 7 pounds

6 to 6½ pounds red cabbage
1 ounce plain or pickling (not iodized) salt
½ ounce black peppercorns

1 ounce (or less, if you like) dried juniper berries
Buttermilk, about 1 cup

1. Remove and set aside several unblemished outer leaves of the cabbage. (This is assuming you grow your own, because "boughten" heads usually lack their outer leaves.) Slice the cabbage fine and place it in a large bowl.

2. Sprinkle the cabbage with the salt and knead it well until the juices begin to be noticeable.

3. Arrange the cabbage, with its juices, in four or five layers in a two-gallon crock, topping each layer with a sprinkling of the peppercorns and the juniper berries. As you make the layers, press each one down firmly and sprinkle it with a few tablespoons of the buttermilk. (This promotes lactic-acid fermentation.)

4. Cover the sliced cabbage with the reserved outer leaves, then with clean cheesecloth, then with a plate or a very clean round board that fits closely inside the crock. The juices must rise up to cover the cabbage completely, and as little air as possible—preferably none—should reach the surface of the juice. Top the plate or board with a weight—a good-sized stone, perhaps—and cover the whole thing with a cloth that reaches down the sides of the crock.

5. Let the sauerkraut ferment in a cool place (about 65° F.) for about two weeks, being sure that the liquid level is satisfactory. When it is ready the sauerkraut will be mildly sour and will be pinkish-purple in color.

6. When fermentation has virtually ceased, the sauerkraut can be frozen, if desired, although it will keep in a cool place for some time. If you prefer to refrigerate it, keep it in glass jars with canning lids screwed into place.

NOTE: If you wish to can the finished sauerkraut, see the directions at the end of the following recipe.

Sauerkraut with Caraway and Peppercorns

PAUL RUBINSTEIN

Makes about 1 gallon

4 to 6 fresh green cabbages (about 7 pounds)
1/4 cup kosher salt or coarse sea salt

1 tablespoon black peppercorns
1 tablespoon caraway seeds
2 cups water

1. Wash the cabbages, then shred them very fine. (This is an ideal time to use the fine slicing blade of a multipurpose food processor, if you own one.)

2. In a straight-sided stoneware crock or wooden barrel of two-gallon capacity, pack very tightly an inch-thick layer of shredded cabbage. Sprinkle with some of the salt, a few peppercorns, and some of the caraway seeds. Repeat until all the cabbage has been used, reserving the seasonings for the top layer. Add the water, then the last of the seasonings.

3. Cover with a plate that fits very snugly inside the crock, and place a heavy weight (a stone, a bowl or jar filled with water, etc.) on top of the plate. The juice will soon rise up to cover the plate, so don't use a metal weight. Cover the crock with a clean linen or muslin cloth.

4. Keep the crock in a cool (about 65° F.) and dry place for at least four weeks, or until no more bubbles arise from the fermentation. The juice must cover the kraut at all times.

5. You may leave the kraut in the crock for up to one year in a very cool place (below 40° F.), but the fermentation process will not stop entirely. It is best to pack the sauerkraut in glass jars and refrigerate it, once it has reached the desired level of fermentation.

NOTE: The finished sauerkraut can be canned: Heat it to simmering (be sure it is uniformly hot throughout) and fill clean, hot canning jars, adding juice to rise to ½ inch of the top. Add lids and process in a boiling-water bath: 15 minutes for pints, 20 minutes for quarts.

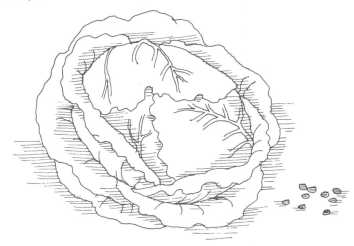

Chunky Chowchow

JANE MOULTON

Use the salad-cutting attachment of your electric mixer, the slicing blade of your grater, or even your meat slicer to quickly cut the vegetables for this relish. The chowchow will mellow in flavor if you allow it several weeks' storage before use.

Makes about 5 pints

6 cups coarsely shredded cabbage (about 2 pounds)

12 cups halved and thinly sliced green tomatoes (about 18 medium tomatoes)

4 sweet red peppers, seeded and slivered

4 sweet green peppers, seeded and slivered

4 cups thinly sliced peeled onions (about 4 or 5 medium onions)

2/3 cup pickling salt or noniodized salt

6 cups cider vinegar

4 cups firmly packed light-brown sugar

1/4 cup mixed pickling spice (remove the hot red pepper pods, if desired)

1. Mix cabbage, green tomatoes, red and green peppers, and onions in a stainless-steel, ceramic, glass, or unchipped enamel container. Let stand for at least 12 hours, but for no more than 28 hours, in a cool place.

2. Drain vegetables in a colander and press out as much liquid as possible without bruising them. Do not rinse them.

3. Combine vinegar and sugar in a large pickling kettle. Place pickling spices in a cheesecloth bag or a stainless-steel tea ball and add them to the vinegar mixture. Bring to a boil.

4. Add vegetables to the kettle and again bring to a boil over high heat, stirring as needed. Cover and cook gently for 30 minutes. Remove spice bag.

5. Pack the hot chowchow into clean, hot pint jars.

6. Add lids and process in a boiling-water bath for 10 minutes.

Chinese Cabbage (Celery Cabbage)

Easily grown and more delicate in flavor and texture than European types of cabbage, Chinese cabbage—sometimes called celery cabbage—is delicious when used in many recipes for the common cabbage. Sliced thin, it makes excellent slaw. It is a light and pleasant vegetable course when cut into 1/2-inch lengths and cooked quickly in very little salted water. Season with butter, salt, and pepper, and accompany with wedges of lemon.

According to those who have tried it, it makes fine sauerkraut. Follow the directions for kraut made with cabbage (see "Cabbage," above), but season the cabbage only with 2 ounces of salt to 5 pounds of cleaned and shredded Chinese cabbage—no spices. Mix well, pack down, and ferment in the same way as ordinary sauerkraut.

Freezing* is the best way to preserve any surplus of Chinese cabbage from your garden. Use only the tender stalks for freezing—the process won't soften or improve old or tough outer stalks, which are better sliced up for the vegetable-soup pot.

For a stir-fry of Chinese cabbage in the Chinese manner, use 2 quarts of fresh cabbage—washed, shaken dry, and cut into 1-inch lengths—in place of the asparagus in the recipe for stir-fried asparagus on page 190. We like the version with ginger and garlic, but these seasonings can be omitted and a final sprinkle of soy sauce used instead. Prepared in either way, this vegetable goes remarkably well with broiled chicken or other non-Oriental main courses. And so does Grace Chu's Creamed Chinese Cabbage (recipe), which can be made with the frozen vegetable.

Creamed Chinese Cabbage

GRACE ZIA CHU

Mme Chu has provided the instructions for making this dish with fresh Chinese cabbage. If you are using the frozen vegetable (2 pints to replace the amount in the recipe), she suggests that you alter the cooking method. Instead of steaming it, cook the still-frozen cabbage quickly in a covered saucepan with very little water—¹/₄ cup or so. Turn it often and break up the mass with a fork so that it cooks quickly and evenly. Cook it just until tender—as little as 10 minutes may be required for this stage to be reached. Then proceed with the recipe as written for fresh, steamed Chinese cabbage.

Serves 6 to 8

2 pounds Chinese cabbage (1 or 2 heads)
3 teaspoons salt
¹/₂ cup milk

2 tablespoons cornstarch
¹/₂ teaspoon sugar
2 tablespoons vegetable oil
¹/₂ cup cooked ham strips

1. Wash and drain cabbage. Quarter each cabbage and then cut into 1-inch lengths.

2. Use a large steamer or pot containing about 4 quarts of water and bring water to a boil. Place cabbage in a bowl or a deep plate and set in the steamer. Steam, covered, for 35 minutes.

3. Add 2 teaspoons of the salt to the cabbage. Pour off liquid and measure, meanwhile keeping cabbage warm. If you do not have enough liquid to make ³/₄ cup, add water.

4. Dissolve the cornstarch in the milk and mix in the remaining 1 teaspoon of salt and the sugar. Mix well.

5. Heat the oil in a saucepan and add the cabbage liquid. Add the milk and cornstarch mixture and stir over heat until thickened.

6. Place cabbage in a serving dish and pour the sauce over it. Arrange the ham strips over the sauce.

Carrots

Probably everyone in the temperate regions of the world has eaten carrots, beginning with the most remote ancestor of the creator of Peter Rabbit, but only those who have grown their own—or pulled carrots in the garden of a friend—have known the remarkable sweetness of the good carrot varieties meant for growing in the home garden, not for long-distance shipping and long supermarket life.

As soon as carrot thinnings are large enough to make half a mouthful apiece, eat them, don't consign them to the compost heap. And do pull some of the main crop while the roots are still small enough to be in the luxury class.

How to cook carrots? In very little water, with a pinch of sugar if they aren't sugar-sweet to begin with, and a little salt; and, to finish, plenty of butter (or cream, boiled down to a final blending with the vegetable juices) and a dusting of minced parsley. The parsley—if it's real parsley that you have grown yourself—lends not only color, but flavor.

Carrots are good when canned* at home, and they freeze* very well, whether whole, cut into strips, sliced, or diced. And see under "Beets" for Beet and Carrot Pickle.

To change the presentation of a vegetable that's too often taken for granted, cook frozen carrots until very tender (or use canned carrots). Drain them and purée them in a food mill—you don't want to use a blender here, which would create too smooth a texture—season them, and reheat them with plenty of butter.

To glaze carrots, cook small whole ones, or cook carrot sticks. Drain well and add to the saucepan butter and brown sugar—say 2 or 3 tablespoons of each to a pound of carrots. Toss and roll the vegetables in the pan over medium heat until a golden, almost-brown glaze is formed. A fine accompaniment for meats—especially pork or ham—or duck or other poultry that responds to a somewhat sweet accent.

Carrots for dessert appear in guises other than the carrot cakes and tortes that begin with raw carrots. Use cooked, drained,

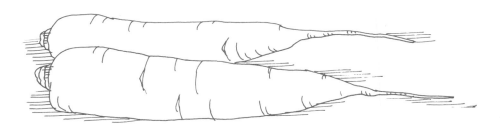

and very smoothly puréed carrots in place of pumpkin in your favorite recipe for pie filling. And if you'd like to try carrots for breakfast, we offer you Pilar Turner's recipe for Carrot Jam, below.

Baby Carrots Canned with Dill

FLORENCE FABRICANT

Yes, these are canned carrots, but they are given added character by the herb. We like to serve them with a dollop of sour cream.

Makes 4 quarts

8 quarts (about 12 pounds) baby carrots, without tops

4 large branches or tops of fresh dill
4 teaspoons salt

1. Scrub carrots and cut off the stem ends. Cover with boiling water and let stand for 2 or 3 minutes. Drain, but save the water.

2. Rinse carrots in cold water, then slip off the skins. Sort carrots for size if necessary.

3. Place one of the branches of dill in each of four clean, hot quart jars. Pack carrots tightly into the jars, leaving 1-inch headroom. Add 1 teaspoon salt to each jar.

4. Bring the carrot liquid to a boil and pour into the jars, leaving 1/2-inch headroom and making sure there are no air pockets. Adjust lids.

5. Process in a pressure canner at 10 pounds of pressure for 30 minutes.

Carrot Jam

PILAR TURNER

In Spain this jam was originally allowed to cool before the jars were filled, and the filled jars were covered with rounds of flannel dipped in brandy. With the generally warmer storage conditions in American homes, it's wiser to seal the jam while boiling-hot in sterilized jars rather than risk spoilage with the more traditional method.

Makes about 8 pints

4 pounds carrots, without their
   tops, peeled or scraped
Water

5 cups sugar
Grated rind of 4 oranges
Juice of 2 lemons, strained

1. Boil the whole carrots in water to cover until they are soft. Drain them and slice, dice, or mash them according to the consistency of jam required.

2. In a porcelainized pot (or other preserving pan) place the sugar and carrots in alternate layers. Add the grated orange rind and the lemon juice and let stand until sugar begins to melt, or overnight.

3. Place over low heat, bring to a boil, and simmer, stirring occasionally, until thick enough, about 35 minutes. (Test by pouring a few drops of the jam onto a thick, cold plate; it is ready when it doesn't run readily when the plate is tilted.)

4. Pour, boiling hot, into hot sterilized jars and seal at once.

Cauliflower

Cauliflower freezes* so well that canning, although a possible way of preserving your crop, is very much a second choice. Both the snow-white cauliflower we're most accustomed to and the purple- and green-headed varieties have much the same flavor, and all freeze equally well.

Besides freezing it, by all means include cauliflower in mixed pickles*—see Elizabeth Colchie's version of Mustard Pickles, below—and see your big cookbooks for other traditional pickle combinations that include this vegetable. For lovers of spicy relishes we offer Monoroma Phillips's recipe for Gobi da Achaar, a traditional pickle from the Punjab.

For cauliflower from the freezer, try a salad seasoned with dill (recipe). Or make one of the many fine French cauliflower soups. Or cook the flowerets, chill them (don't overcook cauliflower if you would enjoy it at its best), and serve them with a herb-flavored mayonnaise. For a substantial garnish for a meat course, thaw very small flowerets, dip them in fritter batter, and deep-fry until golden. Sprinkle freshly cooked cauliflower with bread crumbs browned in a skillet with butter and mixed with freshly grated cheese—Gruyère, for choice. Or place the cooked cauliflower in a shallow baking dish, cover with Mornay sauce, top with crumbs and bits of butter, brown in the oven, and enjoy a classic gratin.

Before you have frozen or made pickles of all of your cauliflower, try a crunchy version of slaw, a pleasant change from cabbage. Slice the small raw flowerets lengthwise as thinly as is feasible—you don't want them to crumble—and mix the slices very gently with a highly seasoned mayonnaise. We add to the mayonnaise Dijon mustard, a drop or two of Tabasco, perhaps some horseradish, sometimes some herbs—this is a taste-as-you-go dressing.

Mustard Pickles

ELIZABETH SUSAN COLCHIE

Makes 6 pints

One 2-pound cauliflower, trimmed and cut into bite-sized pieces (6 cups)
1 pound small green tomatoes, halved
6 carrots, peeled and sliced 1/4 inch thick (2 cups)
1 pound pearl onions, about 1 inch in diameter (3 cups)
1 pound red bell peppers, trimmed, cored, and diced (3 cups)
1 cup kosher salt (or other coarse salt) mixed with 4 quarts water

3 tablespoons dry mustard
1/4 cup flour
1 1/4 cups lightly packed brown sugar
1 teaspoon turmeric
1/2 teaspoon ground ginger
1 cup water
4 cups cider vinegar
1 tablespoon mustard seed
1 teaspoon dill seed
1 teaspoon whole cloves
1 teaspoon whole allspice

1. Soak the cauliflower, tomatoes, carrots, onions, and peppers in the salt and water for 12 hours.

2. Stir together in a saucepan the dry mustard, flour, brown sugar,

turmeric, ginger, and 1 cup water. Add the vinegar and the mustard seed, plus the dill seed, cloves, and allspice, the last three tied in a cheesecloth bag. Bring to a boil, stirring. Simmer, covered, for 10 minutes.

3. Drain the vegetables and place them in a large preserving pot with fresh water to cover. Bring them to a boil, drain, and combine in the large pot with the mustard sauce.

4. Bring the mixture to a boil. Remove the spice bag.

5. Ladle the pickles into 6 sterilized pint jars.

6. Add lids and process for 10 minutes in a boiling-water bath. Store for at least two weeks before serving.

Gobi da Achaar—Pickled Cauliflower

MONOROMA PHILLIPS

"The recipe for this pickle," comments Monoroma Phillips, *"is fairly typical of the Punjab in either Northern India or Pakistan. Frequently, the vegetables used in pickles would be dried in the sun and then made into pickles, but then as now it was a matter of choice.*

"Pickle-making brings back memories of my early childhood, when two Muslim servants would sit out on the side lawn preparing pickles under my mother's supervision. Hindu, Sikh, or Muslim neighbours would drop by and all the ladies would exchange recipes while drinking green tea with cardamom. . . . Every home had a Tandoor or clay oven dug in the ground for baking the daily bread or baking Tandoori Chicken. On pickle-making days the Tandoor was closed and the three-legged clay stove next to it was used for the cooking down of syrups, boiling oil, or toasting garm masala spices."

Makes 3 to 4 pints

2 tablespoons seedless dried
  tamarind (see note on
  ingredients, below)
1 cup boiling water
4 ounces fresh ginger root
6 cloves of garlic, peeled
3 tablespoons salt
2 pounds cauliflower (weighed
  without leaves)

3 quarts water
3 cups malt vinegar
3 tablespoons garm masala (see
  note on ingredients)
1 cup dark-brown sugar
1 teaspoon Cayenne pepper

1. Soak tamarind in boiling water until soft, about 10 minutes. Press tamarind pulp and water through a strainer into a large enameled or porcelain-lined pan.

2. Scrape skin off ginger and grind the ginger and garlic with 2 tablespoons of the salt, using a mortar and pestle.

3. Break cauliflower into flowerets 1 or 2 inches across. Cut the main stem and the larger stems of the flowerets into thin round slices. Place cauliflower in a wire basket.

4. Bring 3 quarts of water to a boil and add the remaining 1 tablespoon salt. Plunge basket of cauliflower into the water and as soon as the water returns to the boil, remove the cauliflower and drain. Pat well with a towel to remove as much moisture as possible.

5. To the tamarind in the preserving pan add the vinegar, garm masala, the ginger-and-garlic paste, sugar, and Cayenne pepper. Bring to a boil and boil 5 minutes, then reduce heat and simmer 5 minutes. Turn off heat, add cauliflower, stir well, and allow to cool. Do not cover the pan.

6. With a clean, dry slotted spoon, place cauliflower in dry, sterilized canning jars, packing it down firmly. Distribute pickling liquid among the jars.

7. Add lids and process in a boiling-water bath for 5 minutes.

8. In India, the filled jars would be set in a warm, sunny place, without the heat processing, and turned every other day to face the sun. Whichever way the pickle is treated, it will be ready to eat in 7 to 10 days.

NOTE: Such ingredients as the spice mixture called garm masala (or garam masala) and the dried tamarind are available in Indo-Pakistani food stores and sometimes in markets catering to Latin Americans. A source (for mail orders only) is Magic Carpet West, 201 West 98th Street, New York, N.Y. 10025.

Cauliflower Salad

FLORENCE FABRICANT

A different cauliflower salad, fragrant with dill, sharpened with onion, enriched with bacon—and served warm. Unusual, too, in that it is made with frozen cauliflower.

4 to 6 servings

4 cups frozen cauliflower, either
  frozen loose or in a block
Boiling water
4 strips bacon
1 cup chopped onion

⅓ cup white vinegar
2 teaspoons salt
Generous amount of freshly
  ground black pepper
2 tablespoons minced fresh dill

1. Place frozen cauliflower in a large bowl. Cover it with boiling water and set aside while continuing with the recipe. (If the pieces are frozen together, pry them apart as the mass begins to thaw.)

2. Fry the bacon until crisp and drain the strips on absorbent paper.

3. Add the onions to the bacon fat and cook over medium heat until they are tender but not browned.

4. Drain the cauliflower thoroughly and place it in a serving dish.

5. Pour the onions and bacon fat over the cauliflower. Add the vinegar and stir gently. Season the salad with salt and pepper and stir again carefully.

6. Crumble the bacon and sprinkle it over the salad, along with the minced dill. Serve immediately.

Celeriac (Knob Celery, Celery Root)

Celeriac is triply related—in name, in flavor, and in family kinship—to our familiar celery, although it would be hard to believe from its appearance—the big, knobby root, the edible part of celeriac, bears little resemblance to the tall ribs of a head of celery. A taste, however, makes the relationship clear. To preserve any surplus, freeze* it.

A European favorite, celeriac is becoming better known in American markets as well as in home gardens. Use it fresh as you would celery, for flavoring soups and stocks. Try it, cooked very briefly (or sometimes left raw), cut into matchsticks and dressed with a highly seasoned vinaigrette or a mustardy mayonnaise—a classic French hors d'oeuvre. Defrosted frozen celeriac and fresh-cooked potatoes are good companions in a hearty salad flavored with anchovies (recipe).

What else? Try simmering celeriac in broth, either in slices or matchsticks (it's easier to peel, by the way, if sliced first). Or cook it, from the freezer or the fresh state, purée it, and mix it with half the quantity of mashed potatoes for an excellent vegetable combination, good with the same meat or fowl courses as a celery and potato purée. Cook the julienned frozen vegetable gently in butter until tender and use it as a garnish or a side dish, or serve it in a cream sauce.

Celeriac and Potato Salad with Cream Dressing

ELIZABETH SUSAN COLCHIE

Serves 6

1 large clove garlic, peeled and sliced
8 canned anchovy fillets, drained and chopped
6 tablespoons heavy cream
2 pounds new potatoes, in their skins
1/4 cup mayonnaise

4 teaspoons Dijon mustard
1 1/2 tablespoons lemon juice
1 teaspoon white pepper
1 pound frozen julienned celeriac, defrosted and dried, if necessary, on paper towels
Minced parsley for garnishing

1. Soak the garlic and anchovies in the cream for 30 minutes or more.

2. Boil the new potatoes for 20 minutes, or until they are just tender. Peel them and cut them into small cubes.

3. Beat together in a small bowl the mayonnaise, mustard, lemon juice, and white pepper. Remove the garlic from the cream and add the anchovy mixture to the mayonnaise.

4. Gently toss the potatoes and celeriac in a bowl with the dressing. Chill for at least two hours.

5. Let the salad warm up slightly before serving. Sprinkle heavily with finely minced parsley as a garnish.

Celery

Familiar as it may be in the bowl of *crudités,* celery is meant for more than munching raw. It has many merits as a cooked vegetable, so it is worth freezing* or canning* when a large supply is available. Little or none of the head of celery need go to waste—the twiggy tops, with their leaves, and any outer stalks that are a bit tough, can be blanched (see Part Two), chilled, frozen on a baking sheet, then packed in plastic bags, ready to have the needed amount removed whenever a soup, a stew, or a stock requires celery as part of the *bouquet garni.*

Pickled celery sticks are an estimable nibble—see the recipe—and celery is an ingredient in many of the mixed relishes* for which recipes are to be found in standard cookbooks and books on pickling. Cooked with leeks and frozen, celery makes a ready-to-use soup base good enough for a party—see the index for Creamed Leek and Celery Soup.

Other suggestions: Cook sliced frozen celery with carrots, and when tender add butter and a good strewing of minced parsley and chives. Cook, drain, and purée celery and blend the purée with about half the quantity of hot mashed potatoes. Whip the purée well, season with salt, pepper, butter, and perhaps cream, and serve with duck, goose, or pork or any other meat or poultry. Cream your cooked celery, or serve it in a cheese sauce, or chill it and add it to a salad of mixed cooked vegetables with a mayonnaise dressing.

Pickled Celery Sticks

ELIZABETH SUSAN COLCHIE
Makes 4 pints

Celery, prepared as directed below
2¹/₂ cups white wine vinegar
2¹/₂ cups water
4 teaspoons kosher or other coarse pure salt

2 teaspoons sugar
2 teaspoons dried tarragon, or 4 to 6 teaspoons minced fresh tarragon
4 shallots, peeled

1. Prepare enough celery to fit tightly into 4 pint canning jars: Remove the leaves and the strings; cut the celery into strips ¹/₄ inch wide and almost the full height of the jars, allowing 1 inch of headspace.

2. In an enamel or stainless-steel saucepan boil together the vinegar, water, salt, sugar, and tarragon for 2 minutes.

3. Fit the celery into 4 clean pint jars and add 1 shallot, sliced, to each.

4. Pour in the pickling liquid to cover the celery, allowing ¹/₂-inch headspace.

5. Add lids and process in a boiling-water bath for 10 minutes.

6. Let stand for a few weeks, and chill before serving as a relish.

Chard (Swiss Chard)

A good mixer, this vegetable with its celery-like stalks and wavy green leaves, both parts edible and especially choice when cut young. Freezing* is the best way to preserve your surplus, which will come toward the end of summer; but canning is satisfactory, too, if your freezing space is limited.

For both processes the younger and more tender the stalks and leaves, the better. But if some of your chard has grown a bit tall and stout, simply chop the stalks coarsely before blanching them, giving them a minute or two longer in the scalding bath than the cut-up leaves; then mix stalks and leaves for chilling, draining, packing, and freezing. Or you may want to pack part of your stalks separately, especially if you have grown the red-stemmed kind, keeping the greens in containers to themselves.

Simple preparations of chard are good: cook it in the minimum amount of water or broth and season it with butter, salt, and pepper, and serve it with wedges of lemon. Or try it, cooked and drained, in a cheese sauce, or perhaps au gratin. It's a good vegetable to include in soups, too, and it combines well with spinach and other greens.

For two unusual dishes, each worthy to be served as a separate course, see Elizabeth Colchie's Aromatic Swiss Chard and Rice and Felipe Rojas-Lombardi's Chard with Herbed Olive Sauce, below.

Aromatic Swiss Chard and Rice

ELIZABETH SUSAN COLCHIE

A versatile dish, to serve hot or cold, as a vegetable course or as a salad.

Serves 6

1 cup minced onions (frozen onions should be thawed before use)
1/4 cup olive oil
6 cups partially defrosted frozen Swiss chard
1/2 teaspoon minced fresh garlic
1/2 teaspoon ground ginger
1/4 teaspoon ground cinnamon

1/8 teaspoon powdered saffron dissolved in 1 teaspoon hot water
1 1/3 cups water
1/2 cup rice
1 teaspoon salt
Lemon juice to taste
Sliced lemon, for garnish

1. In a heavy casserole cook the onions slowly in the olive oil until they are softened.

2. Add the chard, garlic, ginger, cinnamon, and saffron and toss over high heat for a few minutes.

3. Add the water, rice, and salt and bring to a boil, stirring. Cover tightly and cook over low heat for 25 minutes, or until the liquid is absorbed.

4. Add lemon juice to taste. Serve hot, warm, or cold, garnished with lemon slices.

Chard with Herbed Olive Sauce

FELIPE ROJAS-LOMBARDI

Originally devised as an accompaniment for cold meats, the herbed olive sauce recommended here as a dressing for Swiss chard is also delicious over New Zealand-spinach and other greens with a pronounced character, and over green beans cooked al dente, *too.*

Felipe Rojas-Lombardi includes a larger quantity of fresh cilantro (coriander) than he lists below when he makes this sauce to serve with meats, and he recommends the favorite olives of his native Peru—Aceitunas de

Botija—*which are sometimes available as "Alfonso olives" under the Krinos label in specialty food shops or Greek groceries in large American cities. If they aren't to be found, use canned or bottled ripe olives, not the dried Mediterranean black olives.*

Serves 6

HERBED OLIVE SAUCE:

5 tablespoons minced parsley
2 tablespoons minced fresh cilantro (coriander), if available; or substitute fresh basil
1/2 cup pitted and drained ripe olives, measured, then chopped moderately fine

1/2 teaspoon finely minced garlic
1/4 cup fresh lemon juice
1/2 cup olive oil
Salt and freshly ground pepper to taste
Pinch of crumbled dried thyme

THE CHARD:

Small quantity of boiling salted water
4 cups frozen cut Swiss chard

SAUCE:

1. Twist the minced parsley firmly in the corner of a towel to rid it of excess moisture, then repeat the process with the cilantro or the basil. Place herbs in a mixing bowl

2. Add the olives, garlic, lemon juice, olive oil, salt and pepper, and dried thyme and whisk together. Let sauce stand at room temperature for a time to blend the flavors, then whisk again to mix before serving.

CHARD:

1. Bring salted water to a boil in a saucepan and add the frozen chard. Turn the pieces of vegetable frequently as they thaw, in order that they will cook evenly. When thawed, cover and cook over medium heat until the chard is tender—this will take only 5 minutes or so.

2. Drain at once, place in a warmed serving dish, and serve with the olive sauce.

NOTE: Any left-over sauce will keep, refrigerated, for as long as two weeks.

Collards

See "Kale and Collards," below, for suggestions for using this vegetable.

Corn

Poets write of corn, and cookbooks do, too, with a vengeance. This is perhaps the all-American vegetable *par excellence,* having been grown for many ages in North America before the Indians showed the first European colonists how to plant, harvest, and cook it.

With the possible exception of dessert—but no, there's Indian pudding, made with corn meal, so corn appears in that course too—there is no menu category into which corn doesn't fit in one guise or another. Corn in soup or chowder, boiled, steamed, creamed; roasted in the husk, in fritters, in combination with other vegetables; scalloped, in pies, in breads, muffins, pancakes, tortillas, breakfast cereals, pickles, relishes, popped, and parched—there are all these preparations, and more. There may be no such thing as corn jam, but we have seen a recipe for corncob jelly, and it was not a hoax.

Corn is a success when canned*, either in whole-kernel form or cream-style, and perhaps is even more successful when cut off the cob and frozen*. If you have plenty of freezer space, the way to freeze corn on the cob is also described in Part Two.

Because of the wealth of ways to serve corn that are described in every general cookbook, we'll content ourselves here with begging you not to overcook your fresh corn on the cob. Husk it, drop it into a few inches of boiling water (no salt, but a little sugar if the corn isn't as young as you could wish), cover the pot, let it come back to a full boil, cook 1 minute, and that's it. Please do not heed recipes that tell you to boil corn for 15 minutes, or 10 minutes, or even 8 minutes. The writers of those recipes must be thinking of corn that has been sitting in a supermarket for several days and is therefore unfit to eat. Choose fresh corn in the "milk stage," when a kernel will spurt juice when pierced by a thumbnail.

We commend to you the two recipes below for corn relishes—both very American, though different from each other—plus a traditional succotash (you'll find the recipe with others that include lima beans—see the index), a spoon bread with whole-corn kernels in it, and most especially, Jane Moulton's dried corn Ohio-style: she tells how to dry it, how to cook it, and how to make a superlative soup of it.

Corn Relish

JANE MOULTON

This is the clear variety of corn relish, in which the bright-yellow corn is accented with bits of green and red peppers.

Makes about 7 pints

6 cups corn kernels, freshly cut from about 18 ears of tender sweet corn
3 cups seeded, chopped green peppers
2 cups seeded, chopped sweet red peppers
2 cups thinly sliced unpeeled cucumbers
2 cups coarsely chopped onions

4 cups peeled, chopped ripe tomatoes (about 7)
4 cups cider vinegar
2 cups sugar
1/4 cup pickling salt or noniodized salt
2 tablespoons celery seed
1 tablespoon mustard seed
1 tablespoon turmeric

1. Place all ingredients in a preserving kettle holding 6 quarts or more. Stir over medium heat until mixed and sugar is dissolved. Turn heat to high and bring to a full boil, stirring as needed. Turn down heat and let the relish boil gently for 10 minutes, covered.

2. Ladle relish into clean, hot pint jars, making sure corn is packed loosely in the liquid.

3. Add lids and process for 15 minutes in a boiling-water bath.

Another Corn Relish

RUTH ELLEN CHURCH

There are probably as many kinds of corn relish as there are corn-lovers who like to put up summer's surplus vegetables. Ruth Ellen Church's relish contains several ingredients that don't appear in Jane Moulton's, and it would be a brave person indeed who would say which is more "authentic."

Makes 6 pints

5 cups fresh, tender corn, cut from cobs
1½ cups chopped celery
1½ cups chopped cabbage
1 cup unpeeled, chopped cucumbers
1 cup chopped green peppers
½ cup chopped red sweet peppers
1½ cups chopped onions
2 tablespoons salt
1½ teaspoons turmeric
½ cup honey
¼ cup sugar
1½ teaspoons dry mustard
1½ teaspoons celery seed
1½ cups cider vinegar
½ cup water

1. In a large preserving kettle combine all ingredients and stir well to mix. Bring to a boil, then lower the heat and cook at a simmer, stirring occasionally, for 10 minutes.

2. Pour into hot, clean canning jars, leaving ¼-inch headspace.

3. Add lids and process jars in a boiling-water bath for 15 minutes (for pints).

Spoon Bread with Whole-Kernel Corn

ELIZABETH SUSAN COLCHIE

Serves 6

3 cups milk
1 teaspoon salt
1 teaspoon sugar
1 cup stone-ground white cornmeal
2 teaspoons chili powder
4 tablespoons butter
1½ cups frozen corn kernels, defrosted
4 eggs, beaten

1. In a heavy saucepan bring to a simmer the milk, salt, and sugar. Very slowly sprinkle in the cornmeal and chili powder, stirring constantly. Cook for 3 minutes, stirring.

2. Remove from heat and beat in the butter and corn kernels. Beat in the eggs. Turn into a buttered 6- to 8-cup baking dish or charlotte mold.

3. Bake in a preheated 375° F. oven for 30 to 35 minutes, until puffed and golden. Serve immediately.

Oven-dried Corn Ohio Style

JANE MOULTON

"Reconstituted dried corn has a more chewy texture and a sweeter flavor than fresh, frozen, or canned corn. In the early days, drying was the only feasible way to preserve corn, but as other methods developed, drying almost disappeared except in a few farm communities and households in which the dried-corn flavor was considered the true *corn flavor. In recent years, dried corn has been rediscovered and has become somewhat of a delicacy. It's easy to do."—Jane Moulton.*

1. Select sweet, young corn—the same quality of corn you'd enjoy eating fresh off the cob. The average oven will accommodate no more than the kernels from two dozen ears at one time. Dried, that amount of corn will measure about 2½ cups.

2. Husk corn and place in a kettle with a tight lid. Add about 1 inch of water, cover, and set over high heat. After steam fills the kettle, boil for about 3 minutes, then check the corn. When it's done it will have darkened in color just a little. If it isn't ready, steam for up to 2 minutes more, but don't overcook.

3. Place corn in a single layer on paper or terry towels to drain and become cool enough to handle. Cut kernels from the cobs with a serrated knife or a special corn-stripping tool. (Don't worry about any corn silk that may remain—it's easy to remove when the corn has been dried.)

4. Place corn on cookie sheets or jelly-roll pans, spreading it no more than ¼ inch deep. Place pans in the oven and set the thermostat at 140° F. Use an oven thermometer to check the temperature frequently, because it's important to keep it between 140° and 150° F. Some ovens won't hold that low a temperature; if yours won't, prop the door of an

electric oven or of a modern gas oven open about ¹/₂ inch. Doors of older gas ovens should be kept open 6 to 8 inches. Keep checking the heat, and open the door wider, or turn off the heat for a time, if the temperature goes above 150° F.

5. Stir the corn every 30 minutes or so. Every two hours turn the cookie sheets front to back and switch them between the top and bottom shelves, if you are using two shelves. It's difficult to give an exact time for drying corn, but it will be somewhere around 5 to 8 hours, depending upon the size of the kernels, the amount of corn in the oven, and the drying temperature. When dry enough, the corn is almost brittle. (NOTE: Don't leave the house or go to bed with the oven heat on. If your corn isn't quite dry at bedtime, turn off the heat and close the oven door. Finish the drying next day.)

6. Store the dried and cooled corn in glass jars with screw lids that close airtight. (They don't have to actually seal, as they would in canning food, so you can use clean mayonnaise jars or other non-canning jars or decorative jars, so long as their lids are tight.) Keep the dried corn in a cool, preferably dark, place, but it's not necessary to refrigerate it.

7. After a day or two, check the dried corn to make sure no moisture is collecting on the inside of the jar. Moisture indicates that the corn needs further drying, which should be done at once. Otherwise the corn will mold and have to be discarded. Use the corn within a year to enjoy it at its best.

HOW TO COOK OVEN-DRIED CORN:

1. To use dried corn in vegetable soups or in stews, simply toss the kernels into the pot at the beginning of cooking, rather than near the end, when you would add fresh corn. If you prefer a less chewy consistency, soak the corn in water for several hours or overnight. Put it in the refrigerator for overnight soaking.

2. To serve dried corn as a vegetable, combine 1 part corn with 4 parts water. Cover and simmer about 8 minutes for corn of very chewy (but good) consistency. Add salt and butter or other seasonings to taste.

3. For softer kernels—more like those of the fresh vegetable—soak the corn for several hours or overnight in lightly salted water (¹/₄ teaspoon salt to each cup of water, and 1 part corn to 4 parts water). Refrigerate corn if it is soaked for more than an hour or two. Place corn and its liquid in a saucepan and bring to a boil over high heat. Turn down the heat and boil gently until the corn is as tender as you like it—this will

take 5 to 15 minutes. Serve hot, with butter. (Half a cup of corn, cooked in 2 cups of water, will serve 6.)

Ohio Cream of Corn Soup

JANE MOULTON

"Although it takes three to four hours to cook, this soup takes almost no preparation time. It turns a creamy caramel color as it cooks and makes great eating with little effort," says Jane Moulton.

Makes about 3½ cups

½ cup oven-dried corn (see preceding recipe)
1 quart milk, regular or skim
2 tablespoons butter

½ teaspoon salt
½ teaspoon crumbled dried savory or thyme

1. Place all ingredients in the top section of a double boiler and mix well. (Don't worry about the butter—it will melt later.)

2. Place over boiling water in the double-boiler base, cover, and cook for 3 to 4 hours over simmering water, stirring occasionally. Check the base once or twice to see if more boiling water should be added.

3. Adjust seasonings and serve hot.

Cresses

Of the cresses we're considering in this book, all are superb for salads and for eating in sandwiches and as a garnish. Watercress, however, is good when cooked, too, as the Chinese, with their spicy Beef with Watercress, and the French, with their springtime Potage Crème de Cresson, know well.

Anyone lucky enough to be able to grow watercress in or beside a brook or a spring-fed pond, or to gather it wild, is sure to have a surplus to enjoy in cooked dishes. Or, lacking a water-garden source, you can take advantage of greengrocers' specials in watercress season—May through July is the time of abundance—and make and freeze* a purée of the stems (a thrifty use of parts that

sometimes are thrown away), or of the stems and leaves together—
the directions follow. With the purée in the freezer, you'll be
prepared to make Cream of Watercress Soup, below, or a quick cold
soup in which watercress is an alternative to green peas (see the
index).

Watercress Purée for Freezing

FLORENCE FABRICANT

*Try accompanying fish with a velvet purée of watercress, its distinctive
sharpness undiminished. Or use it as a foundation for a cream soup or in a
mélange of vegetable purées.*

Makes 2 pints

3 tablespoons sweet (unsalted)
  butter
1 cup chopped scallions
3 whole bunches watercress or

stems of 5 bunches watercress
(6 cups, packed), picked over,
rinsed, and coarsely chopped
1 teaspoon salt

1. Melt butter in a large, deep saucepan.
2. Add the scallions and cook them over low heat until they are tender
   but not browned.
3. Add the chopped watercress and salt. Cover and cook over low heat
   until watercress has thoroughly wilted, about 20 minutes. Cool.
4. Purée the mixture in a blender or a food processor.
5. Pack into pint freezer containers, leaving ½-inch headroom. Seal,
   label, and freeze.

Cream of Watercress Soup

FLORENCE FABRICANT

6 to 8 servings

2 tablespoons butter
½ cup minced onion
2 cups peeled, diced potatoes
2 cups chicken stock
1 pint frozen Watercress Purée
  (see recipe), thawed

1½ cups milk
1 cup heavy cream
Salt and pepper
Fresh watercress for
  garnishing, if available

1. Melt butter in a large saucepan. Add onion and cook over low to medium heat until tender but not browned.

2. Add potatoes and chicken stock, bring to a boil, and simmer, covered, until the potatoes are tender, about 20 minutes.

3. Put mixture through a sieve or a food mill. Return to saucepan and add the watercress purée and milk.

4. Bring just to a boil, stir in the cream, and season to taste with salt and pepper. Reheat, but do not boil.

5. Serve hot, garnishing each serving with a sprig of fresh watercress, if available.

Cucumbers

Cucumbers get into more kinds of pickles than any other vegetable, which is fortunate for our winter enjoyment of them, because they aren't suitable for canning or freezing.

They *are* suitable for cooking, though, and some summer day when your vines have produced far more fruit than you can cope with, try one of the recipes for a cold cucumber soup, or a hot cream of cucumber soup, that you'll find in big general cookbooks.

For an "icebox pickle" of Scandinavian origin, slice some of your cucumber crop, skin and all, into jars. Fill the jars with a half-and-half mixture of white vinegar and water, plus a lot of sugar—up to 1 cup to 2 cups of liquid—a little salt, a lot of chopped fresh dill, and a little white pepper. These keep well when stored, covered, in the refrigerator, if snack-hunters give them a chance.

When you have 6 to 8 good-sized cucumbers on hand and need a hot vegetable dish, try braised cucumbers. Peel them, halve them lengthwise, scoop out the seeds with a teaspoon, and cut the cucumbers into finger-size lengths. Heat ¼ cup butter in a skillet and turn the cucumbers in it over medium-high heat until they are decidedly golden but not browned. Add a little broth or stock—½ cup or so—cover, and cook until tender. Adjust seasonings and serve with some chopped mint, or chopped parsley, or chopped parsley plus chives, strewn over the vegetables.

Pickles we especially like are those for which we give recipes

---

below: Gloria Pépin's Cornichons, the kind of tiny, sour French pickles that carry astronomical price tags in food specialty shops; Jane Moulton's Bread and Butter Pickles; her Friendship Ring Pickles, which solve the problem of what to do with cucumbers that manage to ripen despite your daily harvesting; and Paul Rubinstein's Polish Dill Pickles, redolent of dill, garlic, and bay leaves.

Cornichons (Sour Gherkins in the French Manner)

GLORIA PÉPIN

Plant cucumber varieties whose seed packets indicate that they are suited for pickling (see "Cucumbers" in Part One). "I like to pick cucumbers for this recipe when they are 1 to 1½ inches in length," writes Gloria Pépin.

"When you start to pick for your first pint of pickles there will not be enough; however, once the plants start to bear well (after two or three days of picking), the yield will be quite large. After that you will be busy every morning or evening gathering. It is important to gather your cucumbers for cornichons either early in the morning or in the evening just before the sun goes down, so that you do not disturb the bees, which pollinate the flowers, and risk losing some of your crop."

1. Wipe each cucumber with a soft cloth to remove the small prickly spines on the skin, so that they are smooth and clean. *Do not wash.*

2. Place them in a bowl and sprinkle with a handful of coarse salt. Allow to rest—turning them once or twice—for 12 to 24 hours. At this point the salt will have melted and you will have liquid in the bottom of the bowl.

3. Wipe each cucumber dry with a clean cloth and place them in a pint (or if you prefer, quart) Mason jar. If you are not able to fill the jar from the first picking, just add to it the next day, but once you wipe them dry and they are in the jar they must be covered with vinegar.

4. Use any ordinary white vinegar, full strength, and fill the jars to the top; or add enough just to cover the cucumbers in a partially filled jar if you plan to add more the next day.

5. Add to each jar a sprig of fresh tarragon and 10 to 12 whole peppercorns. If you are lucky enough to find some tiny pearl onions, peel a few and add to each jar.

The Garden-to-Table Cookbook

6. Put the lid on and store the jar in a cool place. Wait four to six weeks and you can start enjoying the cornichons. We number the jars so that we can keep track of which one will be ready first.

Bread and Butter Pickles

JANE MOULTON

"This is an old family recipe that we have been making since the early 1940s," says Jane Moulton. "Although we have tried a number of other recipes that seem to be similar, we keep returning to this one—the pickles are somehow better. They can be eaten soon after they are made, but they will be more flavorful after they have been stored for a month."

Makes about 11 pints

5 quarts thinly sliced, unpeeled cucumbers (about 9 long, narrow cucumbers)
6 cups peeled and thinly sliced onions (about 1³/₄ pounds)
2 large sweet green peppers, seeded and sliced (optional)
2 large sweet red peppers, seeded and sliced (optional)

¹/₂ cup pickling salt or noniodized salt
1 quart cracked ice
5 cups sugar
1¹/₂ teaspoons turmeric
¹/₂ teaspoon ground cloves
2 tablespoons mustard seed
1 teaspoon celery seed
5 cups cider vinegar

1. In a glass, ceramic, or stainless-steel bowl, combine the cucumbers, onions, peppers, and salt. Mix well.

2. Bury the cracked ice in the middle of the mixture. Cover with a plate that fits inside the container and weight down the plate with a pint jar filled with water, so that the liquid will rise over the vegetables. Let stand 3 hours.

3. Drain vegetables in a colander, but don't rinse them.

4. In a 6-quart or larger preserving kettle, combine the sugar, turmeric, cloves, mustard seed, and celery seed. Bring to a boil, stirring to dissolve the sugar.

5. Add the vegetables to the kettle and again bring to a full boil. Stir well to make sure that the whole mixture is boiling-hot throughout and boil for 3 minutes.

6. Place pickles immediately in clean, hot canning jars.

7. Add lids and process in a boiling-water bath, 5 minutes for pints and 10 minutes for quarts.

Friendship Ring Pickles

JANE MOULTON

"An excellent way to use up the ripe cucumbers that seem to grow big and fat overnight despite your vigilance in harvesting, these pickles with the holes will add material for conversation as well as flavor to the table. You may use overripe cucumbers—those that have turned golden—but don't use any that have any moldy, soft, or slippery spots."—Jane Moulton.

Makes 3 pints

12 large ripe cucumbers
1/4 cup pickling salt or
  noniodized salt
7 quarts cold water, divided (see
  instructions below)
2 tablespoons powdered alum
  (available from some grocers,
  or at pharmacies)

4 cups sugar
2 cups cider vinegar
2 tablespoons whole cloves
2 large sticks cinnamon

1. With a vegetable peeler, peel the cucumbers. Cut them into 1/4-inch slices and, using a small cookie cutter, the inside circle of a doughnut cutter, or some other device, cut out the centers to remove the seeds and leave a clean edge.

2. Place the rings in a 6-quart ceramic or stainless-steel container. Sprinkle with the salt and cover with 4 quarts of cold water. Let stand overnight in a cool place.

3. Drain cucumber rings and place them in a large preserving kettle. Dissolve the alum in 3 quarts of cold water and add it to the kettle. Heat gradually to just below boiling, then turn the heat as low as possible. Cover the kettle and leave over the heat for 2 hours, checking to make sure that liquid doesn't bubble. If it does, put an asbestos pad under the pot, or move the pot partly off the burner.

4. Drain cucumbers, rinse well, and place in a large ceramic or stainless-steel container. Add plenty of cold water plus a tray of ice cubes to chill the pickles quickly.

5. In the large preserving kettle combine the sugar and vinegar. Add the

cloves and the cinnamon (broken up), either tied in a cheesecloth bag or placed in a stainless-steel tea ball. Boil syrup for 3 minutes.

6. Add cucumbers, bring to a boil, and boil gently, covered, for about 15 minutes, or until the rings seem transparent. Pour back into ceramic crock or stainless-steel container, let cool, and cover. Let stand overnight.

7. The next morning, drain syrup into preserving kettle and bring it to a boil, uncovered. Pour hot syrup back over cucumbers and again cool, cover, and let stand overnight. Repeat the process the next day.

8. The fourth day, heat syrup to boiling; fill clean, hot pint jars with the cucumbers, and pour boiling syrup over them, to within 1/2 inch of the top.

9. Add lids and process in a boiling-water bath for 5 minutes for pints. (If recipe quantities are increased and you use quart jars, process for 10 minutes.)

Polish Dill Pickles

PAUL RUBINSTEIN

For these dill pickles you may use any kind of cucumbers if you haven't grown a special pickling variety, and large ones may be cut into chunks of convenient size. Make sure the cucumbers are young—not mature and seedy—and very fresh.

Makes 4 quarts

4 dozen 4-inch-long cucumbers
1 quart distilled white vinegar
3 quarts water
1/2 cup kosher salt or sea salt
2 large bunches of fresh dill,
  with stalks, washed and all
  water shaken off

4 cloves garlic, peeled
4 bay leaves
1 tablespoon black peppercorns

1. Scrub the cucumbers clean and soak them in cold water overnight or longer (12 to 24 hours).

2. Sterilize 4 quart-size canning jars and their lids. (Or you may use 8 1-pint jars, if that size is more convenient.)

3. In a saucepan or kettle with a pouring spout, combine the vinegar, water, and salt and bring to a boil.

4. While the pickling liquid is heating, fold a large dill stalk into each quart jar, and add a garlic clove, a bay leaf, and one-fourth of the peppercorns to each jar. (For pint jars, halve the quantity of dill, garlic, and spices put into each jar.)

5. Pack the cucumbers into the jars. A quart jar takes about one dozen 4-inch cucumbers.

6. Let the brine boil for 5 minutes. Then fill the jars to the top and seal them at once.

7. Store the pickles for at least a month before serving them.

Eggplant

The beautiful, sturdy plant that bears eggplants is not a heavy producer, so it's unlikely that the home gardener will have a large surplus of these vegetables to store away. But if you do—or if you can't resist a good buy at a roadside stand—by all means freeze* them, or even can them if you are fond of dishes in which this vegetable is combined with others—ratatouille, for instance, in which the canned eggplant could be used with acceptable results.

Frozen slices of eggplant, which have of course been blanched and so are partially cooked, are usable in several ways. Be sure to blot all surplus moisture from the slices before you proceed with the cooking, just as you would with fresh eggplant.

For eggplant parmigiana, brown the slices in olive oil, then layer them in a baking dish with tomato sauce (perhaps a sauce from your freezer—see under "Tomatoes" farther along), grated mozzarella cheese, and a seasoning of oregano. Top off the last layer of eggplant with Parmesan cheese and bake in a moderate oven, 350° to 375° F., until the eggplant is tender, half an hour or more, depending on the amount you are baking.

For fried eggplant sticks, excellent with all meats and fowl, cut the thawed slices into fingers, French-fry style. Pat them dry, dredge them with flour, and fry in an inch of hot olive oil until they are well browned.

Some of the best of all ways to enjoy eggplant are described in the recipes that follow: Nicola Zanghi's Insalata di Melanzana, Edward Giobbi's Caponata alla Siciliana, and a peppery-hot pickle from India, Monoroma Phillips's Achaar Vengana.

Insalata de Melanzana—Marinated Eggplant Salad

NICOLA ZANGHI

Makes about 3 pints

2 medium eggplants, about 3
  pounds in all
Boiling water
Salt
1 cup olive oil
1/2 cup red wine vinegar
1 tablespoon crumbled dried
 ·oregano

1/3 cup chopped fresh basil,
  lightly packed into measure
1/3 cup chopped fresh mint,
  lightly packed into measure
Salt and pepper
1 medium onion, diced
2 cloves garlic, crushed

1. Cut unpeeled eggplants into 1-inch cubes.

2. Cover with boiling salted water in a saucepan and cook uncovered for 10 minutes, or until still slightly firm. Drain in a colander and cool thoroughly.

3. Press eggplant cubes gently to remove excess water; place in a bowl.

4. Add olive oil, vinegar, oregano, basil, mint, salt and pepper, onion, and garlic. Taste, and correct seasoning.

5. At this point the salad may be allowed to marinate for a day before it is preserved by freezing.

6. To freeze the salad, remove the garlic and pack the salad into freezer containers, allowing 1/2-inch headspace. Seal airtight, and freeze at once.

NOTE: This is an excellent addition to antipasto. Let it thaw in the refrigerator before serving.

Caponata alla Siciliana—Caponata Sicilian Style

EDWARD GIOBBI

Adapted, with permission, from a recipe published in slightly different form in Italian Family Cooking *(Random House, 1971), this caponata from*

Edward Giobbi's kitchen freezes perfectly. Once prepared and cooled it should be frozen as quickly as your freezer will do the job.

To use the caponata as a first course or as part of an antipasto, thaw it in the refrigerator the day before it will be needed. Near serving time, remove it from the cold and add a 7-ounce can of imported tuna packed in olive oil, mixing the tuna and its oil gently with the vegetables. (If you should have to use tuna packed in water, drain it well before adding it.) Allow the caponata to come to room temperature before serving.

Makes about 4 pints

3/4 cup olive oil
2 medium eggplants (about 3 pounds in all), peeled and cut into 3/4-inch cubes
1 cup chopped celery
2 medium onions, peeled and chopped
1 cup tomatoes (unpeeled), coarsely chopped
3 medium-sized ripe pears, peeled, cored, and diced (optional)

1/4 cup capers, drained
1/4 cup red wine vinegar
1 tablespoon sugar
2 teaspoons pine nuts (pignolias)
Salt and freshly ground black pepper

1. Heat olive oil in a large skillet that has a cover and add eggplant. Cook over high heat until lightly browned, turning often; this will take up to 10 minutes. Remove eggplant and set aside, leaving the oil in the pan.

2. Place celery to one side of the skillet and the onions to the other side. Lower heat, cover, and simmer, stirring occasionally. When celery is tender, add tomatoes. Cover and cook for about 10 minutes longer, turning vegetables to mix them once or twice. Add eggplant (and pears, if used) to the mixture and set aside.

3. Soak capers in cold water for 15 minutes, drain, blot with paper towels.

4. In a saucepan bring vinegar and sugar to a boil. Add capers, pine nuts, salt, and pepper to taste. Simmer for 1 minute.

5. Pour pickling mixture over vegetables and cook over low heat, covered, for 5 minutes.

6. Let cool rapidly, uncovered, and pack into freezer containers, allowing 1/2-inch headspace. Seal and freeze at once.

NOTE: The inclusion of the pears makes a remarkable change in the caponata. This caponata can also be used as a sauce on tubular pasta.

Achaar Vengana—Pickled Baby Eggplants

MONOROMA PHILLIPS

This recipe is spiced in the style of the western and southern regions of India. The pungency of the pickle may be reduced or increased by the quantity of hot peppers used.

24 small eggplants, 3 to 4 inches long
1⅓ cups coarse salt
6 ounces green ginger root
10 cloves of garlic
12 dried, hot red peppers (or to taste)
½ cup malt vinegar
1 tablespoon cumin seed (see note on spices, below)

Makes about 3 quarts

2 tablespoons fenugreek seed
3 tablespoons red mustard seed
1 tablespoon coriander seed
1 tablespoon black peppercorns
Small pinch asafetida (optional)
3 cups sesame oil, either the heavy kind favored in India or light sesame oil

1. Wash eggplants and pat dry. Cut off stems and quarter eggplants lengthwise from the blossom end, without detaching them from the stem end. Sprinkle liberally with salt, making sure that each piece is thoroughly coated. Put in a large bowl and place a dry plate on top of eggplants and press down with a heavy weight. (I generally make my pickles in crocks and therefore use a crock as a weight.) Let stand overnight.

2. Scrape ginger, wash, and dry well. Cut into slices, then into matchstick slivers. Peel garlic and cut into slivers.

3. Place hot peppers and vinegar in the jar of a blender, or in a mortar, and blend or grind to a fine paste. Set aside in a small bowl.

4. Toast the cumin, fenugreek, red mustard, and coriander seed and the peppercorns in a dry skillet over moderate heat. Shake pan frequently to ensure even toasting. After a few minutes, or when you see the mustard seeds crackle, remove to a spice grinder, a mortar, or a blender jar and grind to a coarse powder, along with the asafetida, if you are including it.

5. Remove eggplants from the bowl onto several layers of paper toweling and cover with more layers of paper towels, or wrap in a clean dish

towel, and squeeze gently but firmly to remove as much moisture as possible.

6. Heat the sesame oil in a large pot, preferably an enameled one. Drop in a sliver of garlic and if it rises to the surface immediately, the oil is ready (approximately 395° F., which is very hot). Turn heat off. Add eggplant, ginger, garlic, red pepper paste, and spices and stir gently but thoroughly, then allow to cool. Do not cover.

7. When pickle is cool, place in dry, sterilized jars and seal. Keep the jars in a warm, sunny location if possible, turning them every other day. If you lack a sunny spot, let the pickle ripen in a warm place—near a radiator or a stove. The pickle will be ready to eat in 10 to 15 days. When it is ready, store in a cool place.

NOTE: Such unusual spices as fenugreek, red mustard, and asafetida are available in Indo-Pakistani food stores. A source (mail orders only) for these and other spices is Magic Carpet West, 201 West 98th St., New York, N.Y. 10025.

Kale and Collards

Rich as they are in the elements needed for good nutrition, it is a pity that these two vegetables, which are related as members of the large cabbage tribe, aren't somehow more glamorous. They have their merits, however, and collards especially have their devoted following—they are the "greens" usually meant when Southerners refer affectionately to that favorite dish.

Both can be frozen* and canned* with good results. Collards are traditionally cooked with pork in some form—"fat back," or salt pork, is a favorite in the South—and they benefit in flavor and succulence from the relationship. If you are serving collards that you have canned, try them with a dressing of diced, cooked bacon, some of the bacon fat, salt, and pepper, and pass a cruet of vinegar.

Frozen collards will take up to 20 minutes to become tender when cooked in a little boiling salted water or stock. Cook them, if you wish, with salt pork, bits of bacon, or even ham, and lengthen the cooking time if you like your greens very well done.

Use both kale and collards in recipes as you would cabbage.

Kale, especially, is good when cooked, drained, mixed with a cream sauce, covered with crumbs and bits of butter, and baked until the top is brown.

The recipe below, which the contributor believes is many centuries old, comes from Holland. It bears an interesting resemblance to Colcannon, the Irish dish of cooked kale beaten into twice the quantity of mashed potatoes, then seasoned with cream, butter, salt, and pepper. Sometimes a little minced onion is added, too. The Colcannon is served in a volcano-shaped mound, with melted butter in the crater. With the sausage contributing richness to the Dutch version, the added butter is probably not necessary. Either would be a fine dish for a cold, blustery day.

Kale, Potatoes, and Sausage in the Dutch Fashion

ALLIANORA ROSSE

Potatoes, of a good variety for mashing
Salt
Kielbasa or other smoked ring-shaped sausage, 1½ to 2 pounds

Frozen chopped kale, thawed, enough to amount to about a third of the volume of potatoes when cooked
Butter
Pepper

1. Into a large pan put potatoes, peeled and cut up into large chunks. (Each cook will know how many potatoes will be needed per portion.) Add a little salt and enough water barely to cover the potatoes.

2. Arrange a ring-link of smoked sausage (kielbasa is a fair substitute for the Dutch kind) on top of the potatoes.

3. Add the thawed kale. Cover the pan, bring to a boil, then cook at a simmer until the potatoes are soft.

4. Remove the sausage to a warm platter and keep it warm.

5. Mash the vegetables together. Season with butter and pepper to taste, adding more salt if it is needed.

6. Arrange the mashed kale and potatoes on the platter with the sausage and serve hot.

Kohlrabi

Kohlrabi is very easy to freeze* and it is nearly always enjoyed by those who taste it for the first time, although it isn't as well known as most vegetables. It has a flavor like that of a very delicate turnip. Actually it is a relative of the cabbage, and the pale-green, edible "bulb" is the thickened above-ground portion of the stem. The tender, small leaves are edible, too, and may be frozen (or cooked from scratch, if you're using the fresh vegetable) with the bulbs. Young, small kohlrabi are the best—this vegetable toughens with age and when it reaches too large a size. Kohlrabi isn't especially recommended for canning.

Rather simple ways of cooking kohlrabi are best, suggests Allianora Rosse, who grows this vegetable in her garden and has a repertory of recipes for it. Cook the frozen vegetable—whole, sliced, or diced—in a little salted water or broth just until tender. Either serve it simply with salt, pepper, and butter, or sauce it with a little hot Béchamel sauce and a sprinkling of minced parsley. Cheese is a good addition to the sauce, too.

For a hearty vegetable course, fold kohlrabi into white sauce that has been laced liberally with chopped chives, pour into a baking dish, top generously with grated cheese and a few bread crumbs, and brown the top of the dish in a hot oven.

French-fry lovers will like this: Cook whole or sliced kohlrabi until tender, cool, and cut into sticks. Pat sticks dry and French-fry in deep fat until brown. Salt and serve hot.

For soup, mash cooked kohlrabi and add to chicken stock or other mild-flavored broth. Add a little cream, if you wish, and thicken the soup lightly with a little butter and flour rubbed together (*beurre manié*) and stirred into the simmering soup. Add salt and pepper and garnish with minced parsley, chives, or dill.

Leeks

In most climates leeks keep so well when left in the garden over winter (or in a cool cellar, if you have one) that there is not usually much point in putting them up. However, if you have an abundance of this choice vegetable that you can't leave in place in the ground or put into cool storage, freezing* is your best possibility.

If you plan to use your leeks in dishes—such as vegetable soups—in which they will remain to the end, follow the freezing instructions given for sliced leeks in Part Two. Leeks frozen this way are fine for the Scottish pottage called Cock-a-Leekie Soup, a fine brew originally based on an old hen (or rooster) plus leeks— you'll find a recipe in any good general cookbook, and it's a soup well worth trying, guaranteed to be warming on a winter's day.

For frozen leeks that you will use as seasoning vegetables that will be discarded after they have contributed their flavor to a dish, this way of preparing them is preferable: Cut off the tough parts of the green leaves and the roots. Quarter leeks lengthwise. Wash the strips repeatedly and very well to remove grit, then tie bunches of the strips loosely with string—enough to amount to about two whole leeks per bunch—and blanch them for 1 minute in a large pot of boiling water. Chill for several minutes in a bowl of cold water under the cold faucet, then untie, drain thoroughly, spread the strips on a baking sheet, and freeze, uncovered, until hard. The pieces are then ready to package in plastic bags—you will be able to remove as much as you want without disturbing what remains.

Probably everyone's favorite dish made with leeks is Vichyssoise, that chilled apotheosis of leek-and-potato soup. Freeze a supply of the base, for which we give a recipe, and you'll be ready to serve this delicate soup in no more time than it takes to thaw the base and stir in some cream.

For a frozen base for a hot soup, try Elizabeth Colchie's Creamed Leek and Celery Soup (recipe).

Vichyssoise Base for Freezing

HELEN WITTY

There are two things to notice about this recipe—it's actually a formula—not a recipe—based on the general principles underlying the many versions of this soup that have sprung up since Louis Diat invented it; and it includes no butter. This last is partly personal preference—we have never liked those little clumps of butter floating in Vichyssoise in some restaurants—and the butter is omitted partly because the base freezes better and keeps better without it. With the cream that is to be added at serving time, the soup is quite rich enough.

1. Remove roots and any tough outer leaves and the tough upper part of the green tops from leeks. Slice in ¼-inch rounds and wash repeatedly and thoroughly to get rid of any grit. Drain well and measure.

2. Peel and slice or cube an equal measure of potatoes. Combine leeks and potatoes in a large saucepan with enough fat-free chicken stock (or salted water, lacking stock) to equal the total measure of vegetables: 4 cups of leeks plus 4 cups of potatoes plus 2 quarts of broth.

3. Bring to a boil, lower heat, partially cover, and simmer until vegetables are very tender. Purée through a food mill (use the fine plate) or in a blender or food processor. Cool purée quickly, package with ½-inch headspace, seal, and freeze.

TO MAKE THE SOUP:

1. Defrost the soup base in the refrigerator. (To serve moderate helpings to 6, you'll need about 2 pints).

2. About an hour before serving, stir into the base heavy cream to taste—1 cup or so—and season the soup well with salt and freshly ground white pepper. Return to refrigerator.

3. Serve very cold in soup cups, topped with minced chives, either fresh or frozen.

Creamed Leek and Celery Soup Base

ELIZABETH SUSAN COLCHIE

Here the gardener-cook has two choices: Either use freshly gathered vegetables to make up and freeze a soup base in the tradition of the good French vegetable soups enriched with cream, or use the vegetables that you have frozen earlier to make the complete soup for lunch or dinner today. This recipe can easily be doubled.

BASE:

Serves 4

3 tablespoons butter
1½ cups sliced, washed fresh
  leeks or frozen sliced leeks
4 cups sliced celery ribs, with
  some of their leaves (frozen
  celery may be used)

1 cup sliced parsnips, fresh or
  frozen
3½ cups chicken broth
1 teaspoon salt
1½ cups milk
1½ tablespoons cornstarch

INGREDIENTS TO COMPLETE SOUP:
½ cup heavy cream
Pinch of freshly ground nutmeg

1. In a heavy saucepan place the butter and add the leeks, celery, and parsnips. Stir together over medium heat for 10 minutes, or until the vegetables are wilted, if fresh, or well heated through, if frozen.

2. Add the chicken broth and simmer, covered, for 20 minutes. Add salt.

3. Pour soup base into the container of an electric blender and process to a very fine purée.

4. Strain purée into a saucepan through a fine sieve and add 1 cup milk.

5. Combine remaining ½ cup milk with the cornstarch and mix well. Add to the soup and bring to a simmer over moderately low heat, stirring.

6. If soup base is to be stored in the freezer, pour it into a bowl set into a larger bowl of ice water and stir to chill. When cool, pour into freezer containers, allowing ½-inch headspace, seal, and freeze.

TO COMPLETE SOUP:
1. If base has been frozen, thaw it in the refrigerator.

2. Warm the soup base to a simmer over low heat. Add the cream and nutmeg to taste and serve hot.

Lettuce, Romaine, and Endive

    These three salad plants aren't for canning, obviously, and except for escarole (a variety of endive) frozen for later use in broth (see Edward Giobbi's recipe), they aren't for freezing, either. Or pickling. However, you can make a preserve of romaine—Pilar Turner's Romaine Jam recipe (below) produces a sweet that is most definitely out of the ordinary.

If, despite your best efforts at succession planting, your lettuce crop all seems to be ready at once, there *are* ways to increase your family's consumption of these greens in dishes other than salads.

Wilted lettuce, that old American standby, can be considered a hot vegetable dish, seasoned as it is with a hot sauce of bacon, onions, vinegar, sugar, salt, and pepper—see your favorite cookbook.

You can substitute lettuce for spinach in any recipe for cream of spinach soup, with a lighter and paler result that's worth investigating. If you'd like to try braised lettuce in the classic French fashion, Julia Child and her co-authors have a fine recipe (which can also be used for endive, celery, or leeks) in the first volume of *Mastering the Art of French Cooking* (Knopf, 1961). And *Larousse Gastronomique,* in its English-language edition, contains more than a full page of suggestions for lettuce dishes, including such intriguing preparations as deep-fried lettuce and lettuce soufflé.

Escarole for Freezing

EDWARD GIOBBI

1. Heat to boiling a large pot of water—you'll need 4 quarts to blanch a one-pound batch of escarole, and if your pot holds more than that, you can blanch more at a time (but keep the ratio of 1 pound of leaves to 4 quarts of water).

2. Wash escarole leaves well, removing all grit at their bases.

3. Immerse a batch of leaves in boiling water and start timing; scald them for 2 minutes exactly. It helps to put them in a large salad basket or colander for this step.

4. Remove escarole from pot and immediately immerse in a large bowl of cold water set under cold running water. Let leaves cool completely, then drain very well.

5. Cut up or chop escarole and pack into freezer bags or containers, leaving 1/2-inch headspace if rigid containers are used. Seal and freeze.

TO SERVE THE ESCAROLE IN BROTH:

Serves 4 to 6

1. Thaw 1 pint (or more, if you like) of frozen escarole.

2. Heat 6 cups of well-flavored chicken or beef stock and add escarole. Bring to a boil, reduce heat, and simmer until escarole is tender, a matter of a few minutes. Season, if necessary, with salt and pepper, and add a little lemon juice to taste.

3. Serve hot in soup bowls, topped with freshly grated Parmesan cheese.

Romaine Jam

PILAR TURNER

Like Pilar Turner's Watermelon-Rind Jam, this preserve gives the maker an eminently virtuous feeling, because it makes use of a part of a vegetable or fruit that is often discarded—the rind of the melon or, in this case, the heavy midribs of romaine. Like the melon recipe, this is very old and of Spanish origin.

Makes about 4 pints

2 pounds of ribs of romaine, weighed after greens have been removed and reserved for salads

2 pounds (4 cups) sugar
1/4 cup fresh lemon juice
1-inch strip of lemon peel
1-inch piece of cinnamon stick

1. On a cutting board, cut romaine ribs crosswise into 1/2-inch pieces.

2. Mix romaine with the sugar and lemon juice in an enameled pot and allow to stand, covered, for 12 hours.

3. Add lemon peel and cinnamon and bring to a boil over medium-high heat, stirring, then lower the heat and simmer for 8 minutes.

4. Remove from heat, cool, cover, and let stand overnight.

5. Repeat the heating, simmering, and overnight rest 3 or 4 times, or until the jam has thickened enough: Test by pouring a few drops of the hot jam onto a thick, cold plate. It is ready when it doesn't run easily when the plate is tilted. (In all the cooking steps, be careful not to scorch or overcook the jam, which would cause it to turn brown or become too soft.)

6. Ladle boiling-hot jam into hot, sterile jars and seal at once.

Melons

Melons (including watermelons, which have their own entry farther along) just aren't cannable—too much liquid in their flesh, for one thing—but they freeze* beautifully, whether in slices, or cubes, or balls shaped by a cutter. And some of them are excellent when made into pickles* and preserves*.

Whether you grow muskmelons or cantaloupes, casabas, Cranshaws, honeydews, or Persian melons, all will be delicious when they come out of the freezer—if they were ripe but not overripe to begin with, and if they were quickly and correctly prepared (see Part Two).

Serve melon balls or other shapes while they are still slightly icy at the heart, either in the syrup in which they were packed, or mixed with other fruits, either fresh, frozen, or canned. You might want to try frozen and thawed melon in one of our favorite ways—drained of most of its syrup, then drizzled with a little honey and sprinkled with finely minced candied ginger.

Cantaloupes are popular for pickling, so we include two excellent recipes: one is for Jane Moulton's muskmelon balls, flavored with spice oils so that they retain their natural color, and the other is for Ruth Ellen Church's more traditionally spiced pickles.

A cantaloupe marmalade lightly spiked with fresh green ginger has been devised by Helen Witty, and Marie Hamm has contributed a conserve in which the flavors of honeydew melons, limes, and coconut are blended.

Muskmelon Ball Pickles

JANE MOULTON

"Spicy in a mild manner suitable to melon, these pickles retain a texture reminiscent of the fresh fruit. They also keep their bright color because they are spiced with colorless oils that have to be purchased from a friendly neighborhood pharmacist who caters to his pickling customers. A few food specialty stores also carry the oils. (NOTE: If you can't find a local source, write to Caswell Massey Co. Ltd., a venerable apothecary shop that has been doing business for almost two and a quarter centuries. For a

catalogue, which includes many other products as well as the oils, send $1.00 to 320 West 13th St., New York, N.Y. 10014. The Caswell-Massey retail shop is at 418 Lexington Avenue at 48th St., New York, N.Y. 10017.)

"Don't use distilled white vinegar instead of the wine vinegar in this recipe, as it's too harsh for the melon flavor. Serve these pickles with chicken—and save the pickling juice to use as part of the liquid in molded fruit salads, especially those containing orange."—Jane Moulton.

Makes about 4 pints

4 cups sugar
2 cups white wine vinegar
1 cup water
1/4 teaspoon salt
1/2 teaspoon oil of cinnamon

1/2 teaspoon oil of cloves
2 to 2 1/2 quarts muskmelon or
cantaloupe balls (from about 3
melons)

1. In a large preserving kettle combine the sugar, wine vinegar, water, salt, and spice oils. Bring to a boil, stirring to dissolve the sugar. Boil, uncovered, for 3 minutes.

2. Add melon balls. (You could also use 3/4-inch melon cubes.) Simmer gently, uncovered, for 20 minutes.

3. Pack while boiling-hot into clean, hot pint jars.

4. Add lids and process in a boiling-water bath for 10 minutes.

Cantaloupe Pickles

RUTH ELLEN CHURCH

Makes 3 pints

2 medium-sized, somewhat
underripe cantaloupes (about 3
pounds)
Salt brine as needed (2
tablespoons pickling salt or
noniodized salt per quart of
water)

4 cups sugar
2 cups cider vinegar
1 teaspoon whole cloves
1 teaspoon blade (not ground)
mace
1 small stick cinnamon

1. Cut melons in half, discard seeds and soft membranes around cavity, pare off rind, and cut flesh into balls or strips of uniform size.

2. Place melon in a ceramic, glass, or stainless-steel bowl and cover with salt brine, using enough to cover fruit well. Let stand overnight.

3. Drain melon well. As it drains, combine in a preserving kettle the sugar, vinegar, cloves, mace, and cinnamon, bring to a boil, and simmer for 20 minutes.

4. Add melon to the pickling liquid and cook gently for 10 minutes.

5. Pack melon, without syrup, into clean, hot pint jars. Boil syrup 5 minutes longer, then pour over melon, filling jars to within ¼ inch of top.

6. Add lids and process jars in a boiling-water bath for 5 minutes.

Cantaloupe Marmalade

HELEN WITTY

This marmalade can stand on its own merits—it doesn't aim to deceive—but more than one taster has exclaimed "Apricot!" Use melons of very good flavor—making a poor melon into jam won't transform its character. The color is especially beautiful, a true apricot shade.

Makes about 2 pints

3 to 4 pounds fresh, fully ripe cantaloupe, enough to make 1¾ pounds (5 cups) after paring, seeding, and slicing
1 large lemon

¾ cup water
1 teaspoon finely shredded fresh ginger (or more, if you like)
4 cups sugar

1. Pare and seed the melon and cut into small, uniformly thin slices or strips. The shapes of the pieces don't matter, as the fruit will melt into the jam.

2. Quarter the lemon lengthwise, cut out the white strips of core, and cut the quarters crosswise into very thin slices, removing seeds as you go. Combine the lemon slices with the water and ginger in a saucepan and simmer, covered, until the lemon rind begins to appear clear.

3. Combine the prepared cantaloupe and the lemon-ginger mixture in a preserving pan. Set over medium-high heat and cook, stirring often, until the fruit begins to look clear.

4. Stir in the sugar and boil fairly rapidly until the marmalade thickens. Test by pouring a few drops onto a cold plate and letting the sample

cool, meanwhile removing the pot from the fire. When the liquid part looks jellylike, the marmalade is ready.

5. Reheat marmalade to boiling, if necessary, ladle into hot, sterilized half-pint jars, and seal at once.

Honeydew and Lime Conserve

MARIE ROBERSON HAMM

Makes 6 half-pints

2 whole limes, washed, sliced, and seeded
1 cup water
3 cups sugar

3 cups peeled and diced ripe honeydew melon
3/4 cup white raisins
3/4 cup flaked coconut

1. In the jar of an electric blender, process the lime slices with the water until the lime is finely cut but not puréed.

2. Pour the mixture into a preserving pan and cook, covered, for 10 minutes, stirring once or twice.

3. Add the sugar, melon, and raisins and bring to a boil. Simmer, uncovered, for about 30 minutes, stirring frequently, until the conserve is thick and will fall in a sheet from the edge of a metal spoon (the jelly test).

4. Remove from heat and stir in coconut. Pour at once into hot, sterilized jars and seal.

Okra

One of the most intriguing of home-garden vegetables is okra, which people seem either to love very much or leave very much alone. In the South, especially in Louisiana, it is a staple, and it is included in much of the good cooking of the Caribbean region. Perhaps if it were cooked everywhere as well as it is in New Orleans, for instance, it would rise in the estimation of the okra-ignorant. It freezes* excellently, is equally good when canned*, and makes fine pickles*.

Often, especially in the South, okra is called "gumbo," which is a clue to its most frequent way of appearing—as a thickening (and, not incidentally, a flavoring) for the delectable stews of seafood, or greens, or chicken, or ham, or any combination thereof that are called gumbos in the South.

Your home-canned or home-frozen okra can be used in any recipe calling for fresh okra, if you make allowance for the fact that it is cooked (if canned) or blanched and thus partially cooked (if frozen).

Some suggestions: Thaw frozen, sliced okra and stew it in a little butter in a covered skillet until it is tender. Or cook whole or sliced okra with tomatoes and onions (some cooks add green peppers) for a harmonious vegetable mélange. (The *Ball Blue Book,* that indispensable little bible of home canners, suggests canning this combination: Peel, core, and chop ripe tomatoes. Slice an equal quantity of okra. Boil tomatoes for 20 minutes, with 1 small onion, chopped, added to each quart. Add okra, boil 5 minutes longer, and pack into clean, hot canning jars, leaving 1-inch headspace. Add 1/2 teaspoon salt per pint, 1 teaspoon salt per quart. Add lids and process at 10 pounds pressure for 30 minutes for pints, 35 minutes for quarts.)

Finally, among the best of okra recipes are those for frying it. Precook whole, small pods until tender, cool, pat dry, roll in beaten egg and then in crumbs, and either deep-fry or fry in 1 inch of hot oil in a skillet until browned.

In pickles, okra has an affinity for dill and garlic, both of which are included in Okra Garden Pickles (recipe). Several herbs appear in Cammy Sessa's recipe for Okra Frittatas, which she serves as a vegetarian main course. The frittatas could equally well be an accompaniment for meat, fish, or fowl for those who are not vegetarians.

Okra Garden Pickles

MARIE ROBERSON HAMM

Pickled okra deserves to be better known than it is outside the South, where it has long been a favorite. Gather your okra young for this pickle, and do heed the instruction to leave a short stem on each pod. If the pods are cut when the stems are removed, the mucilaginous juice is lost.

Makes about 6 pints

3 pounds tender fresh okra, with
  $^1/_4$- to $^1/_2$-inch stems left on
6 heads of fresh or dried dill
3 cloves garlic (optional)
4 cups white vinegar
2 cups water

6 tablespoons pure (noniodized)
  salt
$^1/_2$ teaspoon celery seed
$^1/_2$ teaspoon caraway seed
$^1/_2$ teaspoon mustard seed

1. Wash okra in several waters; drain. Prick each pod with a sharp fork to help pickling solution to penetrate.

2. Pack okra into 6 hot, sterilized pint jars or 12 half-pint jars.

3. In each jar place a share of the dill and the garlic, splitting the garlic cloves into the needed number of pieces.

4. Bring to a boil the vinegar, water, salt, celery seed, caraway seed, and mustard seed and boil for 2 minutes.

5. Pour pickling solution, boiling hot, over the okra, filling the jars to $^1/_2$ inch of the top.

6. Add lids and process in a boiling-water bath for 5 minutes. (The time is the same for either pints or half-pints.)

Okra Frittatas

CAMMY SESSA

For people who don't eat meat, vegetable fritters—such as these little frittatas—can serve as a main dish, as they are hearty and well seasoned. For vegetarians and meat-eaters alike, they make a fine luncheon. To serve as hors d'oeuvre, cut into bite-size pieces while hot and serve on a warming tray.

Makes about 18 (3 to 4 inches in diameter)

3 cups frozen okra, cut in 1-inch
  pieces
1 cup boiling water
5 eggs
1 teaspoon salt
$^1/_2$ teaspoon pepper
1 tablespoon crumbled dried
  basil
2 tablespoons minced parsley

Generous pinch dried oregano,
  or to taste
Pinch dried crumbled rosemary,
  or to taste
$^1/_2$ cup coarse, dry bread crumbs
$^1/_4$ cup grated Romano cheese
3 scallions, trimmed and
  chopped (use part of the green
  tops)
Peanut oil for frying

1. Put frozen okra in a bowl and pour the boiling water over it. Let it sit for 3 to 5 minutes, occasionally separating the okra pieces as they thaw. Drain well in a colander.

2. Beat eggs in a deep bowl, using a whisk. Add salt, pepper, basil, parsley, oregano, rosemary, crumbs, and cheese and blend. Add okra and scallions and fold them in.

3. Heat a heavy skillet or electric frying pan (set the electric pan for 375° F.). Add enough peanut oil to cover bottom generously.

4. Scoop up the frittata mixture a large spoonful at a time and drop it into hot oil, allowing some space between the frittatas. Let cook until browned on bottom, 10 to 15 minutes, then turn and brown other side. As the frittatas are done—they will look like fat, brown pancakes— remove them and keep them warm on absorbent paper spread on a pan or platter in a warm oven. Cook remaining mixture in the same way and serve the frittatas hot.

NOTE: Any left-over frittatas are good as a sandwich filling for "brown-baggers."

Onions

Home-canning of onions is feasible, but is somewhat pointless. If you have a good garden crop and follow the simple curing instructions under "Onions" in Part One, you should have no trouble finding an onion in your storage cabinet whenever you want one. Undeniably, though, it is convenient to have a frozen supply on hand when you want a spoonful of chopped onions for a dish being prepared; so freeze* a few containersful, being sure that they are very closely sealed (or, better, double-wrapped) to keep the onion aroma from becoming an all-pervasive and undesirable phantom of the freezer.

Even more than corn, onions are an all-American vegetable—or all-Chinese, or all-Rumanian, for that matter: it is hard to imagine a cuisine that would be palatable without one member or another of the onion tribe. As a seasoning, as a key element in savory vegetable combinations, in soups, stews, salads, and as a solo star—boiled and buttered, creamed with a touch of sage, or French-fried—onions are cooked in countless ways, as any cookbook will show.

In the realm of preserving, onions appear in almost every mixed pickle* recipe you'll come across. They are also excellent when pickled by themselves—see Nicola Zanghi's Cipolline all'Aceto, below. And they are equally excellent as the basis of a relish—witness Elizabeth Colchie's Onion and Pepper Relish, a savory composition in red, green, and white.

Cipolline all'Aceto—Small Onions in Vinegar

NICOLA ZANGHI

Makes about 2½ pints

2 pounds small onions of
  uniform size
Water
Salt and pepper

2 cups white wine vinegar
4 or 5 whole cloves
2 bay leaves, broken coarsely
½ teaspoon dried thyme

1. In a saucepan, cover onions with cold water and add 1 tablespoon salt. Bring to a boil and let simmer, uncovered, for 4 to 5 minutes. Drain and rinse under cold water. Slip off skins.

2. In a preserving pan place onions and all remaining ingredients, including pepper and additional salt to taste. Bring to a boil and let simmer, covered, for 5 minutes.

3. Ladle hot onions and pickling solution into hot, clean jars, leaving ½-inch headspace, and distributing the spices equally.

4. Add lids and process in a boiling-water bath for 10 minutes for either half-pints or pints.

Onion and Pepper Relish

ELIZABETH SUSAN COLCHIE

Makes 4 pints

3 pounds onions
2 pounds sweet red bell peppers
2 pounds green bell peppers
4 teaspoons kosher salt or other
  coarse pure salt
2 cups cider vinegar

1 cup (packed) light-brown
  sugar
2 tablespoons whole pickling
  spices, tied in cheesecloth
⅔ cup dried currants

1. Drop the onions into a large pot of boiling water and boil them for 1 minute. Drain, peel, and slice them.

2. Clean, quarter, and seed the peppers.

3. Pass the onions and peppers through a food grinder into a bowl, using the coarse blade. Sprinkle with the salt, mix, cover with plastic, and let stand in a cool place about 12 hours.

4. Add cold water to cover the vegetables and drain well in a colander.

5. In a preserving pot combine the vinegar, brown sugar, and pickling spices. Bring to a boil and simmer, covered, for 5 minutes.

6. Add the prepared onions and peppers and the currants and simmer for 15 minutes. Remove the spice bag.

7. Ladle into 4 sterilized pint canning jars and add lids. Process in a boiling-water bath for 5 minutes.

Parsnips

No one has ever written a poem about a parsnip, which is a pity. The discriminating souls who love them find in them a sweetness together with an earthy character that is unique, and they therefore welcome the coming of cold weather, which, many believe, improves the flavor of the roots left in the ground.

"This ancient root," says Felipe Rojas-Lombardi, "is the most neglected of all vegetables ... At the end of summer, the solids of the root consist largely of starch, but a period of low temperature changes much of the starch to sugar. The root is hardy and not damaged by hard freezing of the soil ... The parsnip should be treated like the most delicate vegetable. Its sweet quality is ideal in an accompaniment for such diverse things as roasts, pork, lamb, stew, calf's brains, kidneys, chicken, and fish ... and for the making of a good stock."

To which the home gardener says amen, once having learned the merits of this vegetable. Freeze* it, or can* it, if you must; but if possible, simply leave your crop in the ground, digging a supply of roots whenever you need them.

Parsnips are a classic ingredient in many broths and stocks, but they are more valuable as a vegetable. Parsnips purists boil them and butter them, perhaps mashing them for special occasions, or browning them in butter to surround a roast. Fussier souls might envelope them in cream sauce, perhaps, or purée them and combine them with an equal quantity of potatoes, to be shaped into little patties and fried. Felipe Rojas-Lombardi prepares them with basil—Parsnips Alam—and makes an interesting parsnip and turnip purée (recipes). Both these dishes are excellent with roasts.

An ancient British sweet is parsnip pie, traditionally served in spring. Good recipes may be found in Michael Field's *All Manner of Food* (Knopf, 1970) and Alex D. Hawkes's *A World of Vegetable Cookery* (Simon & Schuster, 1968).

Parsnips Alam

FELIPE ROJAS-LOMBARDI   Serves 4

2 cups shredded parsnips (about 2 large parsnips), either fresh or frozen but unthawed
3 tablespoons butter
1/2 teaspoon crumbled dried basil, or 1 to 1 1/2 teaspoons minced fresh basil

Pinch of ground mace
1/3 cup heavy cream or milk
Salt and pepper, to taste
1 teaspoon chopped fresh dill or parsley

1. If fresh parsnips are used, soak them in ice water for half an hour to an hour. If parsnips are frozen, defrost just enough to separate the pieces. Drain the parsnips.

2. In a skillet large enough to hold all the ingredients, melt the butter. When hot add basil, mace, drained parsnips, and milk. Cook for 8 minutes, or until tender, stirring frequently. Season with salt and pepper to taste.

3. Add dill or parsley, mix, and serve hot.

Parsnip and Turnip Purée

FELIPE ROJAS-LOMBARDI   Serves 4 to 6

2 cups fresh or frozen sliced or diced turnips (about 4 medium)
1 cup fresh or frozen sliced or diced parsnips (1 large parsnip)
1 large potato, peeled and sliced or diced
1 quart chicken broth

1 tablespoon sweet (unsalted) butter
1/4 teaspoon finely grated lemon rind
Pinch of freshly grated nutmeg
Salt and pepper to taste
1 teaspoon chopped fresh dill or parsley

1. In a saucepan combine the turnips, parsnips, potato, and chicken broth. Bring to a boil, lower heat, and simmer gently until vegetables are done (soft to the touch of a fork), approximately 30 to 40 minutes.

2. Drain vegetables and allow to cool for a few moments, then press through a fine sieve into a bowl.

3. Add butter, lemon rind, nutmeg, and salt and pepper to taste, and whip with an electric beater or a wire whisk until the consistency is creamy and smooth.

4. Serve at room temperature, garnished with the chopped fresh dill or parsley.

Peas

Any of your fresh garden peas that can't be served within hours of picking should be prepared as quickly as possible for freezing* and put beyond the power of the forces that change their sweetness to starchiness. Canning is also satisfactory for peas, but the quality won't be as high as that of frozen peas.

Once frozen, peas are usable in any recipe calling for the fresh vegetable, if you allow for the degree of cooking they have undergone in the scalding (blanching) process. Cook them from the frozen state, breaking up the mass from time to time so that they cook quickly and evenly.

Something very close to the flavor of *petits pois à la française* can be achieved even in midwinter if you have picked your peas young and rushed them into the freezer. Line a saucepan with leaves of lettuce (or shred the lettuce), put in the peas, some generous chunks of butter, a sprinkle or two of sugar, some salt, a sprig or two of parsley, a small onion or two if you like, and a little salt. Cover with more lettuce and add two or three spoonfuls of water, unless you judge that there is enough water clinging to the vegetables. Cover the pot tightly and steam the peas, shaking the pan from time to time, until they are just done. Fish out the lettuce leaves and onions if they are whole (leave the shredded lettuce), remove the parsley sprigs and add more butter, if you like. Serve the peas in individual dishes, in their buttery juices.

Peas take kindly to being cooked with a little mint, fresh or dried, or with savory, or with a combination of parsley and chervil. If you should have tiny onions on hand, cook them with twice the quantity of peas and butter the cooked vegetables well.

Peas are never better than when they are boiled or steamed quickly and dressed with butter and thick cream. They make a delectable purée (recipe) and an equally delectable base for a cold soup (see below). The flavor of bacon—another affinity—is evident in Edward Giobbi's Piselli con Uova—Green Peas with Eggs—a delicious combination.

Purée of Peas for Freezing

FLORENCE FABRICANT

Nothing could be simpler than a purée of fresh green peas, yet it is an elegant side dish. Keep some on hand in the freezer for a quick and delicious vegetable course, and try combining it with other purées—potatoes, celery root, watercress.

Makes 2 pints

8 cups shelled green peas
2 tablespoons sugar

1. Place peas in a steamer or a colander over boiling water. Cover pot tightly and steam for 25 to 30 minutes, until the peas are tender.

2. Process peas through a food mill (don't use a blender). Stir in sugar.

3. Pack into freezer containers, leaving ½-inch headroom, seal, and freeze.

TO SERVE THE PURÉE:
1. To serve as a vegetable, thaw the purée in the refrigerator and reheat it, adding salt, a little pepper if you like, butter, and perhaps cream. Beat well and serve hot.

2. To use in soup, see Quick Cold Green-Pea or Watercress Soup, for which the recipe is on the opposite page.

Quick Cold Green-Pea or Watercress Soup

FLORENCE FABRICANT   Serves 6 to 8

1 pint frozen Purée of Peas
  (above) or Purée of Watercress
  (see index)
3 cups milk

1 cup heavy cream
Salt and pepper
1 tablespoon minced chives,
  fresh or frozen

1. If purée is still frozen, place it in the top of a double boiler with 2 cups of the milk and heat over simmering water until the purée has softened enough to be stirred into the milk. Remove from heat and add remaining milk. If purée has thawed, stir it directly into the 3 cups of milk.

2. Stir in cream. Season well with salt and pepper—chilling lessens the impact of seasonings—and chill for at least an hour.

3. Stir, taste, adjust seasonings if necessary, sprinkle with chives, and serve.

Piselli con Uova—Green Peas with Eggs†

EDWARD GIOBBI   Serves 4

1 pint frozen green peas
3 tablespoons minced lean
  bacon, or pancetta, if you can
  find it (available in Italian
  markets and some specialty
  food stores)
1 small onion, peeled and
  chopped
1⅓ cups water or chicken stock
  or other mild-flavored broth

½ to 1 teaspoon finely minced
  fresh basil, or to taste
Salt
Freshly ground black pepper
2 eggs, well beaten
Freshly grated Parmesan or
  Romano cheese (optional)

1. Let peas thaw just until they can be separated; do not defrost them completely.

2. In a saucepan, stir the chopped bacon or pancetta over medium heat until it is about half done, but don't let it brown.

3. Add chopped onion and cook until soft and beginning to be translucent, stirring occasionally.

4. Add peas, water or stock, basil, and salt and pepper to taste. Cover and simmer until peas are tender, the time depending on their size and how much frost remains in them.

5. Uncover peas and stir in eggs, blending very well. Remove pan from the heat, cover, and let stand for a few minutes.

6. Serve hot, with grated Parmesan or Romano cheese if you like.

†NOTE: This recipe was published in somewhat different form in Edward Giobbi's *Italian Family Cooking,* Random House, 1971, and has been adapted with the publisher's permission.

Edible-podded Peas (Snow Peas)

These are grown just like the more usual peas that are shelled before they are cooked (see Part One), but they are different in that they are eaten pod and all. Pick them when the peas are barely discernible through the walls of the pods and enjoy them at once, or freeze* them—they're not suitable for canning, as a great point of their delicacy is their tender-crisp texture.

Interestingly enough, edible-podded peas have been grown in America for generations—by the Pennsylvania Dutch, among others, to whom they are known as "sugar peas"—but it has taken the increasing interest in Chinese cooking in recent years to make many cooks and gardeners aware of them.

The frozen peas will never be as crisp as the freshly picked ones, but they are nevertheless delicious. Use them in any recipe from your favorite Oriental cookbook that calls for snow peas, and try Grace Chu's recipe, opposite.

Snow Peas with Water Chestnuts and Bamboo Shoots

GRACE ZIA CHU

"A Chinese vegetable dish that is exotic and easy to prepare—and all ingredients are obtainable in the supermarket, if you haven't grown your own snow peas. The cost is right and the dish is both tasty and nourishing," *says Mme Chu.*

Serves 6

1 pint (or 1 commercial package) frozen snow peas
1 small can (6 ounces) water chestnuts
1 small can (6 ounces) bamboo shoots
1 cup water
1/2 cup carrot slices (2″ × 1/2″)

1 cup fresh Chinese cabbage in one-inch pieces
2 tablespoons vegetable oil
1 clove garlic, crushed
1 tablespoon light soy sauce (see note)
1/2 teaspoon salt
1/2 teaspoon sugar

1. Thaw frozen snow peas and drain.

2. Drain both the water chestnuts and the bamboo shoots well and slice, if necessary.

3. Bring 1 cup of water to a boil. Drop in the carrot slices and bring to a boil. Boil for 3 minutes. Cool and drain.

4. Rinse the cabbage pieces and drain.

5. Heat the oil in a frying pan (or a wok) and add garlic. Let it sizzle for a few seconds, then discard it. Add cabbage and stir-fry for about 3 minutes.

6. Add salt and sugar. Mix well. Add carrots, bamboo shoots, and water chestnuts. Mix a few times and add soy sauce. Add the snow peas. Mix and dish.

NOTE: La Choy, Chun King, and Kikkoman soy sauce are all of the type called light soy sauce. This dish can be eaten at room temperature, or cold.

Peppers, Sweet and Hot

Green, red, yellow, chartreuse, or pimiento-colored, the sweet peppers we grow (or buy for a song at a farm stand in autumn) are valuable candidates for freezing* and canning* as well as pickling* and preserving*, both by themselves and in combination with other ingredients in relishes and mixed pickles.

Until the art of freezing has been further improved, it won't be possible to freeze salad vegetables—such as sweet or bell peppers, scallions, tomatoes, and cucumbers, not to mention greens—so that they will keep their original texture. However, peppers may be cored, seeded, cut up as best suits you, and frozen without blanching—a convenience, especially if you freeze the pieces loose on a baking sheet, then pack them in plastic containers. You can then remove whatever quantity you need without disturbing the rest.

Some experts prefer to blanch peppers, especially if they are frozen in halves for stuffing (see Part Two), but there is general agreement that peppers are the one vegetable for which blanching is not essential. (We'd add another—tomatoes—but read on for that.)

Besides adding your frozen red or green sweet peppers to various dishes as a seasoning, consider using them in the Italian favorites, sweet sausages fried with red peppers, or veal with peppers, both to be found in good Italian (and some general) cookbooks. And then there's Chinese Pepper Steak, too, which has become Americanized by adoption.

Canned or frozen pimientos make a fine antipasto, served criss-crossed with anchovy fillets on a bed of greens. Sweet pepper rings, frozen flat, can be added to salads at the last moment, before they lose the last of their ice crystals, but they won't be crisp, of course. Canned peppers other than pimientos, because of their soft texture, are most useful in soups, mixed vegetable dishes, and as a seasoning.

Suggestions for hot peppers: These, whatever kind you grow, can be dried very simply. When they are ripe, cut them with a short length of stem and either string them through the stems, using needle and thread, or tie the stems with loops to a string. In the Southwest these strings are left out in the sun until dark and brittle; elsewhere, it's more reliable to hang them indoors in a warm, dry place, such as an attic or shed. Dried peppers are ready to add fire to innumerable dishes of the world's many cuisines, but there are other things to do with your fresh hot peppers.

Try pickling them in sherry, the work of a moment (see the recipe for Pepper Wine); or make jalapeño peppers into a hot cocktail jelly according to Helen McCully's directions. Pilar Turner tells how to preserve hot peppers in vinegar in the Spanish way, and, turning to sweet peppers, she tells how a Spanish housewife preserves peppers and tomatoes together in a pickling solution topped with olive oil as a seal.

Roasted red peppers and pimientos have a character all their own, and may be either canned or frozen—see our two recipes, one Spanish, one Italian. And finally, for relishes to accompany a hamburger or a sumptuous buffet of cold meats, see Sweet-and-Sour Red Pepper Jam (below) and Onion and Pepper Relish, which you will find under "Onions" a few pages back.

Pepper Wine

HELEN WITTY

Also called Sherry Peppers, this is a Caribbean condiment of considerable merit. You don't need a recipe, complete with measurements, for this. Just begin with a scalded bottle or jar that has a good tight lid (the lid should be cork- or enamel-lined if it is made of metal).

Use small hot red peppers, or chili peppers, which are somewhat larger, filling the bottle one-fourth to one-half full, depending on how hot you want the resulting liquid to be. Fill the bottle with dry sherry, cap it, and let it rest for a few weeks before using, shaking it once in a while.

Use Pepper Wine with discretion as a condiment—it can be very, very hot. We add more sherry as the liquid level goes down—the peppers don't lose their fire for a long time. When the flavor weakens, it's time to start another bottle with fresh peppers.

Jalapeño Jelly (Hot Cocktail Jelly)

HELEN McCULLY

Serve Jalapeño Jelly with plain crackers and plain cream cheese, or with certain cold meats—lamb, for example.

Makes 4 or 5 half-pint jars

1½ cups cider vinegar
2 tablespoons lemon juice
¼ cup sweet green (bell) peppers, stemmed, seeded, and chopped

¾ to 1 cup jalapeño peppers (fresh or canned), stemmed, seeded and chopped (see note)
5 cups sugar
1 6-ounce bottle liquid pectin (Certo)
Few drops green food coloring

1. Combine the vinegar, lemon juice, and both kinds of peppers in the jar of an electric blender and purée.

2. Pour purée into a saucepan and stir in the sugar. Bring to a boil. Reduce heat and simmer 10 minutes.

3. Skim jelly and, if you wish, strain it.

4. Bring back to a boil and at once stir in the pectin. Take off the heat and add the green food coloring. Skim again if necessary.

5. While boiling hot pour into 4 or 5 sterilized half-pint jars or glasses and seal.

NOTE: The jalapeños are very, very hot, so you may find the lesser amount is sufficient.

Hot Peppers in Vinegar

PILAR TURNER

Pickled peppers, once opened, should be stored in the refrigerator. They may be drained and used as a relish, added to cooked dishes, or served as part of an antipasto. The spicy vinegar should be saved—use it in salad dressings, as a seasoning for fried fish, or as a condiment.

1. Choose perfect hot peppers, green or red, but do not mix green and red peppers in one jar. Clean them thoroughly and wipe dry. Do not remove stems, but trim them if they are too long.

2. Pack the peppers into sterilized pint canning jars, including in each jar, at the side, two sprigs of fresh tarragon. Leave headspace of ¼ inch.

3. For each pint of peppers, bring to a boil in an enameled or stainless-steel pan 1 cup of white wine vinegar, 1 small bay leaf, 1 clove of garlic (peeled), 8 to 10 peppercorns, and 1 teaspoon of salt. Bring to a boil and boil for 1 minute.

4. Distribute seasonings evenly among the jars and pour in the vinegar. If there isn't enough to cover the peppers, bring more white wine vinegar to a boil and add it; the liquid should come to ½ inch of the top.

5. Add lids and process jars in a boiling-water bath for 10 minutes.

Peppers and Tomatoes in Vinegar

PILAR TURNER

Pilar Turner's recipe for preserving tomatoes and peppers in the Spanish manner, without either canning or freezing, is a survival of times when food could be kept only with the help of nature. In this preparation, the olive oil forms a seal and prevents deterioration of the vegetables in their solution of vinegar and salt, which are both preservatives. The method is worth trying if you have a really cool cellar or pantry, but this pickle shouldn't be refrigerated unless necessary, and then should be placed in the least cold part of the refrigerator.

Choose ripe, perfect tomatoes and green (sweet) peppers. Clean them thoroughly, weigh them, and pack them into sterilized canning jars (the wide-mouthed kind would be best). Cover the vegetables completely with a mixture of equal parts of red wine vinegar and water in which you have dissolved 1 tablespoon salt per pound of vegetables. Pour on enough olive oil to form a layer half an inch deep. Cover jars well and set them aside in a cool, dark place.

The peppers and tomatoes may be eaten in 40 days, or they will keep up to two years. If you remove some of the vegetables from a jar, use a very, very clean slotted wooden spoon to prevent contamination of the remaining pickles.

Canned Roasted Red Peppers

PILAR TURNER

1. Choose ripe, perfect red sweet peppers.

2. Roast them, turning continuously. This may be done over charcoal, under the broiler, in a very hot oven (450° F.), or in a heavy skillet on the stovetop. When the skin starts getting black and loose and the peppers soft, transfer them to a dish and cover with a damp cloth—do *not* dip them into cold water or the juices will be lost.

3. Remove the skins, rubbing the peppers with a cloth. Slit each pepper down one side and remove the seeds, saving any juices that run out.

4. Fill clean, hot pint jars with the hot peppers, laying them flat and leaving 1/2-inch headspace. Add to the jars any juices that have run out while preparing the peppers and a little salt, 1/2 teaspoon per pint.

5. Adjust lids and process in a pressure cooker at 10 pounds pressure for 35 minutes per pint.

NOTE: This same method can be used for pimientos, too, if your garden has produced some. For half-pint jars of either kind of peppers, the headspace and processing time are the same as for pints.

Roasted Peppers for Freezing—Peperoni Arrostiti

EDWARD GIOBBI

This delicious way of storing a surplus of red, yellow, or green sweet peppers was described, in somewhat different form, in Edward Giobbi's Italian Family Cooking, *Random House, 1971, and has been adapted by permission.*

For freezing, make the dish without the garlic, which is added at serving time. Serve the roasted peppers either as part of an antipasto or as an accompaniment to a main-course dish or a snack.

Makes 3 or 4 half-pints

8 large sweet peppers, red,
  yellow, or green
3 tablespoons chopped parsley,
  preferably the flat-leaved
  (Italian) kind

3 tablespoons olive oil
Salt
Freshly ground black pepper
Garlic, peeled and sliced (to be
  added at serving time)

1. To roast the peppers, place them one or two at a time directly on the range burner, whether gas or electric, turned to low heat. Turn each as soon as the lower side begins to blister. Roast and turn until they blister all over—you want the skin to be charred, but the pepper flesh shouldn't be scorched.

2. Set aside on a rack to cool. Strip off the charred skin, slit peppers open, and remove seeds from each.

3. Cut peppers into uniform strips about half an inch wide.

4. Mix peppers gently with the parsley and olive oil, adding salt and pepper to taste. Pack into freezer containers, allowing 1/2-inch headroom, cover, and freeze at once.

5. To serve, thaw in the refrigerator, then mix peppers with thinly sliced garlic to taste—about one clove to the equivalent of two peppers. Let stand in the refrigerator for a few hours to blend the flavors, then serve at room temperature. Do not reheat the peppers—if you do, they will become soggy.

Sweet-and-Sour Red Pepper Jam

ELIZABETH SUSAN COLCHIE

Serve as an accompaniment to cold meats, or use as a relish with hamburgers.

Makes 4 half-pints

5 pounds sweet red bell peppers
  (about 14 large)
4 teaspoons kosher salt or other
  pure coarse salt

2 cups white wine vinegar
2 2/3 cups sugar
1/4 teaspoon fennel seed

1. Wash and clean the peppers. Quarter and seed them.

2. Pass peppers through a food grinder, using the coarse blade, into a bowl. Sprinkle with the salt, toss, and let stand, covered, in a cool place for 12 hours.

3. Drain peppers thoroughly. Combine in a preserving pan or a heavy saucepan with the vinegar, sugar, and fennel seed.

4. Boil gently for 45 minutes or more, stirring occasionally, until the jam is quite thick.

5. Ladle the jam into 4 hot, sterilized half-pint jars and add lids. Process for 10 minutes in a boiling-water bath.

Potatoes

Either freezing* or canning potatoes, especially very small ones, can be done successfully, but it seems somewhat pointless for anyone who isn't living off the land down to the last scrap of provender. Directions for both processes are included in Part Two.

For our part, we consider new potatoes a seasonal treat, to be enjoyed immediately after harvesting, when their flavor is a revelation to those who have tasted only market potatoes. If you follow R. Milton Carleton's advice quoted in Part One and plant a "lazy man's potato patch"—quite small—you can enjoy the traditional early-summer combination of the first new potatoes and the first new peas, usually early in July.

Radishes

Radishes aren't for preserving, although winter radishes—the large, often dark-skinned ones—can be held after harvesting for two months or so in very cool storage at high humidity.

The usual spring and early-summer radishes from the home garden—round or finger-shaped, red or white—are meant for eating very fresh, very crisp, with a little salt and perhaps, in the French fashion, a little butter. Radishes aren't suitable for freezing or canning, and they are of little or no interest as a pickle, except in some highly specialized Oriental preparations.

But they *can* be cooked. If you should be faced with a bumper crop, plan to try them as a vegetable course. Trim off tops and tails, slicing or quartering the radishes if they are large (discard any that are pithy) but leaving marble-sized ones whole. Braise them in butter and a little stock, or cook them in broth or salted water, just until tender—15 minutes or so. Sweet marjoram is a good herb with cooked radishes—we like to add it to a little hot white sauce or cream sauce before folding in the radishes. Minced chives or parsley are good, too.

Cooked radishes look something like tiny turnips and taste somewhat like them, too, so they are good with any meat or fowl with which turnips are traditionally served.

Raspberries

Priced like rubies in the market, when you can find them at all, raspberries are one of the most rewarding of all fruits to grow. If you choose a variety that bears in July and again in the fall, you will have weeks of picking, and plenty of berries to put up.

Unless raspberries are dusty (which can be prevented by judicious use of the sprinkler some hours before, or even the evening before, picking time), it is undesirable to wash them before using them fresh or freezing* them: they deteriorate rapidly after they have been washed, so they should be used as soon as possible.

For freezing—the best way to store them—pick the berries right into plastic freezer containers or onto jelly-roll pans if you would have your fruit as perfect as possible. Unless you prefer a sugar or syrup pack (see Part Two), simply seal the containers and set them in the freezer; or freeze the berries in place on the jelly-roll pans, then transfer them carefully into a loose pack in rigid containers, seal, and return to the freezer.

It is feasible to can raspberries, but this method is a distant second choice to freezing.

If your crop is a good one, use part of it to make jam* or jelly* or fruit syrup.* (See Helen McCully's recipe for Fresh Berry Syrup under "Strawberries," farther along, and see below Paul Rubinstein's Raspberry Syrup, made by an unusual method.) Try your raspberry jam as a filling for tiny tartlets, and, most especially, as a filling between layers of your best chocolate cake.

Whole, unsweetened frozen raspberries can be made into a fruit tart that would do credit to the fresh-berry season, but it should not be assembled too far ahead of time. You'll need a 9-inch baked tart shell (to serve 6) in a 9-inch loose-bottomed, fluted tart pan. Make a sweet custard filling or pastry cream (recipes for suitable pastry doughs and custard tart fillings are in general cookbooks) and allow the filling to cool. Melt an 8-ounce jar of raspberry or currant jelly with 2 tablespoons of water and let cool. About 2 hours before serving time, spread a layer of the pastry cream half an inch or more deep in the tart shell and top it with well-arranged, frozen whole berries. Pour the cooled but not stiffened jelly glaze over the berries and set the tart in the refrigerator until serving time. It's beautiful as it is, but a narrow border of whipped cream piped around the edge just before serving gives the tart an attractive finish.

Other suggestions for raspberry desserts: Raspberries in Raspberry Sauce (below); or still-frozen raspberries swirled through sweetened whipped cream, piled into dessert glasses, and topped with shaved bitter chocolate. (Assemble this one a short time before dinner, so the berries will still be very cold, but not hard, when eaten.)

If you have an ice-cream freezer, raspberry ice cream and raspberry sherbet or ice are incomparably good when made with either fresh or frozen berries, summer or winter.

And finally, for a good topping for any number of nonraspberry desserts, see the recipe below for Elizabeth Colchie's Raspberry and Currant Dessert Sauce, a blending of two fruit flavors that go exceptionally well together.

Raspberry Syrup

PAUL RUBINSTEIN

In this recipe of European inspiration, a short period of fermentation serves to develop the flavor of the raspberries.

Makes about 2 pints

3 quarts fresh, ripe raspberries   3 tablespoons citric acid powder
6 cups sugar

1. Wash and drain the berries.

2. Crush them well in a large bowl, cover the bowl with a cloth, and let the berries stand for several days, stirring them thoroughly each day.

3. When all bubbling has stopped and no bits of fruit float on the surface, strain off all juice through three thicknesses of cheesecloth dipped into cold water and wrung out. Discard the pulp.

4. In a preserving pan or enameled saucepan combine the strained juice, the sugar, and the citric acid and bring to a boil. Boil 4 minutes, skimming off the foam and any scum, being careful not to waste any of the syrup.

5. Allow the syrup to cool, then bottle in sterilized bottles and cap closely with sterilized lids. Store in a cool place, but do not refrigerate.

Raspberries in Raspberry Sauce

HELEN WITTY

The beginnings of this recipe go back many seasons, to when we first began to grow our own red raspberries—there's a very good chance that the idea was begged, borrowed, or stolen, not invented. Whatever its source, this is one of the simplest and best of raspberry desserts when only the frozen fruit is available.

1. Thaw frozen raspberries in the refrigerator (allowing 3 pints for 4 persons), just until the berries are separated but still icy. Don't do this too far ahead of time. The berries should still have a few ice crystals in their hearts at serving time.

2. In the jar of an electric blender, purée about one-fourth of the berries, adding superfine sugar to taste. How much sugar to use will depend on the character of the fruit and the taste of the cook; we'd suggest moderation, tasting as you go.

3. If you want a seedless sauce, press the purée through a fine sieve.

4. Add a little kirsch, if you like it, or a little framboise liqueur.

5. Spoon berries into serving dishes and top with the purée. Serve with lightly whipped cream (no sugar) and crisp, simple butter cookies.

Raspberry and Currant Dessert Sauce

ELIZABETH SUSAN COLCHIE

Makes about 2 pints

3 cups sugar
³/₄ cup water
2 cups raspberries, washed, drained, and spread on paper towels

6 cups currants, washed and stems removed
¹/₂ cup eau de vie de framboise

1. Combine the sugar and water in an enamel or stainless-steel saucepan and swirl over low heat until the syrup is clear. Cover and barely simmer over lowest heat for 5 minutes.

2. Add the fruits and simmer, uncovered, for 10 minutes.

3. Strain the syrup into a small saucepan, reserving the fruit. Boil the syrup until it is reduced to about 2¹/₃ cups.

4. Purée the fruit through the fine mesh of a food mill into the syrup. Bring the mixture to a boil and add the eau de vie.

5. Pour the sauce into hot, sterilized jars and seal.

Rhubarb

Rhubarb, a vegetable that is invariably treated as a fruit, has always been a welcome sign of spring and, in fact, was long considered a tonic. Whether it has medicinal value or not, our ancestresses made plain rhubarb pies, rhubarb pies with custard or strawberries, deep-dish rhubarb pies, rhubarb meringue pies, and, rhubarb cobblers. Not to mention cordials, sauces, jams, jellies, conserves, and chutneys.

Recipes for all these rhubarb preparations, and more, are to be found in abundance in American cookbooks, and are commended to anyone who has planted a few clumps of this wonderful plant—called "pie plant" by those ladies of yore. If you can find a red-stalked variety of rhubarb to plant, the color of your desserts and preserves will be more beautiful than if you grow the older, part-green, part-red varieties; but the flavor will be the same.

After the first season or two rhubarb bears heavily, so it can be put up in quantity. Washed, trimmed, and cut up, it freezes* to perfection without sugar, and it is also good for canning*. Use the frozen rhubarb in any recipe calling for the fresh.

Rhubarb "sauce," or stewed rhubarb, is the basis for one of our favorite desserts, Rhubarb Fool (below). Either fresh or frozen rhubarb can be used in the Rhubarb Conserve for which a recipe follows, and for rhubarb jelly, jam, or chutney.

Rhubarb Fool

HELEN WITTY

Easily made with home-grown rhubarb frozen without sugar, this is an old-fashioned dessert, simple but still one of the best.

Serves 6

3 cups frozen sliced rhubarb
2 strips orange peel, each about
  1 inch wide (optional); or 2 or 3
  drops almond extract (optional)

1½ to 2 cups sugar
1 cup heavy cream

1. In a double-boiler top over boiling water, or in a heavy saucepan, combine the rhubarb (it's not necessary to defrost it) with the strips of peel, if you are using them, and 1½ cups of sugar. Cook gently just until rhubarb pieces are tender.

2. Strain off rhubarb syrup and boil over direct flame to reduce it by about one-third. Taste the rhubarb and add more sugar to the syrup if it is needed.

3. Recombine syrup with the rhubarb, from which the strips of peel have been removed, and mash, or process briefly in a food processor, just until a rough purée is formed. Chill.

4. Whip cream to the point of stiffness and beat in almond extract, if you wish to use it and the orange hasn't been included.

5. Fold the cold rhubarb purée into the cream, using a rubber spatula. Pour into dessert dishes or glasses and chill for up to 3 or 4 hours.

6. Serve very cold, garnished with a candied flower or bit of candied fruit, if you like, or with a spoonful of Strawberry Sauce (see index).

NOTE: Frozen in dessert glasses, this makes a refreshing parfait-like dessert.

Rhubarb Conserve

JANE MOULTON

"Good on muffins, toast, or even graham crackers, this conserve would be worth making for its beautiful pink color, even if it didn't taste as good as it does," says Jane Moulton.

Makes about 7 half-pints

3 cups rhubarb cut into ¼-inch pieces (about 1½ pounds) (if frozen rhubarb is used, defrost and save the juice)
¼ cup water
1 large orange
¼ cup maraschino cherries, halved
5½ cups sugar
½ bottle liquid pectin (Certo)
¾ cup white (light seedless) raisins

1. Place rhubarb and water in a preserving kettle or other suitable pan that has a tight lid. Cover and cook over high heat until rhubarb is soft—about 15 minutes. (If you use frozen rhubarb, include the juice that drained from it as it thawed, plus the ¼ cup water.)

2. Using a vegetable peeler, remove just the outer layer of peel, taking none of the white pith, from the orange and place the strips of peel in the container of an electric blender. (If you don't have a blender, grate off the outer layer of the orange peel.) Add a little of the hot rhubarb to the peel and blend in blender jar until smooth, or mix with the rhubarb if you aren't using the blender. Place in a quart measuring pitcher.

3. Peel off all the white pith from the orange and cut the fruit into segments, then into ¼-inch pieces, removing any seeds. Add orange pieces to the measuring cup, then add the maraschino cherries. Fill cup to the 3-cup mark with the cooked rhubarb. If there isn't enough rhubarb to make 3 cups, add water, but don't use more than 3 cups of fruit and liquid.

4. Pour fruit and liquid into a 6-quart preserving kettle and add the sugar. Place over high heat and bring to a full rolling boil, stirring constantly, and boil hard for exactly 1 minute.

5. Remove from heat and immediately stir in the pectin. (The half-bottle measuring mark will be found on the bottle itself, underneath the label.) Add raisins.

6. Skim off any foam and stir the conserve for 5 minutes, then ladle it into hot, sterile jelly glasses or half-pint jars and seal at once.

Roquette (Rugula)

This is principally a salad green (good, too, minced and blended with butter for sandwiches and canapés), so it has few uses in the cooked-foods category. It can't be frozen for future salads, but, if you have an abundance in the garden and it is on the verge of throwing up flower heads and so becoming too strong in flavor to eat, consider Edward Giobbi's way of preparing it for freezing as a pleasantly peppery soup for future use.

Rugula (or Roquette) Soup

EDWARD GIOBBI

Serves 6 to 8

4 tablespoons butter
2 tablespoons olive oil
2 medium onions, chopped
2 cloves garlic, chopped
6 cups water

4 cups cubed potatoes
4 cups tightly packed rugula
  (roquette), stems and all
Salt and freshly ground pepper
  to taste

1. Heat oil and butter together in a pot and add onions and garlic. Cook over medium heat until onions have wilted.

2. Add water, potatoes, rugula, and salt and pepper to taste. Bring to a boil, cover, lower heat, and simmer for about 20 minutes, or until vegetables are tender.

3. Dividing soup into two or three batches, process in an electric blender or food processor until smoothly puréed. Mix batches, cool, and pack and freeze at once; or reheat and serve immediately.

TO SERVE THE SOUP:
    If, after freezing and defrosting, the soup is too thick, add chicken or other stock, or water, to make it the right consistency. Serve hot, with garlic-flavored toast or croutons.

NOTE: Rugula, as anyone who has grown it has noticed, is more or less peppery in flavor according to its stage of growth. A greater or lesser amount can be used in this soup—judge by the flavor of the herb and the taste of the cook.

Rutabagas

See "Turnips (Rutabagas or Yellow Turnips)" for suggestions for using this vegetable.

Sorrel

A fine, tall crop in the garden—it can reach almost 2 feet when conditions are to its liking—sorrel is a shrinking violet when it reaches the pot. Begin with a pound of the leaves, strip away the heavy stems, and you'll have little more than half a pound left. Then cook the leaves and they will wilt startlingly; whether you make a purée or a chiffonade, you'll end up with only around 1 cup of freezable food. Therefore, if you love sorrel and want to put some up by freezing,* plant as much as your space will allow.

A few sorrel leaves, torn small, are good in a mixed green salad, but this distinctly acid-flavored green comes into its own as an accompaniment for fish or pork or poultry, or in a soup or an omelette. If it is too sour for your taste, try mixing it with spinach or other greens in a side dish of vegetables.

When fresh sorrel is on hand, try such a classic soup as that described by Julia Child and her colleagues in the first volume of *Mastering the Art of French Cooking* (Knopf, 1961)—look for Potage Crème d'Oseille in the index. If you have Chiffonade of Sorrel (recipe) in the freezer, try our simpler Chicken Broth with Sorrel (below). And, if you're a dedicated admirer of sorrel, simply add butter, salt and pepper to taste to reheated, frozen Sorrel Purée (below) to make a sauce for baked or broiled fish—salmon, bass, or shad, for instance. If you wish to make a more elaborate sauce, use equal quantities of fish stock or clam broth, defrosted sorrel purée, and heavy cream. Heat, taste, and add more cream to taste. Beat 1 egg yolk to each 1½ cups of liquid and thicken the sauce over medium heat without boiling it; adjust seasonings.

For a sorrel omelette, thaw Chiffonade of Sorrel. Fold 2 tablespoons into a 4-egg omelette mixture and cook the omelette in butter as usual.

Sorrel Purée for Freezing

HELEN WITTY

Makes about 2 cups

1. Wash 2 pounds of sorrel through several waters and shake off all water possible, using a salad basket. With the tip of a sharp knife, cut along the midrib of each leaf and rip away and discard stem and midrib.

2. Place sorrel in a large pot over medium-high heat and cook, without adding water, until leaves are wilted and tender, turning them often with a fork; this will take a very few minutes.

3. In a food mill, blender, or food processor, purée the sorrel. Cool purée quickly, pack with 1/2-inch headspace, seal, and freeze at once.

Chiffonade of Sorrel for Freezing

HELEN WITTY

Makes about 2 cups

1. Wash 2 pounds of sorrel and remove stems and midribs as described for Sorrel Purée (above).

2. Stack the half-leaves of sorrel and cut crosswise with a sharp knife into very thin shreds.

3. Melt 6 tablespoons of butter in a large saucepan and add sorrel. Stir well to coat with butter, cover, and cook over medium heat until tender, stirring once or twice; do not overcook to mushiness—cooking will take only a few moments.

4. Set saucepan in large container of cold water and cool sorrel quickly. Pack into containers, allowing 1/2-inch headspace, seal, and freeze.

Chicken Broth with Sorrel

HELEN WITTY

A refreshing soup, lighter than the more usual creamed sorrel soups, this is a version of a Continental favorite.

Serves 4 to 6

1 quart well-flavored chicken
  broth
1 cup Chiffonade of Sorrel
  (above), thawed
2 egg yolks

2 teaspoons finely cut chives,
  fresh or frozen
Salt and freshly ground pepper,
  if needed

1. Heat broth to a simmer and add sorrel. Return to a simmer and cook
    for a moment or two.

2. Beat egg yolks until well mixed but not frothy, and beat in the chives.

3. Stir beaten yolks briskly into the simmering soup and cook for another
    2 minutes, stirring; do not boil. Taste and adjust seasonings and serve
    hot.

Spinach and New Zealand-Spinach

Despite the development of spinach varieties that can stand
summer heat better than most of the older kinds, spinach is an
early-summer crop for most of us and, as such, has far too short a
season. Frozen spinach from the supermarket isn't to be despised—a clue to the fact that freezing* is the best way to put up
your surplus, with canning coming in second best.

Spinach, like sorrel and certain other greens, is a spectacular
"wilter" in the pot; you will need up to 1½ pounds (depending upon
the thickness of the stems) of spinach to obtain a freezable pint, and
if you purée or chop the blanched spinach, count on getting only
about 1 cup per pound.

New Zealand-spinach, quite a different vegetable from true
spinach in some ways (see Part One), wilts a bit less and has a
different character when cooked. Prepare it in any way you'd cook
your favorite greens, freeze* it or can it, and try a fine Italian
method for sautéeing it (recipe).

Another of our contributors, Paul Rubinstein, likes to prepare spinach purée for freezing (recipe). Thawed, his purée can be
seasoned simply with butter, salt and pepper, or combined with a

velouté sauce to make creamed spinach, or thinned further with stock and milk or cream to make a cream of spinach soup quite different in character from Elizabeth Colchie's unusual Cream of Spinach Soup, Soubise (recipe).

And then there is homemade spinach pasta. Made by our recipe given here, it looks beautiful and it tastes good—so good that its flavor has been known to persuade doubters that there is more than color to distinguish green noodles from egg-yolk-colored ones.

New Zealand-Spinach Sautéed Italian Style

EDWARD GIOBBI

Serves 4 to 6

2 pints frozen New Zealand-spinach (whole leaves or chopped), thawed
3 tablespoons olive oil or butter

2 cloves garlic, peeled and chopped
Salt
Lemon wedges

1. Drain the New Zealand-spinach well in a colander, being sure it is entirely defrosted and free of most of its liquid.

2. In a large skillet heat the olive oil or butter (don't let it smoke) and add the garlic. Cook for a few seconds, stirring.

3. Add the New Zealand-spinach and toss well with the oil or butter. Cover and cook over medium-high heat until the vegetable is just done, turning it with a fork from time to time.

4. Add salt to taste and serve hot, with the lemon wedges.

Spinach Purée for Freezing

PAUL RUBINSTEIN

Makes about 2 pints

2 pounds fresh spinach
2 quarts water
2 teaspoons salt

1/4 cup strained fresh lemon juice

1. Wash the spinach thoroughly and repeatedly through several waters to remove all sand or dirt, drain, then cut off and discard any thick stems.

2. In a large pot bring the water to a boil, add the salt, drop in the spinach, return to a boil, reduce to a simmer, and cook 20 minutes.

3. Strain spinach from the cooking water and cool it.

4. Pass spinach through an electric blender in batches, adding a little of the cooking water to the jar for each batch if necessary. If water is added, drain the puréed spinach in a fine sieve. (If the blender is not used, the spinach may be chopped fine in a wooden bowl with a double-bladed chopper.)

5. Add lemon juice to spinach, pack in freezer containers, allow 1/2-inch headspace, seal, and freeze at once.

Cream of Spinach Soup, Soubise

ELIZABETH SUSAN COLCHIE

Serves 6

3 cups minced onions (frozen onions, thawed, may be used)
6 tablespoons butter
4 cups chicken stock or chicken broth
4 tablespoons raw rice
3 1/2 to 4 cups frozen spinach, defrosted

2 tablespoons minced shallots
Nutmeg, preferably freshly grated
2 cups milk
Salt and pepper
1/2 cup heavy cream
Lemon juice to taste

1. In a large saucepan cook the onions over low heat in 4 tablespoons of the butter until they are softened.

2. Add chicken broth and bring to a boil; add the rice and let come to a boil. Cover and cook on low heat 30 minutes.

3. In a skillet toss the spinach and shallots in the remaining 2 tablespoons of butter for 5 minutes. Add a generous amount of nutmeg to taste.

4. In several batches, purée together the onion mixture, the spinach, and the milk in the container of an electric blender. Mix together the puréed batches and add salt, pepper, and more nutmeg, if needed.

5. Strain the soup through a fine sieve back into the saucepan and simmer for 5 minutes. Add the cream and lemon juice to taste and serve hot.

Green Noodles (Spinach Pasta)

HELEN WITTY

Homemade spinach pasta tastes so much better than the packaged product, no matter how good the brand, that it's a delight to make. A pasta machine to do the kneading and cutting for you is a great help, but the job isn't especially difficult to do by hand. We use a long "noodle pin" to roll the dough; an ordinary rolling pin will serve, however.

Serves 8 to 10

1 cup (packed) frozen spinach, thawed
3 to 4 cups flour, or as needed

Pinch of nutmeg (optional)
3 eggs, slightly beaten
1 teaspoon salt

1. Place spinach in a skillet or saucepan over medium heat and cook it quickly without added water, turning it frequently, just until tender. Pour spinach into a colander to cool and drain.

2. A handful at a time, squeeze the cooled spinach to remove remaining excess moisture. Force spinach through the fine mesh of a food mill, or purée it in an electric blender or a food processor.

3. Beginning with 3½ cups, make a mound of the flour on a pastry slab or board. Make a hollow in the center and add the spinach, the nutmeg, if you use it, the eggs, and the salt.

4. Using your fingers, work the moist ingredients together, gradually working in the flour in an ever-widening circle. When all the ingredients are mixed, form dough into a ball. If the dough is too soft at that point, add enough flour to give it a kneadable consistency. If it is too dry to hold together, add a few drops of water and knead in.

5. Knead dough vigorously for 10 minutes or more, until smooth and elastic. Divide into four portions.

6. One portion at a time, roll dough out paper-thin on a floured board or slab. Roll up each portion into a cylinder and cut crosswise with a sharp knife into wide or narrow noodles, as preferred. Unroll each slice

and toss the noodles onto a spread-out cloth to dry for ¹/₂ to 1 hour before cooking.

7. If using a pasta machine to knead the dough and cut the noodles, follow the manufacturer's instructions, then spread out the noodles on the cloth as described above.

TO COOK THE NOODLES:

1. Bring a large pot of water—at least 8 quarts of water for the amount of noodles made by this recipe—to a hard boil and add salt, if you wish. A few at a time, drop in the noodles quickly and stand over the pot—they will be done remarkably fast. Begin to taste and test after a moment or two and have ready a heated bowl to receive the noodles.

2. Using a large fork or long tongs or a special "spaghetti lifter," a wooden utensil that much resembles a giant hairbrush, lift the noodles from the pot, drain each batch a moment, and drop them into the heated bowl. Toss them at once with softened butter, or butter and grated cheese, or the sauce of your choice, and serve very hot.

NOTE: If you cook only part of the noodles, the remainder will keep for a few days in the refrigerator or for several weeks in the freezer, sealed in a plastic bag or other tightly closed container.

Squash (Summer Squash)

When summer squash of any kind consent to bear in abundance, you'll need to pick daily in order to keep a crop of tender, small vegetables coming. If you let just one or two specimens hide out beneath the leaves until they have grown to the size of young zeppelins, new fruits may not form and, worse yet, the coarse big squash won't be really good eating. So pick on schedule and freeze* or can the surplus, and try making some of the pickles* and preserves* for which squash are suitable.

Yellow crookneck or straightneck squash seem to *taste* buttery as well as looking as if they somehow belong to the dairy world. Fresh, they're superb when shredded very coarsely, cooked in a little butter and as little water as possible, salted, and served with minced fresh basil and sour cream (or sweet heavy cream, if you prefer). This method is also fine for frozen yellow squash, and patty-pans (bush scallops, or cymlings) are good the same way, fresh or frozen. All raw young squash, including zucchini, are a good addition to a mixed salad when sliced paper-thin.

If you have a surplus of golden squash, dedicate it to the preserve cupboard and make Helen Witty's Squash and Citrus Marmalade (recipe), delicately spiced with coriander.

Zucchini that have been cut into sticks, French-fry fashion, before freezing can of course be cooked and seasoned or sauced in any of your favorite ways, but they make a delicious garnish when actually French-fried as an accompaniment for steaks or chops. Thaw the sticks, pat them thoroughly dry, salt them, dredge with flour, and deep-fry to a deep golden brown.

Zucchini frozen in rounds are a good beginning for the cheese-topped flat Italian omelette called a frittata—you will find a recipe in any good Italian cookbook. Frozen zucchini is also suitable for use in Nicola Zanghi's cream of zucchini soup (recipe).

If you should find in your harvest some large but not tough-skinned or too-seedy zucchini, freeze the slices exactly like slices of eggplant (see Part Two), for later thawing and frying, again exactly like eggplant. And finally, if you have frozen and canned your squash and still have zucchini coming, don't forget pickled zucchini rounds (recipe).

Golden Squash and Citrus Marmalade

HELEN WITTY

In our marmalade-loving family we'd value this preserve if it were no more than a citrus-stretcher—note the yield from two lemons and two oranges—but it's more than that. The golden squash gives it a character all its own and a lovely amber color as well. To us it's particularly interesting when the coriander is included. The warm, spicy, somewhat citruslike flavor of the coriander seed is an admirable complement to the preserve. (Coriander, by the way, is the seed of an herb that's easily grown in the home garden. The leaves, too, have culinary uses, so add this plant to your herb garden if you'd like to grow your own supply of a useful "spice").

This recipe calls for spreading your operations over several days, but it's worth it in order to develop the pectin in the citrus fruits and achieve a good consistency and flavor in the finished marmalade. Only a few minutes' work are required at each step except the last, when the marmalade must be watched and stirred carefully lest it scorch toward the end of cooking.

Makes 9 or 10 half-pints

2 good-sized oranges
2 large lemons
2 quarts water
3 pounds (after trimming)
  young, tender yellow summer
  squash

8 cups sugar
2 to 3 teaspoons ground
  coriander seed (optional, but
  strongly recommended)

1. Slice the oranges and lemons thin, remove the seeds, and set the slices to soak in the water, at room temperature, for 24 hours.

2. Put fruit and water into a preserving pan, bring it to a boil, and boil gently for 45 minutes. Let cool, cover, and let stand 24 hours.

3. Strain the fruit from the liquid, returning the liquid to the preserving pan. Chop or grind the fruit coarsely, either in a food processor or in a wooden bowl, using a half-moon chopper. Add the fruit to the liquid.

4. Scrub the squash, trim off ends, and weigh; you should have 3 pounds. Shred the squash coarsely and add to the preserving pan.

5. Stir the sugar into the fruit and squash, cover, and let stand overnight, or 8 to 12 hours.

6. Bring the ingredients to a boil, lower the heat to medium, and cook, stirring often (even oftener as it thickens), until the marmalade is as thick as you like it. The time required will vary according to the moisture content of the squash, but allow an hour or so. Test for consistency either by using the jelly test with a metal spoon (see Part Two) or by spooning out a little marmalade onto a thick china plate and letting it cool, meanwhile setting the pot off the fire. If the clear juice wrinkles and is jellylike when cool, it's ready. If you prefer a softer texture, stop the boiling before this point is reached.

7. If you are using the coriander, add the spice just before taking the marmalade from the fire. Stir the marmalade off the heat for 5 minutes, then ladle into sterilized, hot half-pint containers and seal.

Crema di Zucchini con Mandorle—Cream of Zucchini Soup with Almonds

NICOLA ZANGHI

Cream of Zucchini Soup with Almonds was devised by Nicola Zanghi especially for his Long Island, New York, restaurant. He points out that it is a delight for vegetarians, and that it can of course be made with fresh zucchini as well as frozen—use two pounds of the vegetable in that case, instead of two pints of frozen squash.

He also suggests that you try a delicious summer bonus from the squash plants you grow: pick the flowers, dip them in fritter batter, and sauté them in olive oil as a vegetable course.

Serves 4 to 6

2 pints frozen diced or sliced, peeled zucchini, thawed
6 tablespoons butter
¼ cup diced onion
¼ cup diced celery
8 tablespoons flour, sifted

1 cup heavy cream
1 cup milk
Salt and pepper
1 cup blanched sliced almonds
½ cup toasted sliced almonds

1. Melt butter in a saucepan over a low flame. Add onions and cook until translucent. Add celery and continue cooking until celery has softened.

2. Sprinkle flour over mixture and cook over a low flame for 3 to 5 minutes, stirring with a wooden spoon. Do not let flour brown.

3. Add zucchini and sliced almonds. Stir and cook for 10 minutes over a moderate flame. (If you wish to freeze the soup base for future use, cool it quickly at this point, package, seal, and freeze it. Thaw before proceeding with Step 4.)

4. Add milk and cream, bring to a boil, and reduce to a simmer. Simmer, uncovered, for 1 hour, skimming often.

5. Purée soup and season with salt and freshly ground pepper.

6. Serve hot, garnished with the toasted sliced almonds.

Pickled Zucchini

JANE MOULTON

Makes about 7 pints

5 pounds zucchini, each squash
  about 1½ inches in diameter
4 cups cider vinegar
2 cups sugar
¼ cup pickling salt or
  noniodized salt
1 tablespoon celery seed

1 tablespoon mustard seed
2 teaspoons ground turmeric
1 teaspoon dry mustard
6 cups peeled and thinly sliced
  onions (about 7 medium
  onions)

1. Wash zucchini well, scrubbing with a brush under running water. Cut into ¼-inch slices.

2. In a 6-quart or larger preserving kettle bring to a boil over high heat the vinegar, sugar, salt, celery seed, mustard seed, turmeric, and dry mustard. Remove from heat and add the zucchini and onions. Cover and let stand for 1 hour, mixing every 15 minutes.

3. Bring again to a boil over high heat and simmer, covered, for 3 minutes.

4. Pack immediately into clean, hot pint jars, making sure the pickling liquid is equally distributed and that it covers the vegetables.

5. Add lids and process in a boiling-water bath for 5 minutes. (If quart jars are used, process for 10 minutes.)

Squash (Winter Squash)

From the soup course to dessert, the sweet, orange-colored flesh of winter squash is used in dishes without number. The Indians introduced squash to the European newcomers, and winter squashes have been a staple among the "keeping" vegetables ever since.

The hard-skinned winter squashes—Hubbard, for example—will keep very well if they have been ripened on the vine and stored as described in Part One. But if you don't have good facilities for storage, can* or freeze* the surplus, and make some spiced pickles*, too—see Florence Fabricant's recipe.

Cooked, mashed squash, whether canned or frozen, is a versatile vegetable to have on hand. It is delicious in itself with a minimum of seasonings, and is interchangeable with mashed sweet potatoes or pumpkin in recipes calling for these vegetables. If you'd like to try cream of pumpkin soup—say, the recipe in Louis P. De Gouy's *Gold Cook Book*—and lack pumpkin, make it with squash instead.

Among typically American yeast-raised breads and sweet breads are several containing sweet potatoes or pumpkin. Again, you can substitute: use mashed squash, as James Beard suggests in a headnote to his recipe for sweet-potato rolls or bread in *Beard on Bread* (Knopf, 1973). And developed especially for winter squash is our recipe for Elizabeth Colchie's Winter-Squash Corn Bread (below).

For serving as a vegetable, you can prepare small squash—such as 'Acorn' varieties—in halves or quarters. Remove the seeds from the sections and bake them, covered, in a 400° F. oven until not quite done. Cool thoroughly, then package in foil or plastic, seal, and freeze. At serving time, reheat in the oven with such seasonings as butter (or bacon drippings), salt, and pepper; or use a stuffing of cooked, crumbled sausage and bread crumbs bound with a lightly beaten egg.

For dessert? Squash pie, of course. Use mashed squash in your favorite recipe for sweet-potato or pumpkin pie, or see our own way (below) of making Winter Squash Pie, based on another recipe in this book.

Gingered Winter-Squash Pickle

FLORENCE FABRICANT

Crunchy, spicy chunks of pickled winter squash can take their place beside the chutney served with a curry, or accompany a poultry dish, or delight the recipient of a holiday gift. If your garden has produced pie pumpkins (not the stringy Jack-o'-Lantern kind), this recipe works well with their flesh, too.

Makes 3 pints

6 cups pared, seeded winter squash of a firm-fleshed variety, cut into pieces measuring about 1×1×¹/₂ inches
¹/₃ cup pickling or coarse (kosher) salt

3 cups water
3 cups cider vinegar
2¹/₂ cups sugar
6 whole cloves
6 slices peeled fresh ginger, each about ¹/₄ inch thick

1. Place squash in a bowl or crock, mix with salt, and add water. Set aside for 24 hours. Drain squash, rinse it well, and drain again.

2. Heat vinegar, sugar, cloves, and ginger in a preserving pan and simmer for 15 minutes. Add squash and simmer for 3 minutes, until squash is tender. Do not overcook. Remove from heat and set aside for 24 hours.

3. Remove squash from pickling syrup. Reheat syrup to boiling, add squash, and boil for 1 minute. Ladle into 3 hot pint jars, adding 2 slices of the ginger and a couple of the cloves to each. Leave ¹/₂-inch headroom.

4. Adjust lids and process jars in a boiling-water bath for 10 minutes.

Winter-Squash Corn Bread

ELIZABETH SUSAN COLCHIE

Makes an 8-inch square pan loaf

1¹/₄ cups flour
1 tablespoon double-acting baking powder
¹/₂ teaspoon salt
1 teaspoon ground coriander
¹/₂ teaspoon ground ginger
³/₄ cup stone-ground yellow cornmeal

³/₄ cup (packed) light-brown sugar, lumps removed
2 tablespoons honey
4 tablespoons melted butter
2 eggs, lightly beaten
³/₄ cup frozen winter squash purée, defrosted
²/₃ cup buttermilk

1. Sift into a bowl the flour, baking powder, salt, coriander, and ginger; stir in the cornmeal.

2. In a bowl blend the brown sugar, honey, and butter. Beat in the eggs, squash, and buttermilk.

3. Stir the liquid into the dry ingredients to just blend; do not overmix. Turn into a greased 8×8-inch baking pan.

4. Bake in a preheated oven at 350° F. for 40 to 45 minutes, or until golden-brown and firm.

5. Let cool for a short time on a rack and serve warm.

Winter-Squash Pie

Cooked and mashed or sieved winter squash, freshly prepared or from the freezer, may be substituted for pumpkin in your favorite recipe for pie filling. We like it, too, as a replacement for the rutabagas and apples in Spiced Rutabaga and Apple Pie, page 320. Use 1⅓ cups of the squash, omit the applesauce, and increase the granulated sugar to 2 or 3 tablespoons, depending upon taste.

Strawberries

The index of any good-sized comprehensive cookbook will have several inches of entries for strawberries, the favorite among all American berries and certainly the most widely grown one.

As is true of so many fruits and vegetables, the strawberries you buy in the market are almost certain to be inferior in aroma and flavor to the ones you can grow. Most market varieties have been bred for staying power in the shipping case and at the greengrocer's, not for lusciousness. So if you have, as you are advised to do in Part One, selected and grown the kind or kinds of strawberries best suited to your region, you are to be envied.

Fresh strawberries, if neither tinged with green nor over-ripe, will keep for a day or two, sometimes even three, if stored, unwashed and in shallow layers, in the refrigerator, lightly covered with plastic. The first pickings of your crop are likely to be used as fresh berries, after which it's time to consider putting them up.

Strawberries freeze* perfectly, either sweetened or not. We prefer to freeze the most beautiful berries whole, rinsing them quickly, then hulling them and freezing them on jelly-roll pans. When frozen hard, we pack them into plastic bags or rigid plastic containers. Done this way, even frozen berries can top a wintertime fruit tart (see our directions under "Raspberries"—it's a method that works for strawberries too, if you don't assemble the tart too far in advance).

The run-of-the-patch berries are fine for jam* or jelly* or preserves*—try Maria Friedlander's Sunshine Preserves, for which a recipe is given below—and are good candidates for packing in containers and freezing with or without sweetening. Canning strawberries is feasible, but the fruit tends to float and turn too soft for most tastes.

Once frozen, strawberries are almost as useful as the fresh fruit. They're fine material for Michael Batterberry's Strawberry Mousse with Raspberry Sauce, or could even be used in Nicola Zanghi's Strawberry Sauce for desserts, or in Helen McCully's Fresh Berry Syrup (recipes).

What else? No one needs to tell the owner of an ice-cream freezer about the merits of home-made ice cream made with either fresh or frozen berries and thick, pure cream. Then there's strawberry shortcake, which can be made out of season when you yearn for a taste of June, using berries frozen in sugar or syrup (see Part Two). Then think of strawberry Bavarian cream, or a pool of strawberries in their own juice, surrounding coeur à la crème; or just strawberries and cream; or strawberry cream pie; or strawberry and rhubarb pie, an old-fashioned but commendable combination that turns out very well when frozen fruit is used.

Sunshine Jam

MARIA FRIEDLANDER

"This is an easy, no-cook, gentle way to make jam using freshly picked wild strawberries, such as the large wild strawberry crop our back field used to yield every June. Ruth Christen, a longtime resident of the New City, New York, area, taught us this method," writes Maria Friedlander. It should work just as well with small "tame" berries.

Small strawberries, wild or tame, hulled, washed, and drained in a colander

Sugar, about ½ cup per cup of berries

1. Spread berries in a clear glass baking dish or on a platter so that they are no more than 1½ inches deep. Sprinkle with the sugar, which is less than the amount of sugar usually called for in standard jam recipes.

2. Cover the dish or platter with a sheet of glass (or a glass cover, if the dish happens to have one). Set outside in a spot receiving steady sunshine.

3. Every hour or so, lift the cover, which will have become very wet, and dry it thoroughly with a cloth. (The sun is actually "cooking" the berries, which give off moisture as they would during boiling, only the sunshine method is much gentler and the small berries will retain their shape when done.)

4. In the late afternoon, when the sun is beginning to lose strength, bring in the berries, wipe the cover again, stir the berries very gently, and refrigerate them overnight.

5. Repeat the process each day for several days, until the preserve is as thick as you like it.

6. When preserve is thick, ladle berries into dry, sterilized jars. Seal with a layer of melted paraffin.

NOTE: The making of sunshine jam will not be hampered if a couple of days of rain interrupt the "cooking" process. Just keep the berries and sugar in the refrigerator until the sunshine returns.

Strawberry Mousse with Raspberry Sauce

MICHAEL BATTERBERRY

Serves 6 to 8

1 quart frozen strawberries, frozen without sweetening
½ cup orange-blossom honey
⅓ cup kirschwasser
Juice of 1 large lemon, strained
1 envelope (1 tablespoon) unflavored gelatin
1 pint heavy cream

GARNISHES (optional)
½ cup heavy cream, whipped
Candied violets
Candied mint leaves

RASPBERRY SAUCE (optional)
½ to 1 pint frozen raspberries
2 tablespoons orange-blossom honey
2 or 3 dashes kirschwasser
2 or 3 dashes crème de cassis

1. Defrost strawberries, keeping any juice.

2. Into an enameled saucepan pour, in turn, the honey, the kirschwasser, and the lemon juice. Sprinkle the gelatin over the surface. (The honey will stay at the bottom, allowing the gelatin to soften in the liquids floating on top without fear of disaster.) Allow to soak until gelatin appears to be dissolved, 5 to 10 minutes.

3. Heat mixture slowly over low heat, stirring constantly until a smooth, clear syrup is achieved.

4. Pour half of the syrup into the jar of an electric blender, add half of the strawberries and their juice, and purée. Strain the purée into a handsome glass or crystal bowl. Taste for sweetness; this is crucial, as berries tend to vary in acidity. The flavor should be delicately tart; the cream will more than dull its edge. If the purée is forthrightly sour, however, add a little extra honey to the second batch of purée, then strain it and mix it with the first batch.

5. Whip cream until stiff and fold into purée, gently blending the mixtures with a rubber spatula until uniformly pink. Wipe messy edges of the bowl with a paper towel, cover with plastic wrap, and refrigerate for at least eight hours so flavors can marry.

6. At serving time, to decorate the mousse, you can pipe additional whipped cream onto its surface, or sprinkle it with candied violets and mint leaves, or dribble a little of the Raspberry Sauce over it. (On second thought, we recommend that you make the sauce no matter how you decorate the mousse, and pass it round in a bowl. Delicious.)

RASPBERRY SAUCE:

In the jar of a blender, purée the raspberries with the honey, the kirschwasser, and the crème de cassis. Strain into a serving dish or pitcher and chill before serving.

Salsa di Fragole—Strawberry Sauce

NICOLA ZANGHI

A delectable sauce to pour over ice cream, sponge cake, meringues, frozen soufflés, or perhaps your next hot framboise soufflé.

Makes 2 to 3 pints

1 quart strawberries, hulled,
  well washed, and drained
2 cups water
2 cups sugar

1 tablespoon kirsch, framboise,
  or other fruit or berry liqueur
  (optional)
2 tablespoons cornstarch
A little cold water

1. Cut berries into small pieces and mix them with the water, sugar, and liqueur, if you use it.

2. In a heavy saucepot, bring these ingredients to a boil and allow to simmer, uncovered, for 10 minutes.

3. Dissolve cornstarch in a little cold water and mix into the sauce, stirring. Bring to a boil and cook an additional 3 to 5 minutes.

4. Strain the sauce and let it cool.

5. Pour into freezer containers, allowing ½-inch headspace, seal, and freeze.

NOTE: Other berries may be substituted for or mixed with the strawberries.

Fresh Berry Syrup—Strawberry, Raspberry, or Blackberry

HELEN McCULLY

"These syrups are perfectly delicious and, obviously, should be made at the height of the season when the fruits are at their very best. Fresh strawberries are at their peak in May and June; raspberries in June and July but mostly in July; blackberries in June, July, and August.

"Serve these syrups over ice cream, vanilla pudding, custard, or rice or bread pudding; use as a flavoring for milk shakes and ice-cream sodas; or make a refreshing drink with crushed ice and carbonated water," writes Helen McCully.

Makes about 1 pint

4 cups fresh, ripe strawberries,
  raspberries, or blackberries

1 cup water
2 cups sugar (about)

1. Wash, drain, and hull the berries. Place in a saucepan with 1 cup of water. Bring to a boil, reduce heat, and simmer for *exactly 10 minutes,* no more. The fresh flavor depends on minimal cooking.

2. Now comes the tricky part. You need to strain off all the juice from the fruit through several layers of cheesecloth, if you don't have a jelly bag to use. So you will have to devise some way to hold the fruit in the bag above a large bowl so that it can drip. A little judicious squeezing is allowed to extract the maximum amount of juice.

3. Measure the juice into a saucepan and discard the pulp. Add 1 cup of sugar for each cup of juice. Cook over moderate heat, stirring, until the sugar has dissolved and the syrup comes to a boil. Boil *exactly 2 minutes.* Remove from the heat and skim off all the froth.

4. Pour the hot syrup into hot, sterilized jars, leaving 1/2-inch headroom, and seal.

5. This makes about 1 pint of syrup, more or less—the exact amount depends on the ripeness and the juiciness of the fruit. The recipe can be doubled or tripled with equally good results.

Tomatoes

More recipes and suggestions for using tomatoes are included here than for any other vegetable, for the same reason that more backyard gardeners grow tomatoes than any other crop. This is the vegetable that is the best of all for canning*. When canned as they should be, at the point of perfect ripeness, tomatoes are usable in many recipes designed for fresh tomatoes, as well as in those intended for the cooked vegetable. The canned ones are actually to be preferred to the fresh for use in recipes when the market offers only the tough-skinned, gas-treated, actually unripe kind found in almost every outlet except at farm stands.

So can tomatoes by all means—whole or puréed—even if you can nothing else from your garden (and note the new how-to information on low-acid fruit that is included in Part Two). Plan to can tomatoes in other ways than "just plain." Put them up with basil leaves, or with a seasoning of onion and green peppers, or can them with okra (see under "Okra" farther back in this section).

What about freezing? Some books say "OK," some say "Never." Those who say tomatoes are not for freezing seem to us to be talking about tomatoes intended for use in salads. For, of course, the texture of thawed tomatoes is so changed that they aren't suitable for serving "as is," but their flavor is intact! For dishes in which you'd normally use fresh tomatoes—say chicken in vinegar, in which the tomato chunks are cooked for only a few moments, or for spaghetti amatriciana, or one of the several delicious and virtually uncooked fresh-tomato sauces for spaghetti—we freeze a supply of especially meaty kinds, especially the Italian plum tomatoes. To prepare them, just dip them for a few seconds into boiling water, skin them, cut out the cores, and pack—or, if you wish, cut each tomato in half and squeeze out most of the seeds (there won't be many in the recommended kinds).

Tomatoes are an important ingredient in many of the relishes*, including chutneys, for which you'll find recipes in all preserving books, and we especially commend to you the two quite different versions of chili sauce for which we give you recipes.

Green tomatoes, either at the height of the season or when frost threatens to kill the vines, are wonderful "pie timber" when made into Helen Witty's green-tomato mincemeat (recipe), and are equally marvelous when made into pickles, for which we include Jane Moulton's directions. (For ripe tomatoes pickled with peppers in vinegar in the Spanish fashion, see under "Peppers.")

For ripe tomatoes, again, there are all the possibilities of jams* and preserves*. We include recipes for two—a tomato marmalade, with unusual spicing of ginger and saffron, and tomato preserves, both by Michael Batterberry.

Because tomatoes are used more often in sauces than in almost any other cooked preparation, we offer below a selection of sauces of various types to prepare for the freezer or for canning. There is a basic purée, suitable for use in any kind of sauce you wish to make; Edward Giobbi's notable Marinara Sauce; Nicola Zanghi's Salsa Pomidoro, in the classic Italian pattern; and Carol Cutler's Coulis de Tomates à la Provençale.

With some or all of these good things stored in the freezer and pantry, you will be ready, in terms of tomato supply, to cook wonderfully the dishes of any number of cuisines. And while dinner is cooking, enjoy a glass of Ruth Ann Church's Tomato Cocktail Juice (recipe), which can do double duty as a base for a Bloody Mary cocktail as well.

Old-fashioned Chili Sauce

HELEN WITTY

The name that should be at the head of this recipe is that of the contributor's late Great-Aunt Minnie, who shared this recipe many preserving seasons ago and gave permission for its first publication, in a magazine.

This chili sauce is the nostalgic sort—it doesn't taste like what comes from a bottle from the grocer's shelves, but is a chunky, gently spiced, and mildly tart compound of good garden vegetables—very ripe tomatoes, very sweet peppers, and onions. You can omit the cloves and cinnamon if you wish and substitute for them about a teaspoonful of celery seed, a teaspoonful or more of commercial chili powder, and big pinch or two of Cayenne pepper. Less authentic, but good, too.

Makes 6 to 8 pints, depending on consistency of sauce

About 30 fully ripe tomatoes, or enough to make 3 quarts when peeled and coarsely chopped

8 large onions, peeled and chopped

8 large sweet peppers, half red and half green if possible, stemmed, seeded, and chopped

2 to 3 cups cider vinegar

1/4 cup plain (noniodized) salt, or 1/3 cup coarse (kosher) salt

1/4 cup sugar, or more, to taste

2 teaspoons ground cloves

2 teaspoons ground cinnamon

1. Combine the ingredients, using only 2 cups of the vinegar and 1/4 cup of the sugar, in a large preserving pan.

2. Bring to a boil, stirring. Lower heat and boil gently for about 2 hours, or until the sauce is as thick as you like it. Stir often, and taste as cooking progresses. Add more vinegar if the flavor isn't tart enough, and increase the sugar, too, if you wish.

3. Ladle into hot, clean pint jars and add lids. Process in a boiling-water bath for 15 minutes. If you can the sauce in half-pints, the processing time will be 10 minutes.

Sander Sauce

JANE MOULTON

"Smooth, dark, and quite sweet, this unusual chili sauce was developed by a friend who tired of chopping enough vegetables to provide chili sauce

for her large family, and resorted to the blender to spare her arm muscles. Both of us have been making it ever since.

*   "Use this sauce with meats, and try combining one part of it with three parts mayonnaise for an interesting salad dressing."—Jane Moulton.*

Makes about 7 pints

8 pounds ripe tomatoes, peeled and quartered
2 very large onions (about 1½ pounds), peeled and cut into chunks
6 medium-sized green peppers, seeded and quartered
1 tablespoon ground ginger
1 tablespoon ground cinnamon

1 tablespoon grated nutmeg
1 tablespoon ground cloves
1 tablespoon dry mustard
¼ cup salt
5 cups vinegar, either cider or white
4 to 5 pounds light-brown sugar, according to taste

1. Using the tomatoes to provide the required liquid, purée batches of mixed tomatoes, onions, and peppers in the container of an electric blender, processing until smooth. Pour each batch into a large preserving kettle as it is finished.

2. Add ginger, cinnamon, nutmeg, cloves, mustard, salt, and vinegar. (The cider vinegar gives a more mellow flavor.)

3. Bring mixture to a boil over high heat, stirring constantly. Turn down heat and simmer, uncovered, stirring the sauce frequently as it thickens. Cook until it is of the consistency of very thin catsup, usually about 2 hours. There should be about 3½ quarts in the kettle at that point.

4. Add 4 pounds of brown sugar, stirring constantly over medium heat until sugar dissolves. Taste, taking into account that the sauce will be sweeter as the mixture becomes more concentrated. Add all or part of the reserved sugar, if desired. Continue to cook and stir over medium heat—the mixture will scorch easily.

5. When the sauce has reached chili-sauce consistency, ladle into clean, hot jars.

6. Add lids and process in a boiling-water bath for 10 minutes.

NOTE: If you prefer not to process the sauce after filling the jars, ladle the boiling-hot sauce into sterile jars, using sterile equipment and lids, and seal immediately.

Green-Tomato Mincemeat

HELEN WITTY

Superb for pies and tartlets, this probably should be called something other than "mincemeat." It isn't fake mincemeat; it's a unique blend of green tomatoes with fruits and spices that is no less delicious than the suet- and meat-laden "real thing," but it's considerably easier on the modern digestion. This is how we make it when the frost threatens to end the tomato harvest while unripe fruit is still abundant on the vines.

Makes 8 to 10 pints

About 30 to 40 small-to-average-sized green tomatoes, enough to make 4 quarts when chopped
2 quarts peeled, cored, and coarsely chopped tart apples
Grated rind and chopped pulp of 1 large orange, seeds removed
Grated rind of 1 large lemon
1 pound raisins, or 1/2 pound each dark raisins and light raisins, or 1/2 pound each of raisins, any kind, and currants

1 cup cider vinegar
1 tablespoon salt
2 teaspoons ground cinnamon
1/2 teaspoon ground cloves
1/2 teaspoon ground allspice
1/2 teaspoon ground ginger
4 cups light-brown sugar, packed, or 2 packed cups dark-brown sugar and 1 1/2 cups granulated sugar
1/2 cup dark (Jamaica) rum (optional)

1. Wash tomatoes, cut out the stem ends, and chop tomatoes coarsely in a meat grinder or a chopping bowl. Drain in a colander for 2 hours.

2. In a large preserving pan combine the tomatoes with the apples and all the other ingredients except the rum. Stir well, bring to a boil, reduce the heat, and simmer until thick, stirring often. This will take from 1 to 2 hours, depending upon the juiciness of the ingredients and the heat level.

3. When the mincemeat is thick enough to heap up in a spoon, add the rum if you want to include it.

4. Ladle the mincemeat into clean, hot pint jars.

5. Add lids, and process in a boiling-water bath for 25 minutes. Cool and store in a dark cupboard for several weeks before using.

TO USE THE MINCEMEAT:

The contents of a pint jar, with some added fruit (we like some fresh, chopped apple and a handful of walnut meats) will make an 8-inch pie. Other good additions are muscat raisins, with their seeds removed, and a little freshly grated lemon or orange rind. More rum (or brandy, for that matter) can be added at this point. Make the pie pastry and bake the pie according to any standard recipe for mince pie—our timing is 10 minutes in a preheated 450° F. oven, then 40 minutes at 350° F. If the crust is golden-brown and firm in less time than that, the pie comes out of the oven at once. Serve this pie slightly warm if you want to follow tradition; it can be rewarmed in a low oven.

Dilled Green Cherry Tomatoes

JANE MOULTON

"Originally the specialty of a few members of the Western Reserve Herb Society, this recipe is now widely used in the Cleveland area. The dilled tomatoes are good either as a pickle served with meals, or on an hors d'oeuvre tray. If possible, store the tomatoes for about two months before serving them," advises Mrs. Moulton.

Makes 5 pints

2 quarts green cherry tomatoes,
  washed and stems removed
10 stalks celery, cut into lengths
  to fit into pint jars
2½ teaspoons mixed pickling
  spice
5 seed heads and some of the
  green leaf tips of fresh dill

5 slices sweet or hot pepper,
  preferably red
5 cloves garlic
4 cups cider vinegar
2 cups water
½ cup pickling salt or
  noniodized salt

1. Dry tomatoes thoroughly with paper or terry towels.

2. Use 5 clean pint jars. In each place 2 lengths of celery, ½ teaspoon
    pickling spice, 1 head of fresh dill and some of the foliage, if you have
    it, 1 strip of pepper, and 1 clove of garlic, cut into quarters. Fill jars to
    within ½ inch of the top with cherry tomatoes.

3. Combine vinegar, water, and salt in a saucepan. Place over high heat
    and stir to dissolve salt. Bring to a full rolling boil and pour over
    tomatoes in jars, being sure to cover them.

4. Add lids and process in a boiling-water bath for 10 minutes.

Red or Yellow Tomato Marmalade

MICHAEL BATTERBERRY

*A gloriously colored jam, with saffron among the spices raising the
tomato to uncommon delights.*

Makes about 5 half-pints

2½ pounds tomatoes, red or
  yellow
1 orange
1 lemon
Sugar
1 cinnamon stick

10 to 12 cloves
4 tablespoons chopped
  crystallized ginger
1 teaspoon loosely packed
  saffron strands

1. Peel tomatoes and slice thin. Slice orange and lemon, remove the seeds,
    and either grind or chop the slices fine.

2. Mix the citrus fruit with the tomatoes and measure into a preserving
    kettle. Add an equal quantity of sugar, measuring cup for cup. Tie
    cloves in a scrap of cheesecloth and add, along with the cinnamon stick.

3. Stir over medium heat until sugar dissolves. Cook 1 hour, stirring often and skimming as foam rises. Add ginger and saffron and cook another 10 to 15 minutes, or until the marmalade is thick enough.

4. Remove kettle from the heat, remove the cinnamon and cloves, and seal the marmalade at once in hot, sterilized jars.

Yellow Tomato Preserves

MICHAEL BATTERBERRY

Makes about 2 pints

2 quarts small yellow plum
  tomatoes, skinned
1½ lemons, sliced thin and
  seeded
2 to 4 sticks cinnamon,
  depending on size
1½ cups sugar
Water sufficient to soften sugar
  (about ½ cup)

1. Combine ingredients in a preserving kettle and let stand until sugar dissolves.

2. Cook over low heat, stirring occasionally, until thick, watching carefully to keep from sticking; time will be about 1 hour. Skim off foam as it rises.

3. Pour into 2 sterilized pint jars, seeing that a cinnamon stick or two and some lemon slices are in each, and seal. Makes about 2 pints and a "taster."

Basic Tomato Purée for the Freezer

MICHAEL BATTERBERRY

This purée may be used in the making of more complicated sauces or, with or without the addition of herbs, may be used "as is" on pasta or in omelettes or other dishes.

Makes about 1 quart

6 tablespoons butter, preferably
unsalted
6 tablespoons good olive oil
2/3 cup tightly packed minced
onion
2 1/2 pounds coarsely chopped
ripe tomatoes, with their skins
(plus extra peels—see note)

2 to 3 teaspoons kosher (coarse)
salt (use the lesser amount if
salted butter is used)
1/2 teaspoon sugar

1. In an enameled cast-iron pot or pan, sauté the onions slowly in hot butter and oil until they are translucent. Do not let them brown.

2. Add the roughly chopped tomatoes, skins and all, along with the extra peels, if any, the salt, and the sugar. Bring to the bubbling point, stirring patiently. Cover with a lid set askew to permit steam to escape, reduce the heat, and simmer gently, scraping the bottom of the pot occasionally to prevent sticking. Depending on the ripeness of the tomatoes, it will take from 20 to 30 minutes for them to mellow and soften sufficiently to be forced through a coarse sieve or food mill. Avoid overcooking, however; the sauce should not lose its garden fragrance.

3. Sieve or press through a food mill into a clean bowl. Cool quickly and freeze the purée in whatever size containers best suit your needs.

NOTE: Particularly at the peak of their season, when tomatoes are cheap, ripe, and abundant, save their peels when preparing salads, relishes, or whatever. Wrapped in plastic, they'll keep for up to a week in the refrigerator—or longer, of course, in the freezer. These sorry-looking scraps will dramatically intensify the flavor of the purée.

This recipe can easily be doubled if you have a large enough pot of the right kind.

Marinara Sauce for Freezing

EDWARD GIOBBI

Described by Edward Giobbi as the best marinara sauce he has ever tasted, this sauce is worth making in a good-sized batch for the freezer. The recipe is adapted, with permission, from one given to him in Florence. It was published in somewhat different form in his book Italian Family Cooking *(Random House, 1971). Amounts can be doubled, if you wish.*

Makes about 4 pints

2 quarts, packed down firmly, of
fully ripe, skinned fresh plum
tomatoes
1/2 cup olive oil
4 cups coarsely chopped onions
1 cup sliced carrots

4 cloves garlic, minced
Salt and pepper
2 to 3 teaspoons dried oregano
2 to 3 tablespoons minced fresh
basil, or 2 to 3 teaspoons
crushed dried basil

1. Work the tomatoes through a sieve or a food mill, removing all the seeds. Set pulp aside.

2. In a large skillet, heat the olive oil and add the onions, carrots, and garlic. Cook, stirring often, until the vegetables are golden brown.

3. Add the puréed tomatoes to the browned vegetables and season with salt and pepper. Cover the skillet with a lid set partly to one side and simmer until the vegetables are soft, 20 to 30 minutes.

4. Again purée the sauce through a sieve or food mill, pushing all the vegetables through.

5. Return the sauce to the skillet or a saucepan and add the oregano and basil. Cover partially and bring to a boil, lower the heat, and simmer again for 30 minutes.

6. Cool, uncovered, and pack into pint freezer containers, allowing 1/2-inch headspace. Cover and freeze.

7. When using the sauce, allow it to thaw completely, then heat slowly. Check the seasonings and adjust if necessary—herbs sometimes lose flavor during frozen storage—and blend in 2 tablespoons butter for each pint of sauce.

Salsa Pomidoro—Classic Italian Tomato Sauce

NICOLA ZANGHI   Makes 4 quarts

4 quarts water
1/4 teaspoon baking soda
5 quarts plum tomatoes
1 cup olive oil
1 cup vegetable oil
1 1/2 cups diced onions
16 cloves garlic, crushed

2 tablespoons salt
1 teaspoon crushed dried red
pepper
Herb bouquet: 6 to 8 parsley
stems, 1 bay leaf, 1 tablespoon
oregano, and 6 sprigs basil, all
tied in a cheesecloth bag

1. Bring 4 quarts of water and the baking soda to a boil.

2. Divide tomatoes into three batches and, one batch at a time, plunge them into the boiling water and leave them for 1 minute. Let water return to the boil before blanching each of the remaining batches.

3. Peel skins from tomatoes with the aid of a small paring knife. Split tomatoes, remove seeds, and allow halves to drain upside down to remove excess juice.

4. In a large saucepot (minimum 6-quart capacity), heat oils, add onions, and cook over a low flame until limp. Add garlic and continue to cook until onions and garlic are lightly browned.

5. Add salt, red pepper, and herb bouquet, bring to a boil, and reduce to a simmer. Allow to simmer for at least 1 hour. Skim often and stir often with a wooden spoon, being careful not to scrape the bottom of the pot.

6. Remove from fire and strain sauce.

7. Cool sauce, pour into freezer containers, allowing ½-inch headspace, seal, and freeze at once.

NOTE: If sauce is desired in which the tomatoes are in small pieces (Salsa Pomidoro a Pezzi), remove the garlic cloves after they have browned, and break tomatoes while cooking with a potato masher. Do not strain the sauce when cooking is complete.

Coulis de Tomates à la Provençale— Thick Provençal Tomato Sauce†

CAROL CUTLER

"Pack away some of the heady flavors of Provence when tomatoes are at their reddest and ripest—it would be a shame to put out all the work and time if the raw material is inferior. Coulis de Tomates à la Provençale is a thick tomato sauce perfumed with onion, garlic, orange, and a fragrant mingling of herbs. The resulting flavor cannot be bought in any commercially produced can or bottle, nor will any amount of 'doctoring up' canned tomatoes recapture it. The zest of this sauce must be there from the very beginning.

"There is also a great bonus to preparing this sauce at home," Carol Cutler goes on—"fresh tomato juice. Since the juice is squeezed out of the

---

tomatoes before they are cooked, it can be saved for an unheard-of treat: drinking uncanned tomato juice. A word of caution: since there are no preservatives in the tomato juice, it will ferment in a few days, even in the refrigerator. To avoid that pour the juice into single-portion-size plastic glasses, cover, and freeze. Even in the dead of winter, this juice will bring back bright memories of summer sunshine.

"The coulis itself goes well with any pasta or rice, with boiled chicken, veal, or beef, or on hamburgers or with meat loaf. It's really too fine a sauce to put on pizza. The recipe can be halved, but since the sauce is versatile, this larger quantity is suggested."

Makes about 5 pints

6 pounds fresh tomatoes
$1/3$ cup polyunsaturated oil
1 cup finely diced onions
$1/3$ cup flour
$1/2$ teaspoon sugar
5 cloves mashed garlic
3 1-inch pieces orange peel (no white)
1 large herb bouquet (6 parsley sprigs tied around 2 bay leaves)

$1/2$ teaspoon fennel seed
$1/2$ teaspoon dried basil
$1/4$ teaspoon ground coriander
1 teaspoon salt
$1/2$ teaspoon pepper
$1/2$ teaspoon celery salt
Pinch saffron
2 to 4 tablespoons canned tomato paste

†This recipe is adapted, with the permission of the publishers, from *Haute Cuisine for Your Heart's Delight,* by Carol Cutler, Crown Publishers, 1973.

1. Plunge tomatoes into boiling water for a few seconds and remove skins, then cut in half and gently squeeze out the seeds and juice. Coarsely chop the remaining pulp. There should be 7 to 8 cups of tomato pulp.

2. Heat the oil in a heavy pot, add onions, and cook slowly for about 15 minutes with cover on. Do not allow onions to brown; they should just be transparent.

3. Remove lid and stir in flour, cook together 2 to 3 minutes, still not allowing the mixture to brown. Add the tomato pulp, all the seasonings and herbs, cover pot, and simmer slowly for 15 minutes.

4. Add 2 tablespoons of the tomato paste and simmer the sauce very slowly, partially covered, for 1 to $1/2$ hours; stir occasionally, making certain to scrape the bottom of the pot so the mixture does not stick or scorch as it thickens. As you stir, press the tomato pulp against the sides of the pot to make the sauce smoother. If there is any risk of

scorching, add a little tomato juice or water. Cook until the sauce is very thick and will stand up in a mass on a tablespoon.

5. Remove herb bouquet and orange peel. If color seems a little pale, or you would like to intensify the tomato flavor, add the remaining two tablespoons of tomato paste. Taste for seasoning and add more salt and pepper if necessary.

6. To freeze, spoon the cooled coulis into 1- or 2-cup plastic containers, allowing ½-inch headspace, cover with lids, and freeze.

7. To can, spoon the cooked coulis while still hot into clean, hot canning jars, allowing ½-inch headspace, seal, and process for 45 minutes in a boiling-water bath (the time is the same for either pints or half-pints).

Tomato Cocktail Juice

RUTH ELLEN CHURCH

Served chilled with a splash of lemon juice in each glassful, this is a delicious cocktail in its own right. It also serves as a good base for Bloody Marys.

Makes about 3 quarts

4 quarts quartered tomatoes, stem ends cut out
2 onions, peeled and quartered
6 or more sprigs parsley
1 green pepper, quartered and seeded
2 or 3 small hot peppers
3 or 4 ribs celery, with their leaves

2 teaspoons crumbled dried basil or, better, several large sprigs fresh basil
1 tablespoon salt
1 tablespoon sugar
½ teaspoon black pepper

1. Put all ingredients into a large preserving kettle and bring to a boil. Lower heat and simmer, stirring occasionally, until very soft, then press through a fairly fine-meshed sieve.

2. Return juice to kettle, taste, and add more seasonings, if you wish. You may need more salt.

3. Bring juice to the boiling point and pour at once into hot, clean jars, filling them to within ¼ inch of the top.

4. Add lids and process jars in a boiling-water bath for 10 minutes.

Turnips (White Turnips)

Turnips are at their best when only a couple of inches in diameter. They can be kept for a time in cool storage (root-cellar conditions), which of course are not available to most of us, but they freeze* so well, either whole (if tiny) or cut into slices or diced, that we recommend this way of storing a surplus. Canning is feasible, too (see Part Two). (If you like turnip greens, be sure to can or freeze* them, too, using the youngest leaves available.)

Turnips as a vegetable dish complement many other foods, points out Felipe Rojas-Lombardi, mentioning especially meats, sausage, fowl, fish, and especially game. "They can be served as a purée," he writes, "made into soufflés, cut into little flowerettes and cooked gently in broth, or cut into cubes, boiled or steamed, and served with sweet butter, salt, and a touch of garlic. They can be baked alongside a roast in its drippings, and in any good stew or any honorable vegetable soup, a turnip or two is always welcome."

Turnips enter into a delectable combination when puréed with parsnips (see the Rojas-Lombardi recipe under "Parsnips" in this section), and they ring an interesting change on potatoes in the same expert's recipe for Turnips Lyonnaise (below). For a gently flavored dish of young turnips in a lemon and egg sauce, see Elizabeth Colchie's recipe. And don't fail to try an experiment if you have self-declared turnip-haters in your house. Cook young turnips, drain, purée them very smoothly (you could use a blender here), and beat them together with an equal quantity of mashed potatoes, with the usual butter, salt, and pepper. Serve this with roast duckling, or perhaps turkey, and receive the diners' compliments before disclosing the secret ingredient.

Turnips with Lemon and Egg Sauce

ELIZABETH SUSAN COLCHIE

Serves 4 to 6

4 cups partially defrosted frozen turnips
1½ cups chicken broth
2 eggs
1½ tablespoons lemon juice
1 teaspoon arrowroot

½ teaspoon salt
Big pinch nutmeg
Big pinch white pepper
Finely minced parsley for garnishing (optional)

1. In a heavy saucepan gently boil the turnips and chicken broth for 10 minutes, or until turnips are fully cooked.

2. Beat together in a bowl the eggs, lemon juice, arrowroot, salt, nutmeg, and pepper.

3. Strain the broth from the turnips and gradually beat it into the egg mixture.

4. Pour the sauce back over the turnips and stir sauce and vegetable continuously and gently over low heat until sauce thickens, about 3 to 4 minutes.

5. Turn the vegetables into a hot serving dish and sprinkle with the finely minced parsley, if desired. (We like them better pale and pure.)

Turnips Lyonnaise

FELIPE ROJAS-LOMBARDI

Serves 4 to 6

4 cups frozen sliced turnips, thawed (or about 4 medium-sized fresh turnips, peeled and sliced)
1 medium onion, peeled and sliced
3 tablespoons butter
2 tablespoons flour
1/4 teaspoon finely chopped garlic (about 1 small clove)

1 cup chicken broth
1 cup milk
1/8 teaspoon sugar
Pinch of freshly grated nutmeg
Salt and pepper, to taste
2 tablespoons freshly grated Parmesan cheese

1. Preheat oven to 400°F.

2. Arrange sliced turnips and sliced onions, separated into rings, in a shallow 1 1/2- or 2-quart baking dish, beginning with turnips; you should have a total of 3 layers of turnips and 2 layers of onion rings. Set aside.

3. In a saucepan, melt butter but don't allow it to brown. Add flour, stirring constantly with a wire whisk for 1 minute. Add garlic and stir vigorously. Add chicken broth, milk, sugar, and nutmeg, stirring the sauce constantly until it is lightly thickened. Remove from heat and add salt and pepper to taste.

4. Pour sauce through a strainer over the vegetables in the baking dish,

making sure the turnips are coated. Cover dish with foil or a sheet of waxed paper.

5. Place baking dish in oven and lower heat to 375°F. Bake for 45 minutes. Uncover and sprinkle top with Parmesan cheese. Continue cooking until top is lightly browned, approximately 30 minutes, and vegetables are tender when pierced with a skewer or knife tip.

6. Remove from oven and let stand for 5 mintues before serving.

Turnips (Rutabagas or Yellow Turnips)

As we point out in Part One, calling a rutabaga a "yellow turnip" is sometimes considered incorrect, but that name is so well known that we have grouped rutabagas with turnips in this book, as you have seen.

Like white turnips, rutabagas (interestingly enough, called "swedes" in some parts of the world) keep well in cool storage. But, as root cellars are unavailable to most of us, any surplus of this vegetable might best be frozen*. Freeze it steamed or boiled and mashed, or blanched and diced, as best suits you. (Some cooks like to bake the vegetable whole in a medium oven—350° to 375° F.—then mash the pulp after scooping it from the skin. Cool and freeze.)

This is a vegetable with a pronounced character, somewhat turnipy, somewhat squashlike. Those who like it are fond of it indeed—it is an excellent companion for turkey (witness its traditional role at Thanksgiving) or duck or goose, and it's fine with pork, or in fact with any food that is complemented by an assertive vegetable.

Mash your rutabagas and season them with butter, salt, and pepper; or add some cream, or sour cream, and sprinkle the top of the dish with parsley. There are those who combine the mashed vegetable with mashed potatoes, as we recommend for white turnips (above), and another good combination is mashed rutabaga beaten with mashed yams or sweet potatoes.

Our only formal recipe for this vegetable is for a most unlikely dessert, remarkably delicious. It's a pumpkinlike pie whose filling can be baked as a custard: simply pour the filling into a baking dish, set the dish into a larger pan or dish, pour hot water into the pan to rise two-thirds up the sides, and bake in an oven preheated to 350°. Remove from the oven when the center is not quite firm—a suggestion that applies to the pie as well. The custard, after cooling, should be served with lightly sweetened (or unsweetened) whipped cream.

Spiced Rutabaga and Apple Pie

HELEN WITTY

Although rutabagas are a traditional part of the Thanksgiving menu, they are often given only token attention when served as a vegetable, despite—or perhaps because of—their unique character.

Baked in a pie with spices and a flavor-smoothing measure of applesauce, rutabagas might well replace pumpkin in the Thanksgiving dessert. This pie evolved from the recipe for a favorite made with sweet potatoes but no apples. We especially like the optional topping of a little coconut, but a drizzle of honey or a sprinkling of nuts is good, too.

Serves 6

Unbaked 9-inch pie shell, chilled in its pan
3 eggs
1 cup cooked, mashed, and cooled rutabagas (if frozen, thaw and allow to come to room temperature)
1/3 cup applesauce
1/2 teaspoon salt
1 teaspoon ground cinnamon
1 teaspoon ground ginger
1/4 teaspoon ground cloves

1 tablespoon sugar (increase to 2 tablespoons if unsweetened applesauce is used)
1/2 cup (packed) dark-brown sugar, sieved to remove lumps
1 cup evaporated milk or light cream
2 to 3 tablespoons flaked coconut (optional), or 1 to 2 tablespoons honey, or 2 to 3 tablespoons coarsely chopped pecans or walnuts

1. Preheat oven to 400° F.

2. Beat eggs in a mixing bowl until well mingled. Add rutabagas, applesauce, salt, cinnamon, ginger, cloves, sugar, dark-brown sugar, and evaporated milk or cream. Whisk or beat well together until no lumps remain—sieve the mixture if in doubt.

3. Pour filling into the unbaked pie shell and bake at 400° F. for 10 minutes, then lower heat to 350° and bake 20 minutes longer.

4. Sprinkle coconut or nuts, if used, on top of pie and return to oven until center is almost but not quite set (it will continue to firm up after pie comes out of the oven). About 10 minutes' additional baking should be enough, but jiggle the pan to be sure.

5. Drizzle the honey over the top of the pie if coconut or nuts have not been used, and cool on a rack. Serve at room temperature.

Watermelon

Beyond freezing* watermelon balls or cubes in syrup (or without, if you prefer), either with other melons, a mixture of several fruits, or alone, there isn't much to do by way of preserving the delectable pulp of these melons.

The rind, however, is another story. Today's improved breeds of watermelon have thinner rinds than those of many plant-generations ago, but there's still enough of the thick, white rind on the average melon to make a good-sized batch of sweet-sour watermelon-rind pickle. Recipes for this delicacy abound, but pickled watermelon rind is especially good when it is crisp. The recipe that follows is for such a pickle, made with either "pickling lime" or calcium hydroxide, harmless substances long used in preparing home-made preserves.

One of the most unusual of the preserves in this book is Pilar Turner's Watermelon-Rind Jam (below), a Spanish sweet that has the modern-day merit of recycling what otherwise might go to waste. Flavored with a little lemon juice and peel, it is commended to those who would like something different for the breakfast toast.

Crisp Watermelon-Rind Pickle

JANE MOULTON

A favorite especially in the South, this type of watermelon-rind pickle owes its crispness to the use of pickling lime or calcium hydroxide.

Makes about 5 pints

Water, in quantities required for the various steps outlined below

½ cup pickling lime (available from some grocers) or 1 tablespoon calcium hydroxide USP (available at pharmacies)

2 quarts watermelon rind, cut in ½-inch pieces, with all green skin and pink flesh removed (the rind from half of a large melon, approximately)

4 cups cider vinegar

6 cups sugar

1 tablespoon whole allspice

1 tablespoon whole cloves

1 four-inch stick cinnamon

2 lemons, sliced thin and seeded

⅔ cup quartered maraschino cherries, with their liquid

1. In a glass, unchipped enamel, ceramic, or stainless-steel container make a solution of 2 quarts of water and the pickling lime or calcium hydroxide USP. (Not all the lime will dissolve.) Add the prepared watermelon rind and let it stand for at least 12 hours, or for as long as 24 hours.

2. Rinse rind in at least three changes of cold water, lifting the pieces out of the water each time and leaving any residue behind.

3. Place rind in a 6-quart or larger preserving kettle with 2 quarts fresh water. Bring to a boil and boil gently, covered, for 1 hour. Drain rind in a colander.

4. In the preserving kettle combine 6 cups water, 1 cup of the vinegar (reserve 3 cups), and 3 cups of the sugar (reserve 3 cups). Place the allspice and cloves in a cheesecloth bag or a stainless-steel tea ball and add to the kettle, together with the cinnamon stick and lemon slices. Boil over high heat, stirring as needed, until the sugar dissolves.

5. Add watermelon rind. Bring to a full boil and then cover, lower heat, and simmer for 30 minutes. Turn off heat and let stand for 24 hours—there's no need to refrigerate the pickle.

6. Add the remaining 3 cups of vinegar, 3 cups of sugar, and the maraschino cherries and their juice and bring to a boil. Lower the heat and simmer, uncovered, until the rind becomes slightly translucent— about 2 hours. Add a little water if the syrup becomes too thick before that point is reached.

7. Remove spice bag and cinnamon stick. Pack the boiling-hot pickle in clean, hot pint jars.

8. Add lids and process in a boiling-water bath for 5 minutes.

Watermelon-Rind Jam

PILAR TURNER

Makes about 4 pints

2 pounds watermelon rind, trimmed of all skin and pink pulp

2 pounds (4 cups) sugar
Juice of 1 large lemon
2-inch strip of fresh lemon peel

1. Cube finely or shred the watermelon rind and mix it with the sugar in a heavy enameled pot. Add the lemon juice and allow to stand for 12 hours, or overnight.

2. Add lemon juice and lemon peel and set pot over medium-high heat. Bring rind and sugar to a boil, stirring. Reduce heat and simmer for 10 minutes.

3. Remove from heat, cool, cover, and let stand for 1 day.

4. Repeat the heating and 10 minutes' simmering, following by standing for 1 day, for a total of 3 or 4 times, until the jam is sufficiently thick: Test by pouring a few drops of the hot jam onto a thick, cold plate. It is ready when it doesn't run easily when the plate is tilted.

5. When jam has thickened enough, bring it to a full boil. Ladle it into hot, sterilized jars and seal at once.

Herbs

All herb growers, even those who have only a few pots of plants on a window sill, have favorite methods of preserving any surplus of these seasonings. For the herbs in this book, we prefer drying for the strong-flavored ones—dill foliage and seed, oregano, rosemary, sage, savory, sweet marjoram, tarragon, and thyme. Either drying or freezing is good for the various mints and for green heads of dill seeds for pickling. Our vote goes to freezing for basil, chervil, chives, and parsley, none of which dries as well as it freezes. But, of course, just to come full circle, you can, if you wish, freeze any of the herbs for which we prefer drying. Or vice versa.

Farther along are instructions for drying herbs, freezing

herbs, making herb-flavored vinegars; for preserving tarragon in vinegar, making basil jelly, and making Marcella Hazan's pesto for the freezer; and for sweet-and-sour mint sauce and an Indian chutney based on dried mint. You may want to make jellies from herbs other than basil, too—check the recipe booklet that comes with liquid pectin to find out how to make such standards as mint jelly, and see your jam-and-jelly cookbooks.

Drying Herbs

If herbs to be dried don't require rinsing before processing, so much the better. If they're dusty or show signs of the presence of insects (very rare), rinse thoroughly and shake or swing vigorously to rid them of water, then pat them with towels. Cut the stems of flowering types just before they bloom, if possible—the flavor is most intense then.

PAPER-BAG DRYING. Good for tall herbs—oregano, for instance, or tarragon. Bunch a dozen or more stems together and place them, heads down, in a large paper bag. Tie the bag closely around the stems, leaving the ends protruding. Hang in a dry, airy, preferably warm place—an attic is traditional and excellent, but a shed or even a closet may serve. Lacking such a space, hang near a hot-air vent or even outdoors in the shade in dry, hot weather. (Take indoors at night.) Drying time will vary according to the herbs' moisture content and the size of the leaves and stems. Let dry until brittle, then strip off leaves and store airtight and out of the light for the best preservation of flavor. Crumble the leaves when you use them.

OVEN DRYING. This should be done at a very low temperature, otherwise the herbs actually cook and lose all character. If you can set your oven to hold a temperature as low as 100° F., use the automatic control. If not, and the oven has a pilot light, rely on the warmth produced by the pilot light and don't turn on the burner at all. The third possibility is to set your oven at its lowest setting—140° F. is quite common—and turn it off for 15 minutes after every 20 or 30 minutes of operation. Herbs dry better if the oven door is propped open an inch or two.

For this drying method, strip the leaves from the stalks and spread leaves on wire cake racks set on cookie sheets. (This lets you catch all the tiny bits, while letting air circulate around the leaves being dried.) Watch the herbs—some dry very fast, some take hours. When they're brittle, they're done. Pack the cooled leaves airtight in jars and store as described above.

DRYING HERBS OUTDOORS. Hot, dry weather is needed, sometimes for several days in a row. Spread herbs, preferably removed from main stalks (this speeds up drying) on a clean window screen or a rather coarse cloth tacked over a frame or spread on a wire refrigerator shelf or some such support. Prop your frame on supports so that air reaches the underside, and take the frame indoors at night. The frame method works well indoors, too, in an attic or any similarly warm, dry area.

DRYING HERB SEEDS. You may want to harvest your dill crop in the form of seeds. Watch the heads—just as the seeds begin to turn brown, clip the entire heads and enclose them, a few to a bag, in brown paper bags. Tie the mouths of the bags and hang them to dry as described above for "Paper-Bag Drying." The same method works for any other seed herbs you may grow—anise, caraway, or coriander, for instance.

Freezing Herbs

It is possible to freeze most culinary herbs so that they keep much of their flavor (while of course losing their looks), but experts differ on methods. (Frozen herbs, by the way, are about equal to the fresh in strength, while you'd use only about one-third to one-half as much of a dried herb as the fresh.)

As noted above, whether you dry or freeze is a matter of taste. Try both and see which is more satisfactory and more convenient for you.

THE BLANCHING METHOD. Some experts swear by this, saying it extends the freezer life of herbs. You may want to rinse, dry, and package some unblanched herbs and also blanch some of the same ones to compare results.

To blanch, tie herbs together by the ends of their stems in

small bunches and dip the bunches *for a few seconds only* into boiling water. Then drop bunches into a bowl of water and ice cubes and leave them until chilled through. Blot gently on towels and package the bunches in rigid plastic containers, or plastic bags, or screw-top glass jars. If preferred, strip off the leaves and store them in small jars (but you'll be losing the potential flavoring contributed by the stems).

HOW TO FREEZE PARSLEY AND CHIVES. These freeze and keep very well without blanching, and supplies as much as a year old are full of flavor if kept (as all frozen food should be) at zero degrees F. Rinse the parsley well (it can be very gritty) and pull the small sprigs from the main stems. (Bundle the stems into a plastic bag and freeze them for use in seasoning stocks and soups.) Pat the foliage as dry as possible on paper towels and mince it with a chef's knife on a board. Don't, please, use any kind of mincing gadget, or even a bowl and a half-moon cutter—you want to keep the juice (and the flavor) in the parsley.

Spread the minced parsley on a jelly-roll pan and place the pan in the freezer. As soon as the pieces are frozen, scoop them into containers, excluding as much air as possible without packing down the parsley too much, and return at once to the freezer.

Treat chives in exactly the same way, but bunch the stems closely and cut them by slicing through the bunch—don't chop at random.

DILL FOR PICKLERS. Here's a useful idea if your dill heads are ripe before your cucumbers are: Clip the ripe but not dry dill heads, rinse, shake dry, and drop them into glass jars, cover, and freeze until you need them.

Herb-flavored Vinegars

HELEN WITTY

Tarragon is the best-known of the herb vinegars—see the separate recipe farther along, which lets you eat your tarragon and have your vinegar, too—but there are several other herbs that can be used to flavor vinegars worthy of a place among your salad condiments.

CHIVE VINEGAR:

For a delicate oniony flavor this is to be recommended. Wash the chive spears and pat or shake them thoroughly dry. Cut them into 1-inch lengths and pack them loosely into a scalded wide-mouthed jar. Bruise the chives thoroughly with the handle of a wooden spoon or other wooden implement, freeing as much juice as possible. Bring to a boil enough white wine vinegar (or, if you can get it, Japanese rice vinegar) to fill the jar almost to the top. Pour in the vinegar, let it cool, then cover the jar closely.

Let the chives and vinegar stand for at least a week, giving the jar a shake when you think of it. When the flavor is strong enough to please you, strain out the leaves and filter the vinegar into a clean bottle through a funnel lined with filter paper. Cork or cap the vinegar, using an enamel-lined or glass lid, and store at room temperature.

BASIL VINEGAR:

Make this the same way as chive vinegar, but you needn't cut the leaves up—simply bruise them well in the jar. If you have grown the basil variety 'Dark Opal,' the vinegar will be garnet-colored; made with any variety of green basil, it will be a light green-tinged gold.

As the basil steeps in the vinegar, taste often after the first few days—filter it before the flavor becomes too strong. For a variation, add a bruised clove of garlic or a bruised shallot to the jar with the basil.

OTHER HERB VINEGARS:

If you like mint sauce with lamb, preserve spearmint in cider vinegar, following the directions for tarragon leaves in vinegar (recipe below). Dill vinegar is made from fresh dill foliage in the same way as chive or basil vinegar, but use cider vinegar in preference to white wine vinegar or rice vinegar.

Dill vinegar can also be made by steeping dried dill seed in vinegar, say 2 or 3 tablespoons of seed to a pint. When the flavor is pleasing, simply strain out the seeds.

Tarragon Leaves in Vinegar

HELEN WITTY

If you'd like to have both tarragon vinegar and a supply of tarragon leaves to use as seasoning in preparations—Béarnaise, for example—where their slight acidity won't matter, here is how to avoid paying the price of the luxurious little bottles of tarragon in vinegar sold in fine-food shops.

1. Rinse large sprigs of tarragon, shake off all the water possible, and pat the leaves thoroughly dry with paper or terry towels.

2. Scald a clean wine bottle or a jar that has a cork, or else an enamel-lined or glass lid. Pack the tarragon branches fairly closely into the container.

3. Bring to a boil enough white wine vinegar (or our own favorite for this condiment, Japanese rice vinegar) to fill the bottle. Pour vinegar over the tarragon, making sure leaves are covered (poke them down into the liquid if they try to emerge). Let the vinegar cool, then cap or cover the container and set aside in a dark cupboard.

4. The vinegar will have enough flavor to use in two weeks or so, and the tarragon, fished out when needed, can be used at any point. As the level of the vinegar lowers, keep the tarragon leaves covered, adding plain, unscalded vinegar for the refills. We kept one bottle of "perpetual" tarragon vinegar going in this fashion for more than two years, and the liquid was delicious to the last. The leaves were too soft to be pleasant after the first year or so, however.

Basil Jelly

HELEN WITTY

Pale amber in color and delicate in flavor, basil jelly is one of the few non-fruit jellies we think worth making; it is enjoyed by people who "hate" mint jelly, for instance. It is pleasant as a change on breakfast toast when bacon and eggs are on the menu, and it is more than acceptable as an accompaniment to meat or poultry.

Makes about 6 half-pints

Enough fresh, unblemished
  basil leaves to make 1 cup,
  packed
2¼ cups water

2 tablespoons strained fresh
  lemon juice
3½ cups sugar
½ bottle liquid pectin (Certo)

1. To prepare the basil for measuring, pull the leaves from the stems and rinse them quickly; pat them dry with paper towels and pack them well into the cup when measuring.

2. Place the measured basil in a preserving pan and crush it, using a wooden potato masher or a similar implement to bruise the leaves thoroughly.

3. Add water, bring to a boil, remove from the heat, cover pan, and let the basil steep for 10 minutes.

4. Strain the liquid into a measuring pitcher. Return 1¹/₂ cups of the infusion to the preserving pan.

5. Stir in the lemon juice and sugar and bring to a hard boil over high heat, stirring constantly with a wooden spoon as the mixture heats.

6. As soon as a hard boil is reached, pour in the pectin, still stirring. Return to a hard boil and cook for exactly 1 minute.

7. Skim off any froth and pour the jelly into sterilized half-pint jars or jelly glasses. Seal immediately.

Marcella Hazan's Pesto for the Freezer

In her Classic Italian Cook Book: The Art of Italian Cooking and the Italian Art of Eating *(Alfred A. Knopf, Inc.), Marcella Hazan comments that "Like much good poetry,* pesto *is made of simple stuff. It is simply fresh basil, garlic, cheese, and olive oil hand ground into sauce. There is nothing more to it than that, but every spoonful is loaded with the magic fragrances of the Riviera."*

When basil is plentiful, Mrs. Hazan recommends that a blender be used to make a supply of pesto to be kept in the freezer. To make it in the traditional way, with mortar and pestle, would be too laborious.

The recipe that follows, adapted from one in her cookbook, is given in terms of proportions: obviously, some gardens will yield more of the basic herb than others will, and some families will want to store just a little pesto, others a lot.

When multiplying the ingredients listed below in order to make a large batch of pesto, divide the ingredients into manageable portions for the blender, using no more than 2 cups of leaves, with the correct amounts of other ingredients, to a batch. When all batches have been blended, stir them together in a bowl before spooning the pesto into slant-sided glass freezer jars or rigid plastic containers for freezer storage.

For each cup of basil leaves, torn into pieces if large, and packed fairly lightly into the measuring cup, use:

¹/₄ cup olive oil	1 clove garlic, lightly crushed,
1 tablespoon pine nuts	then peeled
(pignolias)	¹/₂ teaspoon salt

1. Put ingredients into the blender jar and process at high speed, scraping down the sides of the jar from time to time, until you have a

smooth purée. (This job can also be done in a multipurpose food processor, using the steel blade.)

2. Make additional batches, if any, and mix with the first batch.

3. Pour into containers, allowing ½-inch headspace, and freeze at once.

TO USE THE PESTO:
1. Allow the pesto to thaw in the refrigerator.

2. For each batch based on 1 cup of leaves, beat into the pesto the following additional ingredients:
   4 tablespoons freshly grated Parmesan cheese
   1 tablespoon freshly grated Romano pecorino cheese
   1½ tablespoons butter, softened to room temperature.

3. The pesto is now ready to use as an addition to vegetable soup, especially minestrone. If it is to be used as a sauce for hot pasta or potato gnocchi, beat in 1½ tablespoons of the hot cooking water from the pasta or gnocchi before using the sauce. This helps melt the butter and thins the sauce so that it coats the food more effectively.

NOTE: A batch made with 1 cup of leaves and frozen in a container holding about a half-pint will, after the cheese, butter, and hot liquid are added, be enough sauce for pasta for 3 or 4, depending upon appetites.

Salsa Menta—Sweet-and-Sour Mint Sauce

NICOLA ZANGHI

What to do with that delicious weed. A mint sauce that's absolutely excellent with hot or cold roast lamb.

Makes about 2 pints

3 cups (packed) spearmint leaves that have been rinsed and shaken dry
2 cups granulated sugar

2 cups white wine vinegar, or 1½ cups white vinegar and ½ cup dry white wine
1 cup water
Salt and pepper

1. Purée the mint: pulverize it with mortar and pestle, or whirl it in a blender until puréed.

2. In a heavy preserving pan, melt the sugar over a low flame, stirring, and continue to cook it until light caramel in color. Add vinegar and water and boil 5 minutes.

3. Remove the caramel from the fire and pour over the mint purée. Season with salt and pepper to taste.

4. Bring to a boil again. At this point Salsa Menta may be cooled and refrigerated for use within the next few days.

5. To freeze the sauce, cool it, then pour it into freezer containers, allowing 1/2- to 1-inch headspace, and freeze at once.

Pudine ki Chutni—Mint Chutney

MONOROMA PHILLIPS

This, says Monoroma Phillips, is "a basic 'Lakhnavi' recipe (from my father's home in Lucknow, in the haute-cuisine region in Northern India) which I have adapted for dried mint, since fresh mint is not always available here. For variations, yogurt or coconut milk can be used instead of water, thereby making it a mint chutney from another region of India . . . Mint chutney can be served not just with Indo-Pakistani dishes, but is an excellent complement for lamb chops, hummus bi tahina, kibbi [both Middle Eastern], or even chicken croquettes."

Makes about 1 cup

3 ounces dried mint (spearmint) leaves (about 2 cups)
Water for soaking mint
1 small onion
1-ounce piece fresh ginger root
1 or 2 long, green hot peppers, or more, to taste
2 green limes or 1 tablespoon green mango powder
1/2 clove fresh garlic, peeled
1/2 teaspoon freshly ground black pepper
3/4 cup water
2 teaspoons sugar (my choice, but optional)
1 teaspoon salt

1. Place mint in a bowl of water and allow it to soak for 15 to 20 minutes.

2. Peel onion and cut in quarters. Scrape skin from ginger and cut into small pieces. Seed the hot peppers if you do not want your chutney very hot, otherwise cut in halves.

3. Halve limes, squeeze out juice, and place juice in jar of an electric blender.

4. Gently remove mint from water with a slotted spoon and drain. Drop into blender jar and add all other ingredients—the mango powder, if lime juice has not been used, the garlic, black pepper, water, sugar, and salt.

5. Blend at highest speed for 5 minutes. Place in a small glass dish and chill until serving time.

Exotica: A Selection of Special Recipes

In one part or another of the country there are home gardeners who are fortunate enough to have backyard plantings of fruits or vegetables that are difficult or impossible to grow in other regions, or that take up more space than the average garden can spare.

To those who don't or can't grow them, we recommend buying these "exotica" in the market in order to try this bonus section of good preserves. In the recipes that follow, our contributors—among them Barbara Acosta, Allianora Rosse, Michael Batterberry, Harvey Steiman, Maggie Waldron, and Helen McCully—have dealt in varied and intriguing ways with apricots, avocados, boysenberries, cherries, cranberries, currants, figs, gooseberries, grapes, guavas, kumquats, mangoes, mushrooms, olives, bitter (Seville) oranges, peaches, pears, plums, and quinces. And finally, in the recipe for Tutti-Frutti, are directions for preserving, in one brandied crockful, as many fruits as you can grow or buy week by week throughout the summer.

Apricot Preserves

HELEN WITTY

In California and other mild-climate areas where apricots grow in back yards, jams and jellies made from this beautiful fruit are among the everyday homemade preserves. In recent years hardy strains of apricots have been developed, so that they can be grown far beyond their earlier climate range. But even if you have to go to market for the fruit, this delicious preserve is worth making as much for its color as its flavor, which is incomparable.

Makes about 5 pints

5 pounds apricots, firm-ripe but not soft
5 pounds sugar (10 cups)

Juice of 3 lemons, strained, or to taste

1. Using a wire basket, dip a few apricots at a time into a pot of boiling water, let them remain a few seconds, then turn them into a large container of cold water, set under running cold water, to cool quickly.

2. When all the fruit has been scalded, strip off skins, cut apricots into halves lengthwise, and remove the stones. Place in a large preserving pan and stir in the sugar, then the lemon juice. Cover and let stand for several hours in a cool place.

3. Set pot over medium-low heat and bring fruit and sugar to a boil, stirring occasionally. Adjust heat so that the mixture merely simmers and cook, stirring frequently, until the apricot halves look translucent and the syrup is thick enough to suit you. (If the fruit is ready but the syrup is not, strain off syrup and reduce it rapidly in another pan; recombine with the fruit and return both to the boiling point.)

4. Ladle into hot, clean half-pint or pint jars, add lids, and process in a boiling-water bath for 10 minutes for either half-pints or pints.

Chinese Apricot-Plum Sauce

ELIZABETH SUSAN COLCHIE

Makes about 4 half-pints

1 pound apricots, halved and stoned
1 pound plums, halved and stoned
2¼ cups cider vinegar
¾ cup water
1 cup sugar
¾ cup (packed) brown sugar
½ cup strained lemon juice
¼ cup peeled, chopped fresh ginger
1 tablespoon salt

1½ tablespoons mustard seed, lightly toasted in a hot skillet
1 small onion, peeled and sliced
1 small fresh green chili, seeded and chopped
1 teaspoon minced garlic
1 cinnamon stick
A 6½-ounce jar pimientos, rinsed, drained, and chopped (or ¾ cup grilled, peeled, seeded, and chopped red peppers)

1. Combine the apricots, plums, 1½ cups of the vinegar (reserve the rest), and the water in a preserving pan, bring to a boil, and simmer for 5 minutes, covered. Uncover and simmer for 15 minutes, or until the fruit is soft.

2. Combine the remaining vinegar, the granulated and brown sugars, and the lemon juice in a large stainless-steel or enamel saucepan or another preserving pan and boil the mixture for 10 minutes.

3. Add the fruit mixture, ginger, salt, mustard seed, onion, chili, garlic, and cinnamon stick. Simmer for 45 minutes, stirring once in a while.

4. Add the pimientos and simmer 45 minutes longer, stirring often. Remove the cinnamon stick.

5. Press the sauce through the coarse mesh of a food mill, then return it to the pan and simmer until thick, stirring often.

6. Ladle into hot, sterilized jars and seal. Let stand at least two weeks before using.

Avocado Purée for Freezing

Freezing these subtropical fruits at first thought seems to involve undue violence, but in fact when puréed the buttery flesh of perfectly ripe avocados freezes very well. Thawed, avocado purée is useful in any way the freshly mashed flesh would be used: in a cold soup, in a cocktail dip, in a jelled salad, or in guacamole, for example.

Paul Rubinstein, one of our contributors, likes to freeze the purée with a large quantity of lemon juice—up to 3 tablespoons per large avocado—and later make his own version of guacamole by combining the thawed purée with minced fresh onion and garlic, Tabasco sauce, and salt to taste. Other versions of guacamole would include some or all of these ingredients plus, perhaps, chopped ripe tomatoes, free of seeds and juice; or chili powder; or chopped canned green chilies.

For use in desserts, the purée should be frozen with less lemon—1½ to 2 teaspoons per avocado—to avoid distorting the flavor of the final dish. Or, if you prefer, use ascorbic-acid powder (see Part Two) instead of lemon to prevent discoloration—use ⅛ teaspoon of the crystals, dissolved in very little water, to each 3 large avocados. This non-lemony purée is suitable for inclusion in ice cream, or it can be sweetened and served "as is," or, best of all, it can be used in Allianora Rosse's Indonesian Avocado Dessert (the recipe is farther along).

1. Choose completely ripe but not mushy avocados and work quickly once

they are cut open. Scoop the flesh from the shells and mash it well, or purée it quickly in a food mill.

2. Blend in the lemon juice or ascorbic acid solution (see the notes above) and pack in freezer containers, leaving ½-inch headspace. Seal and freeze at once.

3. Use the purée fairly soon—it can be kept frozen for up to 1 year at zero degrees F., but it's at its best when kept for not more than about 4 months.

Indonesian Avocado Dessert

ALLIANORA ROSSE

The ingredients of this unusual dessert may sound very strange indeed, but the preparation is incredibly delicious. It can be made either with fresh avocados or with frozen avocado purée that has been mixed with a little ascorbic acid (see the purée recipe above) before freezing.

Avocado purée (see recipe), about ⅓ cup per person, thawed if frozen
Granulated sugar, preferably superfine

Strong coffee, liquid coffee essence, or freeze-dried coffee dissolved in a very little water

1. The proportions for this dessert are a matter of taste. To the purée add a little sugar and a little coffee, beat well, and taste. Add more of either or both until the flavor is pleasing.

2. Beat the mixture well, until the consistency of thick cream. Let stand for a few minutes to permit the flavors to blend.

3. Serve in rather small portions in dessert glasses, as this delicacy is rather rich. It can be topped with whipped cream or vanilla ice cream, but to me that would be gilding the lily.

Blackberries

For a recipe for blackberry syrup, see the index for the recipe for Fresh Berry Syrup.

Boysenberry Jam

PAUL RUBINSTEIN

This recipe for boysenberries—enormous, juicy, and easily grown in the home garden—also works well with youngberries, a California favorite, and loganberries.

Makes 7 half-pints

8 cups ripe boysenberries   ½ cup water
6 cups sugar

1. Wash and drain the berries, removing any stray bits of stem.

2. Place the berries with the sugar and water in a large preserving pan and stir over medium heat, using an asbestos pad between the burner and the pan. When the mixture boils, lower the heat and let it cook for about 45 minutes, or until the jam thickens, stirring occasionally. Do not overcook—once a little of the jam holds its shape on a cold plate without spreading out, it is ready.

3. Pour boiling-hot jam into warm, sterilized half-pint jars or jelly glasses and seal or cover with paraffin at once.

Cherry Marmalade

PILAR TURNER

Makes 6 to 8 pints

1 egg white   6 pounds ripe but firm cherries,
2 cups water   pitted (either black cherries or
4½ pounds (9 cups) sugar   sour cherries may be used)
1 cinnamon stick

1. Whip egg white together with water in a preserving pan. Add the sugar and cinnamon stick. Bring to a boil. When foam starts rising, remove from heat.

2. Strain through two layers of cheesecloth and return to the pan. Bring

again to a boil. Gradually add the cherries to the syrup, which should continue to simmer as you add them.

3. Allow to simmer until marmalade is ready. This is determined as follows: Pour a tablespoon of the syrup onto a cold porcelain plate and allow it to cool. (Meanwhile, set the marmalade off the heat.) Push the edge of the syrup gently with a finger and the surface of the syrup will wrinkle when it has been cooked enough.

4. When the marmalade is finished, cool it slightly, stirring often, for 5 to 10 minutes, then seal it in sterile jars.

NOTE: This recipe may be done with unpitted cherries, if so desired.

Cherry Bounce

MICHAEL BATTERBERRY

In certain quarters this is considered as great an American classic as corn sticks. Today you can prepare cherry bounce in a variety of ways, in contrast to a century ago, when only the best quality of bourbon was considered an adequate base.

In any case, start with the kind of cherries you'd normally eat raw. Discard stems and any blemished fruit. Put the cherries in a colander or a salad basket of fine mesh and dip them for a couple of seconds, no longer, into a pot of boiling water. Drain.

Pack the cherries into sterilized jars, leaving a good inch or so of space at the top. Cover the fruit completely with either bourbon, an economical house brand of vodka, or pure grain alcohol. Seal jars and leave them in peace in a cupboard for at least a year.

The resulting cherry liquor can be taken neat in snifters, or on the rocks, or over ice cream, preferably homemade. If vodka is used, it produces a pleasant cherry-scented eau de vie. The grain-alcohol product, because of its very high proof, should be diluted, at least by half, with distilled water.

When decanting the finished Cherry Bounce, be sure to strain it through several thicknesses of cheesecloth. The fate of the cherries themselves is up to you—some find the bourbon- or vodka-soaked fruit delicious; others, with a lower tolerance for the taste of alcohol, do not concur. If the fruit was packed in grain alcohol, consider that it has performed its function as a flavoring agent and throw it away.

Spiced Cranberries

BARBARA ACOSTA

Makes about 2 pints

2¹/₂ cups sugar
¹/₂ cup water
2 sticks cinnamon
1 teaspoon whole cloves, tied
  loosely in cheesecloth

Grated rind of 1 lemon
2 tablespoons strained fresh
  lemon juice
4 cups fresh cranberries, picked
  over and washed

1. In a preserving pan combine the sugar, water, cinnamon, cloves, lemon rind, and lemon juice. Bring to a boil and simmer 5 minutes, stirring occasionally. Let stand overnight at room temperature.

2. Heat syrup, add cranberries, bring slowly to a boil, and cook slowly, stirring occasionally, until the skins pop open.

3. If the cranberries are to be sealed in jars for fairly long storage, remove the cinnamon stick and bag of cloves. Pack the berries, boiling hot, into clean, hot pint or half-pint jars, leaving ¹/₄-inch headspace. Adjust lids and process for 5 minutes in a boiling-water bath.

4. If the cranberries are to be served within two or three weeks, leave the spices in (you can omit the cheesecloth bag for the cloves and simply leave them loose). Store, covered, in the refrigerator or, for longer storage, in the freezer.

Spiced Red Currants

HELEN McCULLY

An excellent condiment with hot or cold chicken, turkey, ham, duck, goose, lamb, or veal.

Makes about 10 half-pint jars

5 pints red currants
1 teaspoon ground cloves
1 teaspoon ground cinnamon
¹/₄ cup cider vinegar

¹/₂ cup water
7¹/₂ cups sugar
¹/₂ bottle fruit pectin (Certo)

1. Wash the currants and strip off the stems. Place in a large preserving kettle and stir in the cloves, cinnamon, vinegar, and water.

2. Cook over moderate heat, stirring constantly, until mixture comes to a boil. Reduce heat to a simmer, cover, and cook for 10 minutes.

3. Strain through a jelly bag back into the kettle. A little judicious squeezing is allowed to extract all the juice. Mix in the sugar, stirring thoroughly.

4. Bring to a rolling boil and *boil 1 minute exactly,* stirring constantly.

5. Take off the heat and stir in the pectin. Spoon off any foam that rises to the surface. Continue stirring and skimming for 5 minutes.

6. While boiling hot, ladle into sterilized 8-ounce tapered jars, leaving about 1/8-inch headroom, and seal.

Currant Sauce

For a dessert sauce made with currants, see the index for Raspberry and Currant Dessert Sauce.

Fig Preserves

CAMMY SESSA

Makes about 8 half-pints

2 quarts ripe figs, either light or dark, washed, stems removed, and chopped (measure after chopping)

6 cups sugar
1 lemon, sliced thin and seeds removed
1/2 cup water

1. In a large preserving pan, mix the figs, sugar, lemon, and water and allow to stand for about half an hour.

2. Place over low heat and bring to a boil, stirring occasionally. Cook slowly until mixture thickens, about an hour and a half, stirring as often as necessary to prevent sticking.

3. Pack into hot, sterile jars and seal at once.

Pickled Figs

CAMMY SESSA

Makes 9 to 10 pints

4 quarts of firm, ripe figs,
  unpeeled
Boiling water, as needed
5 cups sugar
2 quarts water

3 cups cider vinegar
2 sticks cinnamon, broken up
1 tablespoon whole cloves
1 tablespoon whole allspice

1. Pour boiling water over figs, covering them well, and let them stand until cool, then drain.

2. In a preserving kettle, add 3 cups of the sugar (reserve 2 cups) to 2 quarts water and cook until sugar dissolves. Add figs, bring to a boil, lower heat, and cook slowly for 30 minutes.

3. Add the reserved 2 cups sugar, the vinegar, and the spices, tied loosely in a cheesecloth bag. Cook gently until figs are clear. Remove from heat, cover, and let stand 12 to 24 hours in a cool place.

4. Remove spice bag and heat pickles and syrup until simmering-hot throughout.

5. Pack into clean, hot pint jars, leaving 1/4-inch headspace. Add lids and process 15 minutes in a boiling-water bath.

Gooseberry Purée for Fools

MICHAEL BATTERBERRY

The name of this recipe does not indicate the character of the potential user, but it does refer to the dish in which the purée is intended to be used. (Elsewhere in the book will be found another Fool, that one made of rhubarb.) Gooseberries, beloved in Britain, aren't commonly met with in the United States, more's the pity, although they are easy to grow. They make excellent preserves as well as this excellent dessert.

For each pound of gooseberries,
  use:
4 to 5 tablespoons of butter
Sugar, as needed

Pinch of salt

1. Top and tail gooseberries and place them in a heavy, lidded enameled-iron pot with the butter. Cook them over a low flame, covered, until they start to collapse.

2. Crush them down with a wooden spoon, bring to a brief boil, and add the sugar to taste—a pungent sweet-sourness is what you'll need. Add salt.

3. Purée gooseberries in an electric blender, a food processor, or a food mill. Cool, pack in freezer containers, seal, and freeze at once. Because of the perishability of butter, the purée should be used within a few months.

TO MAKE GOOSEBERRY FOOL:
1. Measure defrosted gooseberry purée and measure out an equal amount of heavy cream (allow about 1 cup of each to serve 4 to 6).

2. Whip cream and fold into the purée. Pile onto a serving dish or into individual dessert glasses and chill thoroughly before serving.

NOTE: If you would like to make a purée that will keep longer in the freezer, omit the butter during the cooking, substituting 2 or 3 tablespoons water to prevent sticking. When preparing the fool, reheat the purée with the appropriate amount of butter, cool, then fold in the whipped cream.

A Sorcerer's Sauce

MAGGIE WALDRON

Makes 2½ pints

2 lemons
2 oranges
1 cup butter (2 sticks)
¼ cup sugar
2 tablespoons red wine vinegar
Salt and freshly ground pepper
2 tablespoons curry powder
½ cup currant jelly

1 cup sweet Marsala
½ cup golden (white) raisins
1 package (8 ounces) mixed dried fruit
2 cups chicken broth
2 cups seedless grapes, pulled from stems, rinsed, and drained (about ¾ pound)

1. Remove the thin outer peel of the lemons and oranges and cut into slivers. Extract the juice of the fruit and strain out any seeds. Reserve peel and juice.

2. In a large saucepan, melt the butter. Stir in sugar, vinegar, a little salt and pepper, the curry powder, currant jelly, the slivered citrus peel, citrus juices, and Marsala. Bring to a boil; then cook over medium heat, stirring occasionally, until mixture is reduced by half.

3. Add dried fruits and broth. Cook, uncovered, until fruits are tender (about 30 minutes).

4. Add grapes and poach for 2 or 3 minutes, just until the grapes are heated.

5. Ladle into hot, clean freezer jars, leaving ½-inch headspace, and cover. Cool before freezing.

6. To use the sauce, thaw it in the refrigerator, then bring to a boil, thinning with a little wine or water, if necessary. Serve over game, pork, or fowl.

Guava Jelly

PAUL RUBINSTEIN

Makes about 8 half-pints

4 dozen slightly underripe
  guavas

Water
About 8 cups sugar

1. Wash the guavas well, drain, and slice them very thin.

2. Place the fruit in a large preserving pan and add enough water to cover it by about half an inch. (This should work out to about a cup of water to a cup of fruit.)

3. Bring the fruit and water to a boil, reduce the heat, and simmer until the guava slices are very soft, about 30 minutes.

4. About 1 cup at a time, ladle the fruit into a strainer lined with at least three thicknesses of cheesecloth wrung out in cold water. (Or use a jelly bag.) Do not attempt to press the pulp through, but let the juice drip at its own speed. Occasionally remove accumulated pulp from the strainer before adding more from the pot.

5. When all the pulp has been strained, measure the juice (you should have about 8 cups). Return juice to the washed preserving pan.

6. Add an equal measure of sugar and bring to a boil over high heat,

stirring, and cook until a candy thermometer reads 220° F., or until the jelly passes the "sheet test" (see Part Two).

7. Pour the hot jelly into warm, sterilized half-pint jars or jelly glasses and seal at once.

Kumquat Preserves

HELEN McCULLY

Makes 3 pints

2 pounds (2 quarts) kumquats
2 tablespoons baking soda
Boiling water

4 cups sugar
4 cups water

1. Pull stems and leaves off the fruit, wash well, and drain.

2. Place in a deep kettle and sprinkle with baking soda. Cover with boiling water. Allow to stand until the water is cool. Pour off the water and rinse the fruit 3 times in cold, fresh water. Drain well.

3. Pierce each kumquat with a fork to prevent it from bursting during cooking.

4. Have ready a kettle of rapidly boiling water. Add the kumquats, bring to a boil again, reduce heat to moderate, cover, and cook for about 10 minutes, or until tender. Drain fruit well and return to the kettle.

5. Meanwhile, combine the sugar with the 4 cups of water in a preserving pan. Bring syrup to a boil and boil 10 minutes.

6. Add the drained fruit. Place back over the heat and cook until the fruit is clear and transparent and the syrup thickens (226° F. on a candy thermometer).

7. Take off the heat, cover, and allow to stand overnight.

8. The following day, bring to a rolling boil again. Pack the hot kumquats into 3 sterilized pint jars, leaving 1/2-inch headroom, and seal.

Loganberries

Consult the index for the recipe for Boysenberry Jam, which can be followed to make loganberry jam.

Mango Chutney

HARVEY STEIMAN

Many South Floridians have the enviable problem of an annual surplus of mangoes. Large numbers of suburban backyards have trees, most of which produce early in the season, during May and June. Commercial varieties are available from May into August and September, the later varieties actually being sweeter and more flavorful than the early ones.

Makes about 8 pints

5 pounds ripe but still firm mangoes, peeled and chopped
2 large onions, peeled and chopped
2 green peppers, seeded and chopped
1/2 cup chopped dates
1 cup raisins
4 ounces crystallized ginger, chopped
2 cloves garlic, peeled and minced

1 whole lime, seeds removed, chopped
1 tablespoon ground cinnamon
1 teaspoon ground allspice
1 teaspoon ground cloves
2 teaspoons salt
1/4 teaspoon Cayenne pepper
3 cups dark- or light-brown sugar, packed down
1 quart red wine vinegar
1 cup blanched and chopped almonds

1. Combine mangoes, onions, green peppers, dates, raisins, ginger, garlic, and lime in a large preserving pot. Stir in the cinnamon, allspice, cloves, salt, Cayenne pepper, brown sugar, and vinegar.

2. Bring to a boil, stirring, and add the almonds. Simmer for 1 hour, stirring occasionally.

3. Pour into warm, sterilized pint or half-pint canning jars and seal.

Mango-Pineapple Jam

HARVEY STEIMAN

Makes about 6 half-pints

3 cups chopped ripe, soft mango pulp
1 1/4 cups crushed canned pineapple, drained

Juice of 1 lime, strained
1 box powdered fruit pectin (Sure-Jell or other)
5 1/2 cups sugar

1. Combine the mangoes, pineapple, and lime juice in a wide, heavy pan or a preserving pan. Stir in the powdered pectin.

2. Bring to a hard boil, stirring. Add sugar all at once, continue to stir, and bring again to a hard rolling boil. Boil for exactly one minute, stirring all the while.

3. Remove from heat and alternately stir and skim off foam for 5 to 7 minutes to prevent floating fruit.

4. Ladle into warm, sterilized half-pint canning jars and seal at once.

NOTE: This can be stored in plain heat-resistant 8-ounce water glasses, sterilized before filling. Seal with paraffin.

Pickled Mushrooms

MARIA FRIEDLANDER

Although it is possible to pressure-cook in the jar mushrooms pickled in this fashion, so that they may be stored like other canned foods, we don't recommend it. Mushrooms pickled this way will keep well, covered completely with olive oil to exclude air, in a really cool pantry. If the weather is warm or cool storage is lacking, keep the mushrooms in the refrigerator. Set them out to reach room temperature before serving.

Maria Friedlander's recipe for pickled mushrooms comes from her mother's family in the Apennines, above Sestri Levante on the Italian Riviera. She recommends them as an accompaniment for simply prepared meats, as an hors d'oeuvre, or with salad, or as a simple lunch with Italian bread and cheese.

Makes a scant 2 pints

2½ to 3 pounds of very firm mushrooms, preferably small, bite-sized ones
2 cups white vinegar
Pinch of dried rosemary
2 bay leaves
Olive oil, as needed
Salt and freshly ground pepper to taste

7 cloves garlic, peeled and minced
1 teaspoon crumbled dried oregano
Additional dried rosemary
Additional bay leaves

1. Trim ends of mushroom stems and wipe mushrooms with a damp cloth, if they are quite clean, or rinse them quickly, not allowing them to soak up water.

2. In a preserving pan heat the vinegar with a pinch of rosemary and 2 bay leaves. When the mixture boils add the mushrooms (whole, or cut into bite-sized pieces if large) and boil slowly for 5 minutes.

3. Drain mushrooms, discarding liquid and seasonings. Place mushrooms in a clean cheesecloth or towel and squeeze them carefully but firmly to remove excess moisture. Let them dry off thoroughly and cool to room temperature on the spread-out cloth.

4. While mushrooms are cooling, sterilize well-washed jars (half-pint, 12-ounce, or pint size) by boiling for 15 minutes in water to cover; drain jars just before filling with mushrooms.

5. When mushrooms have cooled, place them in a large bowl. Add enough olive oil to coat them, plus salt, pepper, garlic, and oregano. Toss gently as you would a delicate salad.

6. Spoon the mushrooms into the sterilized jars, filling them to within 1½ inches of the top. To each jar add a pinch of rosemary (a small pinch for small jars, a larger pinch for larger sizes), plus a scrap of bay leaf. Fill jars almost to the top with olive oil and screw on caps.

7. Store in a very cool pantry, or in the refrigerator if pantry storage isn't available. Allow mushrooms to come to room temperature before serving.

Marinated Cracked Green Olives

PILAR TURNER

"One of my most vivid childhood memories," reminisces the contributor of this recipe, "is that of harvest time in my grandmother's house . . . the time of canning, preserving, and pickling. Neighbors would bring partridges and quails for preserving and making confit; *hams and sausages were made for the winter; and olive oil was bought in huge barrels for the entire winter. The canning of olives was my favorite, and we always had a large supply available for our frequent visits. I became such a zealous aficionado of this delicacy that I frequently stuffed eight at a time into my mouth, and became known as the champion olive-consumer of the Pyrenees."*

5 pounds raw green olives, free
  of any dark spots
Cold water, as needed (see
  directions)
1 whole head of garlic,
  separated into cloves

3 bay leaves
2 tablespoons dried rosemary
2 tablespoons dried thyme
½ cup salt
Boiled and cooled fresh water

1. Wash and dry olives thoroughly.

2. Place a few olives at a time on a wooden chopping board and crack each olive, using a metal meat pounder or a small rock. Wear clean, new rubber gloves for this operation, or staining of your hands will result.

3. Place the cracked olives in a large glass or ceramic container and cover them with enough cold water to rise 3 or 4 inches above the olives. Set in a dark, cool place for 2 days.

4. Pour off water, refill the container with fresh, clean water, and return to the cool spot you have chosen. Repeat this operation for about 20 days, changing the water after every 2 days' soaking. This removes the bitter taste from the raw olives.

5. At the end of the soaking period drain all water from the olives. Add the garlic (each clove, unpeeled, should be slightly crushed first); the bay leaves, rosemary, thyme, and salt. Cover the olives with boiled, cooled water, enough to cover them by 2 to 3 inches.

6. Store, loosely covered, in a cool, dark place. The olives will be ready to use in about 2 weeks, but their flavor will continue to improve for as long as a year. When removing them from their container, use a spoon or a strainer, never your hands. If a film should appear on the top of the liquid, just skim it off. The olives will not be affected.

Seville Orange Marmalade

PILAR TURNER

Makes 6 pints

12 Seville oranges (bitter oranges)

Water
3 pounds (6 cups) sugar

1. Soak 12 Seville-type (bitter) oranges in cold water for 1 hour. Remove and scrub thoroughly with a brush. Cover again with cold water and let stand for 24 hours.

2. Place oranges in a large preserving pot and add enough cold water to cover. Cook, but do not boil, until oranges are easily pierced with a fork. Remove the oranges and save the water.

3. Add 3 pounds of sugar to the liquid. Bring to a boil and cook until a medium-thick syrup is obtained.

4. Cut the oranges into fine slices, removing all seeds, and add to the syrup.

5. Cook, stirring from time to time, until all orange slices become translucent. Remove from heat and let stand for 20 minutes. Stir, then seal in hot, sterile jars.

Peach Chutney

MICHAEL BATTERBERRY

Makes about 3 pints

4 pounds peaches, scalded, peeled, and cut into small pieces
½ cup seedless raisins, chopped
½ cup chopped onion
2 small cloves garlic, peeled and minced
1 cup fresh ginger roots, peeled and coarsely chopped (see note)

2 tablespoons powdered mild red chilies (see note)
2 tablespoons mustard seed
1 tablespoon salt
4 cups cider vinegar
1½ pounds (4 cups, packed) dark-brown sugar

1. Put the peaches and all remaining ingredients in a large preserving kettle and stir.

2. Bring mixture to a boil and cook, stirring gently occasionally, until fairly thick; the time will be about 1 hour.

3. Pour into hot sterile jars and seal.

NOTE: My mother, whose family recipe this is, says that 1 cup of preserved or crystallized ginger (rinsed of excess sugar) may be substituted for fresh, producing a slightly different but equally delicious flavor. The ground chilies may be found in markets catering to Latin-American cooks. Do *not* use the common spice blend called "chili powder," and do not, Heaven forbid, use Cayenne pepper.

Gingered Pear Spread

ELIZABETH SUSAN COLCHIE

Makes 4 half-pints

2 pounds hard (winter) pears
2 lemons, seeded and sliced paper-thin

2 ounces fresh ginger, peeled and very thinly sliced
2 cups water
4 cups sugar

1. Core and thinly slice the pears. There should be 4 to 5 cups.

2. Combine half the pears with half the lemon, ginger, and water and whirl briefly in an electric blender to chop fine. Pour the mixture into a preserving pan. Repeat the blending procedure with the remaining pears, lemon, ginger, and water. Add to the pan and add the sugar.

3. Bring the mixture to a simmer over low heat, stirring to dissolve the sugar. Turn up the heat and boil gently for 30 to 40 minutes, stirring often, until the spread is thick and registers 228° F. on a candy thermometer.

4. Ladle into four sterilized, hot half-pint jars and seal immediately.

Brandied Plum Conserve

ELIZABETH SUSAN COLCHIE

Makes 2 pints

3 cups sugar
3/4 cup water
2 pounds red plums, stoned and
  sliced

1 1/2 cups chopped walnuts
1/2 cup brandy

1. Combine the sugar and water in a stainless-steel or enamel saucepan and swirl the pan over the heat until the syrup is clear. Cover and simmer for 5 minutes.

2. Add the plums and cook over low heat for 25 minutes, stirring occasionally. Let the mixture stand overnight, or for about 12 hours.

3. Simmer for 30 to 40 minutes, or until the conserve thickens. Add the walnuts and brandy and bring to a boil.

4. Ladle the conserve into 4 hot, sterilized half-pint canning jars and seal.

5. Serve the conserve, after it has ripened for two weeks or more, over ice cream or fresh fruit.

Quince Paste

ELIZABETH SUSAN COLCHIE

8 cups peeled, cored, sliced
  quinces

2 cups water
1 cup honey

1. Combine the quinces and water in a heavy saucepan or baking dish and bake them, covered, in a 300° F. oven for about 2 hours, or until they are very soft.

2. Force the quinces into a smaller, heavy saucepan through the finest mesh of a food mill. Add the honey and simmer for 30 minutes, stirring occasionally. Lower the heat and cook, stirring very often, for about 1 hour more, or until the paste forms a thick mass that holds its shape in the spoon.

3. Remove from the heat and beat to cool the paste.

4. Spread paste on a baking sheet or aluminum foil and let it dry overnight in a cool, dry place. Turn over and let dry another 12 hours or so. Place on a rack and let dry for another day, or until the surface is no longer sticky.

5. Cut into strips and store in an airtight tin. Dried spices or herbs, such as stick cinnamon, cloves, allspice, or bay leaves, may be added to the tin if additional perfume is desired.

Quince Chutney

ALLIANORA ROSSE

This is a very spicy and hot condiment. The quinces replace the more usual mangoes, with interesting results.

Ginger preserved in syrup, or candied ginger, may be used in place of the fresh root, but in that case add the ginger after the fruits are soaked in brine and either reduce the quantity of sugar slightly, or rinse the surplus sugar off the preserved ginger.

Makes about 5 half-pints

3 or 4 large quinces, pared, cored, and sliced as thin as possible
3 or 4 limes, sliced paper-thin and seeds removed
2 fairly large single joints of fresh ginger root, peeled or scraped and sliced paper-thin
2 large onions, peeled and sliced thin
2 large cloves of garlic, peeled and sliced thin
1/4 cup pickling salt or plain (noniodized) table salt

Water
1 cup white vinegar
1 cup granulated sugar or light-brown sugar (packed), or 1/2 cup of each
1/2 teaspoon turmeric
1 teaspoon Cayenne pepper
1 teaspoon whole black peppercorns
1/2 teaspoon ground cloves
1 teaspoon mustard seed
1 teaspoon ground cardamom

1. In an enamelware or crockery container combine the quinces, limes, ginger, onions, and garlic. Add the salt and water to cover and let soak overnight.

2. Drain the fruit and vegetables well and place them in a large preserving pan. Add the vinegar, sugar, turmeric, Cayenne pepper, peppercorns, cloves, mustard seed, and cardamom.

3. Bring to a boil, stirring occasionally, then cook at a simmer, with occasional stirring, until about the consistency of jam or preserves.

4. Pour into clean, hot jars, adjust the lids, and process in a boiling-water bath for 10 minutes.

Tutti-Frutti

HELEN WITTY

Whether you call this tutti-frutti, the familiar name, or "Rumtopf," the name lettered on the storage jars made especially for compounding it with rum, this fruit sauce is delectable—made with many fruits, sugar and your choice of brandy or rum, mixed and mellowed the summer long and let ripen until the Christmas season. Then you serve it over ice cream, pudding, plain cake, or anything else that would be better for a baptism of transcendental fruits. To make tutti-frutti ice cream, stir some of the mixture into softened vanilla ice cream, then refreeze.

For assembling tutti-frutti you need a large container, traditionally a stoneware crock, but a vessel of glass or enamel will do just as well. A close-fitting cover is needed.

We like to start with a fifth of Cognac or good domestic brandy, pouring it into a 2-gallon stoneware crock that has been well washed and thoroughly scalded. Strawberries go in first, about a quart, hulled, washed, well drained, and weighed. An equal weight of sugar is stirred in, the crock is covered, and the whole thing is left alone for at least a week except for a daily stirring.

As other fruits are ready they go into the crock in whatever amounts come to hand, but never more than a quart at a time and never more often than once a week. Each time an equal weight of sugar is added with the fruit, and the daily stirring continues. If the fruit tends to float, a heavy china plate smaller than the inside of the crock will hold it down.

The fruits we like to use are pitted and halved cherries, soft-seeded and tender berries such as raspberries (and some kinds of blackberries, but not all), grapes, halved (and seeded if necessary), peeled and sliced peaches, nectarines, and apricots, quartered plums, and peeled and cut-up pears. Such tough-skinned or seedy fruits as huckleberries and blueberries aren't suitable. Some people add pineapple and other tropical fruits, some add strips of citrus peel for their unique flavor, and there is a school of thought that favors spices—whole cinnamon, cloves, allspice, and so on—we don't. If the liquid level seems low at any point, add more brandy (or rum, if you have chosen the Rumtopf version).

When the crock is full—or the fruit season is over—stir the sauce well again (the sugar should be all dissolved by now), and cover it very closely for storage. Alternatively, ladle the tutti-frutti into sterile jars and cover with canning lids. Let the tutti-frutti rest for three months before serving it. It will keep indefinitely.

Youngberries

See the index for the recipe for Boysenberry Jam, which can be followed for youngberry jam.

Bibliography: Some Books for Additional Information and Inspiration

Part One: Growing Your Own . . .

All About Vegetables, Edited by Walter L. Doty. 1973. Chevron Chemical Company, Ortho Division, San Francisco, California 94104. The contents live up to the title.

The Complete Illustrated Book of Garden Magic, Edited and Revised by Marjorie J. Dietz. 1969. J.G. Ferguson Publishing Company, Chicago. Vegetables, fruits, soils, and basic gardening techniques.

Farming in a Flowerpot, by Alice Skelsey. 1975. Workman Publishing Company, New York. Help for city and apartment gardeners.

The Edible Ornamental Garden, by John E. Bryan and Coralie Castle. 101 Productions, San Francisco, California 94103. Imaginative growing and cooking ideas.

Gourmet Gardening, by Hamilton Tyler. 1972. Van Nostrand-Reinhold Company, New York. Serious food growing for dedicated cooks.

Growing Vegetables in the Home Garden, by Robert E. Wester. 1975. Dover Publications, Inc., New York. A useful compilation of information from the United States Department of Agriculture.

The Home Vegetable Garden. 1972. Brooklyn Botanic Garden, Brooklyn, N.Y. 11225. Down-to-earth approach with no nonsense.

Mini-Gardens for Vegetables, Home and Garden Bulletin No. 163. Available for 15¢ from Superintendent of Documents, Government Printing Office, Washington, D.C. 20250.

Natural Gardening Handbook. 1975. Brooklyn Botanic Garden, Brooklyn, N.Y. 11225. Includes list of soil-testing labs and organic-fertilizer alternatives to chemical fertilizers, along with information on other basic subjects.

The Postage Stamp Garden Book, by Duane Newcomb. 1975. J.P. Taplinger, Inc., Los Angeles, California 90069. The organic-gardening approach for very small gardens.

10,000 Garden Questions Answered by 20 Experts, Edited by Marjorie J. Dietz. 1974.

Doubleday & Company, New York. Many, many questions and their answers on vegetables, fruits, soils, and virtually every kind of gardening.

Vegetables for Today's Gardens, by R. Milton Carleton. 1967. D. Van Nostrand Company, New York. Gardening for better food, by a man who knows and appreciates the arts of both the garden and the kitchen.

Part Two: Putting Up Food

The Ball Blue Book. Frequently revised, this inexpensive but invaluable handbook of canning and freezing techniques also covers pickling and preserve making and has many recipes. Published by the Ball Corporation, Muncie, Indiana 47302.

The Ball Freezer Book. The companion volume to the *Blue Book.*

The Complete Book of Home Freezing, by Hazel Meyer. Revised edition, 1970. J.B. Lippincott Company, Philadelphia. As readable as it is informative, chockablock with the fruits of the author's experience with every aspect of freezing and with every food that is freezable (and some that, she says, are debatably so).

Complete Guide to Home Canning, Preserving and Freezing. 1973. Dover Publications, Inc., New York. A reprint, in one softbound volume, of the U.S. Department of Agriculture pamphlets entitled "Home Canning of Fruits and Vegetables," "Home Canning of Meat and Poultry," "How to Make Jellies, Jams, and Preserves at Home," "Making Pickles and Relishes at Home," "Home Freezing of Fruits and Vegetables," "Home Freezing of Poultry," and "Freezing Meat and Fish in the Home." The separate pamphlets are also available from the Government—write to Consumer Information, Public Documents Distribution Center, Pueblo, Colorado 81009.

"Fresh Foods for the Freezer," Booklet, 1974. Cooperative Extension Service, Rutgers University, New Brunswick, N. J. Basic methods for getting food from the garden to the freezer.

"Home Canning of Fruits and Vegetables," by Isabel Wolf. Booklet, 1974. Agricultural Extension Service, University of Minnesota, Minneapolis, Minnesota. Basic methods.

Kerr Home Canning and Freezing Book, 1974, and "10 Short Lessons in Canning and Freezing," both issued by the Kerr Glass Manufacturing Corporation, Sand Springs, Oklahoma 74063.

Make Your Summer Garden Last All Year, by Patricia Shannon Kulla. 1975. Lyceum Books, Wilton, Connecticut. How to dry everything dryable and how to succeed with cool winter storage of a wide range of foods. Also contains a section on winter growing of vegetables and herbs, either indoors under lights, or in a cellar or a cold frame.

The Pleasures of Preserving and Pickling, by Jeanne Lesem. 1975. Alfred A. Knopf,

New York. A collection of unusual recipes by a prominent food editor. There is also detailed information on techniques, ingredients, and equipment.

Putting Food By, by Ruth Hertzberg, Beatrice Vaughan, and Janet Greene. 1973. Stephen Greene Press, Brattleboro, Vermont 05301. Admirable and also indispensable, especially for anyone who wants to go beyond its excellent coverage of fruits and vegetables. Includes canning, freezing, jelly and preserve making, pickling, smoking, drying, root-cellaring, and other methods of preserving an array of foods that includes dairy products, meats, and poultry.

Stocking Up: How to Preserve the Foods You Grow Naturally, by the Staff of *Organic Gardening and Farming*; Edited by Carol Stoner. 1973. Rodale Press, Emmaus, Pennsylvania. With emphasis on the organic aspects of the foods they recommend we eat, the editors cover harvesting, freezing, canning, drying, underground storage, pickling, jam and jelly making, and making fruit juices and vinegars. Plus handling dairy products and making cheese; storing eggs; butchering, canning, freezing, and curing meats and poultry; and handling nuts, seeds, and grains.

Part Three: Recipes

In our text we occasionally suggest a way of preparing a food without giving a complete recipe, relying on your own knowledge or on the recipes to be found in a large general cookbook. Most cooks, whether novices or accomplished professionals, need cookbooks. Which ones? A highly personal matter.

The short list that follows emphasizes books that are especially good for the foods we write about in this book. In addition to those we list, there's another cookbook that no kitchen should be without—the latest edition of *Joy of Cooking*, by Irma S. Rombauer and Marion R. Becker (Bobbs-Merrill). This isn't recommended especially because of its recipes (which are always usable, if not always inspired), but because of its wealth of basic information about foods themselves, the raw materials with which you'll be working.

America's Best Vegetable Recipes, Selected and Tested by the Food Editors of *Farm Journal*; Edited by Nell B. Nichols. 1970. Doubleday & Company, New York. Judging from the varied and delicious dishes included here, there's still mighty good cooking, some of it quite sophisticated, being done down on the farm. Recommended.

Fruits in Cooking, by Robert Ackart. 1973. Macmillan Publishing Company, New York. Billed as "an imaginative guide to the unexplored world of fruit cookery," this cookbook matches fruits to a wide range of foods, including other fruits, in interesting combinations. Gives botanical and historical background of fruits. Some preserving recipes are included.

The Gold Cook Book, by Louis P. De Gouy. 1948. Chilton Book Company, Philadelphia. Long a success, and deservedly so, Chef De Gouy's biggest book is especially rich in imaginative and elegant ways to use vegetables. Covers the international cuisine, but also includes basic information for the novice as well as material for the advanced cook or the professional.

The Escoffier Cook Book and Guide to the Fine Art of Cookery, by A. Escoffier. 1941. Crown Publishers, Inc., New York. Not for the novice, perhaps, but, like *Larousse* (below), full of ideas, especially for those who like the French ways with vegetables. This is the American edition of Escoffier's famous *Guide Culinaire*.

The Gourmet Cookbook, by the Editors of *Gourmet* Magazine. Vol. I, 1950; Vol. II, 1957. Gourmet Distributing Corporation, New York. Still a standard: two big books, each with a large offering of fairly well-detailed recipes for every section of the menu.

Larousse Gastronomique, by Prosper Montagné. 1961. Crown Publishers, Inc., New York. Consider this English translation of Montagné's *magnum opus* a marvelous source of inspiration rather than a book of recipes. On the other hand, there are those who cook from it.

Vegetable Cooking of All Nations, Edited by Florence Schwartz. 1973. Crown Publishers, Inc., New York. Some 700 recipes, selected from those in 14 ethnic cookbooks, deal with fifty-odd vegetables. The recipes are intriguing, and each is annotated as to country of origin.

A World of Vegetable Cookery: An Encyclopedic Treasury of Recipes, Botany and Lore of the Vegetable Kingdom, by Alex D. Hawkes. 1968. Simon & Schuster, New York. Beautifully illustrated by Bill Goldsmith, this book lives up to its title billing. Not only are all the usual vegetables here, complete with botanical and other background lore plus good recipes, but there are uncommon vegetables in plenty: consider akee, many odd kinds of beans, breadfruit, cardoon, water chestnuts, and on and on. Both fascinating and usable.

THE GARDEN-TO-TABLE COOKBOOK

Index

357